ML
2075
.D38
1999

Davis, Richard

Complete guide to film
scoring

D1057797

Alfred Newman Scoring Stage
Twentieth Century Fox, Los Angeles
Courtesy Milroy and McAleer ©1998

Watkins College

Complete Guide to Film Scoring

*The Art and Business of Writing
Music for Movies and TV*

Richard Davis

berklee
press

Complete Guide to Film Scoring
by Richard Davis

Edited by Jonathan Feist

BERKLEE PRESS
Dave Kusek, Director
Debbie Cavalier, Managing Editor
Ola Frank, Marketing Manager
Jonathan Feist, Senior Writer/Editor
David Franz, Contributing Editor

Cover Design: Moore Moscowitz
Book Design: Dancing Planet MediaWorks™

ISBN 0-634-00636-3

1140 Boylston St.
Boston, MA 02215-3693 USA
(617) 747-2146

Visit Berklee Press Online at:
www.berkleepress.com

DISTRIBUTED BY

HAL•LEONARD®
CORPORATION
7777 W. BLUEMOUND RD. P.O. BOX 13819
MILWAUKEE, WISCONSIN 53213

Visit Hal Leonard Online at:
www.halleonard.com

Copyright © 1999 by Berklee Press
All Rights Reserved

No part of this publication may be reproduced in any form or by any means
without prior written permission of the publisher.

Praise for Richard Davis's
Complete Guide to Film Scoring

"From his technical discussions to his fascinating interviews, Richard's book is one of the best resources on film/television scoring I have ever read. I wish I'd read it twenty years ago. It should be mandatory reading for everyone in the business—newcomers, veterans, students, and movie buffs."
—*Mark Snow, Composer for the* X-Files *and* Millennium

"Richard Davis's book, *Complete Guide to Film Scoring*, is very concise and thorough. It is excellent both as a novice's introduction to the subject and as a reference for professionals."
—*Mark Isham, Academy Award nominated film composer and Grammy winning recording artist for* A River Runs Through It

"This book gets right down to business. Clear, concise, comprehensive, and up-to-date, this is the most well written book on the subject of film scoring. I highly recommend it to music students, lovers of film, or anyone who has an interest in film scoring."
—*Richard Stone, Emmy winning Musical Director of* Animaniacs *and* Pinky and the Brain

TABLE OF CONTENTS

ACKNOWLEDGEMENTS

No book is a solo effort, and there have been many who have given invaluable help to me on this project.

This book would not be the same without the participation of the composers, music editors, and agents who gladly offered their time. And I can't thank Nancy Knutsen of ASCAP and Doreen Ringer-Ross of BMI enough for the help they gave me in setting up many of the interviews.

In transcribing and preparing over 200 pages of interview transcripts, I had the very enthusiastic and gracious help of my student "elves": Haddon S. Kime, Michael Wasserman, Joseph Pondaco, Erica Weiss, Matt Koskenmaki, Sha-Ron Kushner, Daniel Davis, Marijke Van Niekerk, Alvin Abuelouf, Thanh Tran, Nina Edelman, Susan Lim, Jason Getzel, and Michael Albers. Their effort and feedback was wonderful. In Los Angeles, my former student, Alfonso Chavez was a great help in facilitating interviews, giving superior computer/technical advice and feedback on the manuscript. David Franz was the go-to details guy, efficiently helping with many different areas of production.

The Film Scoring Department at Berklee College of Music gave important feedback and guidance: Eric Reasoner, Jack Freeman, Don Wilkins, Michael Rendish, and Jon Klein. Also Richard Grant, creator of the Auricle software, helped steer me in the right direction on several issues.

In securing clearance to use copyrighted materials and photos I had the help of Jonathan Watkins of Fox Music Publishing, Carol Farhat of Fox TV Music, Antonia Coffman of *The Simpsons*, Stacey Robinson at Twentieth Century Fox Productions, and Richard Hassanian of Todd-AO Studios.

Finally, I'd like to thank the staff at Berklee Press. Senior Writer/Editor Jonathan Feist devoted countless hours to meticulously editing and assembling this manuscript. Jonathan, Managing Editor Debbie Cavalier, and Director Dave Kusek all facilitated getting a huge project through the pipeline in a very short amount of time (not to mention gentle encouragement when I felt I'd never make it). And for additional help in proofing the manuscript, the eagle-eyed editor, Larry Davis.

—*Richard Davis*

INTRODUCTION

This book is for anyone interested in writing music for movies or television. It takes the reader step-by-step through the art of film scoring, from the history of the field, through the process of writing the score, and finally to an explanation of the music business as it pertains to film and television composers. As a composer myself, I have worked with some of the top people in the business. In preparing this book, I interviewed over 20 of my colleagues—composers, music editors, music supervisors, and agents—and included their observations and anecdotes.

Successful film scoring is not a matter of just writing good music; it is writing good music that supports a dramatic situation. After teaching film scoring for several years at the Berklee College of Music, I have realized that the most important thing for the beginning composer to learn is how to approach writing this kind of music. This means finding the heart of the film, the soul of the film, and expressing that in music. No one can get inside a composer's head and tell them which notes to write. Every musician brings his own personal experience and musical point of view to a composition. But they can be guided and pointed in a certain direction, either by a teacher, a director, or simply a gut reaction to a particular scene. I have found that the best creative guidance I can give is to help someone find that heart of the picture in order to know what they want to express about it. That expression can then combine with other skills—compositional, technical, creative, business, and communication skills—to make a successful film score and a successful composer.

This is our approach in the Film Scoring Program at Berklee, and there are several dimensions to our program that are reflected in the structure of this book. First, it is invaluable to have an appreciation of the masters of film scoring, past and present. The chapters on the history of the field give an overview, and hopefully will inspire the student of film music to further study.

Second, every composer hoping to work in film scoring must know the process of film making and the evolution of a film score. The chapters on topics such as spotting, syncing, and music editing will give the reader an understanding of this process that many established composers had to learn on the job.

Third, and the most difficult to impart in a book, are the chapters on creating the score. With the help of my composer colleagues, I focus on the important concepts in writing a film score. Again, my aim is to point the reader in the right direction, and hopefully the interested student of film scoring will take the advice of several of the composers in this book, and study, study, study.

The final chapters discuss an issue that is necessary to the livelihood of every professional musician: the music business. Royalties, agents, attorneys, copyrights, and other topics of the film music business are addressed at length. This provides a basic understanding for anyone entering the field.

The book concludes with 19 interviews with some of the top composers and agents in Hollywood. These interviews provide an illuminating glimpse into the careers of those who are successful in this field. Their relationships with directors, stories of how their careers began, the ups and downs along the way, anecdotes about how specific scenes were written, and many other issues are discussed.

How does this music end up on the silver screen? What does it take to be able to compose it? Who chooses the composer? Who chooses what the music should sound like? How long does it take? How do the finances work? This book answers these questions and many others about the art and business of film scoring.

—*R.D., Boston, May 1999*

The History of Film Music

PART I

CHAPTER 1

Early Films and Music: The Silent Movies

Music in film is a vital necessity, a living force.
—Bernard Herrmann[1]

Music and drama. Drama and music. Either way, these two branches of the performing arts have been linked together for thousands of years in many cultures around the world. There is Japanese Kibuki, Indian Bharatnatyam, and the Balinese Monkey Dance. The early Greeks and Romans used choruses and orchestras to accompany their dramatic plays. In Europe, during medieval times there were pagan festivals that used music to accompany stories of gods and heroes, as well as liturgical dramas that portrayed various biblical stories through singing and dramatic action. During the Renaissance, music was used in various scenes in the plays of Shakespeare and others. In the Baroque period of classical music we find early opera and ballet, forms of musical drama that continue today. And finally, in this century we have the huge popularity of Broadway plays and film music.

In all these examples, the music and drama can be separated into independent entities, but their combination as a whole is greater than the sum of their individual parts. Overtures and arias from Mozart's or Verdi's operas are often performed independently and are musically satisfying. Some of these same operas exist as plays or books. But hear the aria as part of the staged opera and the effect is profound in a way that the play or music by itself cannot approach. Music for film is similar. Certainly a film composer can write good music that stands up on its own without the film. John Williams' Suite from *E.T., The Extra-*

Terrestrial is frequently performed in concert to great acclaim. But when heard in conjunction with the visual of the film, it is awesome and the whole film takes on another dimension.

It is often difficult for the modern 1990s audience to appreciate the experience of the film audience of even the 1940s or 1950s, much less the audience of the turn of the 20th century, when the technology of moving pictures was new. But try, for a moment, to put yourself in the shoes of the filmgoer in 1895. The common forms of long-distance communication were letters and the telegraph. The cutting edge of communication technology was the telephone, and only a tiny percentage of city dwellers had one in their homes or had ever used one. Horses and trains were still the primary modes of travel; automobiles were about as common as telephones, and the flight of the first airplane was still 10 years away. Electric lights were only 15 years old and gas lamps were still the prevailing method of artificial light. Einstein had yet to propose his Theory of General Relativity. Stravinsky was only 13 years old and Schoenberg's twelve-tone system of music was more than two decades in the future; music lovers were most familiar with Brahms, Wagner, Mozart, Verdi, Beethoven, and other 18th and 19th century composers.

Imagine now that you enter a small theater, or even a café with curtains closed against the light. A very noisy machine in the middle of the room starts up, and across a screen in the front you see the images of people, animals, and buildings. To you, the almost turn-of-the-century filmgoer, this is like a miracle. And yet at the same time the images seem disembodied, for there is no accompanying sound. The mouths might move, the horse might gallop, the car spews its fumes, but there are no words, there is no clippity-clop, and there is no chugging and banging of the engine. All is left to your imagination, for the only sounds you hear are the loud and noisy rotations of the projector's motor.

However, imagine you are in the same room and there is a pianist or small group of musicians playing while the picture moves on the screen. This adds another dimension to your experience, and even if the music is just background music with no dramatic importance, your previous impression of empty, disembodied images is transformed into a more complete experience. There are still no words, no hooves, no automobile engine noises. But the addition of music somehow makes the images on the screen more complete and less like two-dimensional shadows.

From the very beginning, there were probably musical accompaniments to films, though the first documented incidents were in 1895 and 1896 when the Lumiére family screened some of its early films in Paris and London with musical accompaniment. These were a great success, and soon orchestras were accompanying films in the theaters.

At first, the music that went with these films was taken from anywhere: classical favorites, popular songs, folk songs, or café music. There was little or no attempt to give the music a dramatic importance; it was there to enliven the audience's experience.

As the film industry grew and became more sophisticated, music in the theaters grew as well. Depending on the size and location of the theater, there could be anywhere from one piano or organ to a small orchestra. The player or music director would choose various pieces from the already existing literature and prepare them for performances.

In 1908, again in France, Camille Saint-Saens was commissioned to write what is believed to be the first film score tailored for a specific film, *L'Assassinat du Duc de Guise*. This score was successful, but because of the added expense of commissioning a composer, preparing the music, and hiring the ensemble, the concept of scores specifically composed for a film did not take hold.

However, many people in the industry were becoming aware that there was a need for standardizing music for films, if not specifically composing for them. Music was not yet an integral part of the drama on the screen; it was still simply an adjunct with little or no dramatic significance. And because of the logistical problem of composing for as many different kinds of ensembles as there were theaters, scores were only rarely composed for specific films.

Music Fake Books

What did take hold, however, was a method of standardizing the musical experience of the audience, and a way of codifying what the musicians played. This happened with the publication of several books that provided many different pieces of music with different moods that could cover almost any dramatic situation. These books, of which the most well-known are the *Kinobibliothek* (or *Kinothek*) by Guiseppe Becce, *The Sam Fox Moving Picture Music Volumes* by J.S. Zamecnik, and *Motion Picture Moods,* by Erno Rapée, organized the musical selection to be played by dramatic category. The music director could simply determine the mood or general feeling of a particular scene, look up that idea in the book, and choose one of several possibilities. If, for example, he needed music for a very dramatic scene set in an evil castle, he might have seen these listings under "dramatic expression":

> Night: sinister mood
> Night: threatening mood
> Magic: apparition
> Impending doom
> Pursuit, flight
> Heroic combat
> Disturbed nature: fire, storm

In addition, there were many other moods and also other main categories: Love, Lyrical Expression, Nature, Nation & Society, and Church & State. (See Figs. 1.1, 1.2, 1.3.)

The use of these books could be a cumbersome process, especially if there was more than one musician playing. The music director in each theater would view the film several times with a stopwatch and time each scene. He then would choose the individual pieces to be played, knowing how many seconds each piece should run. Much was dependent on the ability of the conductor or player to anticipate a scene change and to be able to extend or compress a piece. One of the most problematic areas became the transitions between scenes that had different pieces of music. A change in key center, tempo, instru-

MOTION PICTURE MOODS

For

Pianists and Organists

A Rapid-Reference Collection
of Selected Pieces

Arranged By

ERNO RAPÉE

**Adapted to Fifty-Two
Moods and Situations**

G. SCHIRMER, INC., NEW YORK

Fig. 1.1. Rapeé.
Reprinted by Permission of G. Schirmer, Inc.

Table of Contents

[vi]

Fig. 1.2. Rapeé.
Reprinted by Permission of G. Schirmer, Inc.

Fig. 1.3. Rapeé.
Reprinted by Permission of G. Schirmer, Inc.

mentation, or overall mood could be very awkward without a written-out transition. Therefore, many musical directors created such transitions themselves.

The fake books were successful since they created a set musical script that any musician could follow. However, their dramatic effectiveness was limited by the ability of each theater's musical director.

A concurrent system whose inception actually predates the use of fake books was developed by Max Winkler, a clerk at Carl Fischer Music Store and Publishing Company in New York. Winkler realized that if he could see the films before they were released, he could then make up what he called "cue sheets" for each film (similar to modern-day cue sheets or timing notes, but not to be confused with them). These cue sheets would lay out the choice of music and give timings for how long to play each piece, as well as present guidelines for interpretation, in order to stay synchronized. The publisher would preview the film, create a cue sheet, then organize and sell a book for each film that was provided to the musical director of a theater. This benefited the film maker, for it provided a set musical script with rough timings. It also benefited the publishers of the music, for they could make a profit selling or renting the music itself to the theaters. Here is the cue sheet for an imaginary film that Winkler drew up the night he got the idea:

Music Cue Sheet for
The Magic Valley
Selected and compiled by M. Winkler
Cue

1. Opening—play *Minuet No. 2 in G* by Beethoven for ninety seconds until title on screen "Follow me dear."

2. Play—"Dramatic Andante" by Vely for two minutes and ten seconds. Note: play soft during scene where mother enters. Play Cue No. 2 until scene "hero leaving room."

3. Play—"Love Theme" by Lorenze for one minute and twenty seconds. Note: Play soft and slow during conversations until title on screen "There they go."

4. Play—"Stampede" by Simon for fifty-five seconds. Note: Play fast and decrease or increase speed of gallop in accordance with action on the screen.

Copyright © Carl Fischer

This is clearly imprecise, with the effectiveness of the mood and the accuracy of the timings dependent on the pianist or conductor's ability to interpret these instructions. However, the response from producers and from musicians was overwhelmingly positive. It gave them a musical script to follow that ostensibly followed the wishes of the film makers.

In actuality, both the *Kinothek* and Max Winkler methods were destined for short lives. Winkler's system debuted in 1912 and the *Kinothek* was published in 1919. By the late 1920s the revolution of "talkies," the first movies with their characters actually speaking in synchronized sound, were being distributed. It was this technological advancement that began the modern use of music in movies.

CHAPTER 2

The First Talkies:
The Beginning of Synchronized Music

There was a time in this business when they had the eyes of
the whole wide world. But that wasn't good enough for them,
oh no, they had to have the ears of the world, too. So they
opened their big mouths and out came talk. Talk! Talk!
—*Norma Desmond in* Sunset Boulevard

The use of sound in films revolutionized the way movies were made. Not only was there an amazing new dimension to the audience's experience, but the way a story was communicated had to be completely rethought. Previously, when the actors were silent, the film maker often had to convey or amplify an emotion, or make a certain point by use of lighting or camera angles. Because the actors were now talking on-screen, directors felt that they had to highlight them with clear, bright light. In addition, the camera angles stayed more static in order to focus on the speakers and the reactions of those listening. (Actually, this was also a technological requirement because the cameras were still very noisy and had to be enclosed in bulky, soundproof cubicles that were cumbersome to move around the set.) The effect of all of this was that the dialogue became the focal point of the film. The imagination of the audience was curtailed as the actors explained everything happening.

This meant several things for the musicians. First, a composer could provide needed insight into the emotional and psychological drama through the music. Second, he could compose a piece of music that would accompany the film wherever it was shown. Third, the shift towards sound pictures meant that thousands of theater musicians would be put out of work.

One of the interesting side-stories to the development of the film industry is that in the late 1920s there were quite a few studio owners who believed that the talkies were a passing fad. However, there were others who saw the commercial possibilities of movies with synchronized dialogue. During the mid-1920s several different technologies were being experimented with to synchronize picture and dialogue. In 1925 and 1926, several shorts were screened to the public by the Warner Bros. Studio to gauge the audience reaction. These were not dramatic films; they simply showed opera singers, trains, or other mundane events that included synchronized sound.

In 1927, nervous Warner Bros. executives premiered *The Jazz Singer* in New York. Starring vaudeville singer Al Jolson, this film had several musical numbers featuring synchronized sound. With seventy years of hindsight, it is easy for us to think, "What was the big deal? Of course everyone would love this new technology." But the reality of the time is that no one knew how audiences would react after thirty years of silent pictures. Although much of the spoken dialogue was still silent and the story told by narration "cards," when Jolson sang "Blue Skies" and "My Mammy," and the sound appeared to come from his mouth, the audience was thrilled. *The Jazz Singer* did terrific box-office business and became the film that showed the industry the way to go. It opened up a whole new era.

For several reasons, both commercial and technical, many of the first successful talkies were to be musicals. For about three years, until about 1931, a steady stream of musicals was produced. This was probably because of the entertainment value of musicals; not only did the actors speak, they also sang and danced. In addition, there was the logistical advantage of having the musicians on the set and often on camera. However, as with any fad, after several years of a steady diet of musicals, the public's interest in them soon waned. When this happened many studio executives thought there was no longer a need for musicians, and many of the studio orchestras were laid off. A yearlong period of adjustment ensued until the same executives found out how much they really did need the music.

Adding music to films at this time was an expensive, cumbersome, problematic process. In the very early days of talkies, there was no way to record the music separately from the rest of the production. All the musicians had to be present on the set, positioned in such a way as to be heard but not cover up the actors' lines. They could not make a mistake lest a whole take be ruined. This was a nightmare for all involved: musicians, actors, director, and soundmen. Sometimes a short song could take two or three days to record. In addition, there could be no edits afterward or the music would be ruined: the soundtrack would have jumps and blips.

The technology that was to free the music from the confines of the shooting set was the ability to record the music at a separate time, or "re-record" as it was known then. Developed about 1931, this allowed the music to be recorded on its own scoring "stage," so-called to distinguish the music recording building from the "sound stage" or film set building. It allowed the film maker to be able to put the music anywhere he wanted in the film, and it created the process we now call "dubbing," when the music, dialogue and sound effects are mixed together. Dubbing was yet another major technological advance, as it gave the director or producer control not only over where the music and sound effects would go, but also over how loud they would be in relation to the dialogue.

This new technology made the process of including music in films much more flexible and less expensive, and by the early 1930s, directors and producers began to accept that the film's underscore was a critical component. However, many still believed that the source of the music needed to be accounted for visually. Max Steiner, one of the giants of the early days of film scoring, described the situation:

> But they felt it was necessary to explain the music pictorially. For example, if they wanted music for a street scene, an organ grinder was shown. It was easy to use music in a nightclub, ballroom, or theater scene, as there the orchestras played a necessary part in the picture.

Many strange devices were used to introduce the music. For instance, a love scene might take place in the woods and in order to justify the music thought necessary to accompany it, a wandering violinist would be brought in for no reason at all. Or, again, a shepherd would be seen herding his sheep and playing his flute, to the accompaniment of a fifty-piece orchestra.[1]

Such examples show the naiveté of many film makers at that time. Audiences had been accepting music with no need for a visual justification from the beginning of films. However, it was a period when the industry was finding its way and discovering what worked and what did not work in these new sound movies.

To address the perceived necessity that all music be justified visually, two distinct and diametrically opposed solutions of music use came into vogue. One was the use of constant music—a score that started at the opening credits and did not stop until the picture ended. The other was no music at all. Neither of these solutions was ideal, and it took some trial and error on the part of film makers to find one that worked. Ultimately, a system of bringing the music in and out of the picture as the drama required became the standard practice, and still is adhered to today.

It is interesting to note that between these early days of talkies and the contemporary films of today there have been very few successful movies that had absolutely no music. A revealing anecdote is that of *The Lost Weekend*, a 1945 film starring Ray Milland. This intense film about an alcoholic on a weekend bender was originally released without any music at all. When first shown in the theaters, at the most dramatic scenes of Milland's descent into an alcoholic blur, the audience snickered and giggled—exactly the opposite of the film maker's intent. It was quickly pulled from circulation, and almost permanently shelved. However, composer Miklos Rosza was brought in to do a score and the movie was re-released to great acclaim. It went on to win best actor, best picture, and best director, but the score was not acknowledged even though it was the only thing added to the original, failed version.

During the period of film music's infancy between 1927 and 1931, a clear progression can be seen. At first, the most common and obvious use of music in the talkies was as part of a musical with song and dance numbers. Upon the arrival of re-recording, producers went to the extremes and thought they didn't need music at all or had to have it all the time. Experiments were made with various kinds of *source music* (music that comes from a "source" on-screen), as in the Marlene Dietrich film, *The Blue Angel*. Theme songs were used, just as they are today, in order to promote the film and sell records and sheet music. And finally, directors began to play with the idea that music could come in and out of the soundtrack to support various types of scenes. Watching old films, you will notice that the concept of constant music was slow to die and was used in many films. However, the notion that music was a necessary part of film took hold and the underscore as we know it today began to take shape.

CHAPTER 3

The Studio System and The Studio Music Department

Music, one of our greatest art forms,
must be subjugated to the needs of the picture.
That's the nature of movie making.
—Sidney Lumet[1]

Much has been written about the Hollywood "studio system" in effect from the silent film era until the 1960s. Although we are primarily concerned with how this worked in relation to composers and musicians in general, it is worthwhile to briefly describe the overall "studio system."

In the early days of Hollywood, there were several large movie studios that produced the majority of films. These studios grew up during the days of the silent films, and the system of production they established then carried over to the talkies. Warner Bros. Studios, Metro-Goldwyn-Mayer (MGM), Universal Studios, Paramount Studios, RKO, Twentieth Century-Fox, and United Artists were the most productive and longest lasting. As still happens today, many of these entities were constantly shifting in ownership and had varying degrees of profitability. They were also each known for having certain kinds of films. For example, Warner Bros. was known for swashbuckling adventure stories, Universal for steady production of "B" horror and comedy movies, and MGM for grand dramas.

This was the most productive time in the history of the film business in terms of the sheer numbers of films produced. It has been said that in contemporary times Americans go to a movie, in the 1930s Americans went to the movies. Back then, people would frequently spend the afternoon seeing a double feature, whereas today going to the movies is an occasional evening out. In the 1930s approximately 80 million Americans (65% of the population) went to the movies *once a week*. Today, a much smaller percentage (under 10%) of the population goes to theaters regularly.[2]

In the summer of 1998 more people bought more tickets to movies (541.9 million) than any summer in history. However, since the population of the U.S. has grown so substantially since the 1940s, these statistics better reflect the movie-going public when expressed in terms of proportions to the general population.[3]

Because of the volume of films needed to satisfy the appetite of the movie-going public, the studios developed a system that was like an assembly line. It was efficient, streamlined, and somewhat insulated from the possibility of the temperamental manipulations of one creative individual. In other words, it was difficult for one person involved with the production, whether screenwriter, director, composer, editor, or others, to derail, hold up, or change the thrust of a production if they disagreed with the others. A new person would simply be brought in from the ranks of the studio staff, and work would continue. The only person with somewhat absolute power was the production executive, compared to whom even the stars had only limited power. If a particularly temperamental actor attempted to sabotage a production, the producer could control him by threatening not to give him any further projects for the remainder of his contract.

Each studio was a completely self-contained film-making factory where every aspect of the process was owned and controlled by the individual studio. The studio employed full-time contracted staffs of screenwriters, directors, producers, actors, extras, costume designers, hairdressers, carpenters, electricians, musicians, publicity agents, and others, spanning every possible job necessary to the making of a film. They had their own labs to develop the film and had complete post-production facilities for editing and dubbing. In addition, the individual studios also owned chains of theaters that showed only their films. The studio controlled not only the making of the film in every aspect, but also where, when and for how long it would be shown. (This ownership of the theaters was deemed illegal in 1949 and the studios were forced to sell off their theaters. It was only recently that Sony and others have found a way to own chains of movie theaters without violating U.S. antitrust laws.)

When a film started its journey through this studio assembly line, the producer pulled the strings and guided the process as it went through all the different departments. First, a group of writers would be assigned to create, complete, and polish the script. Note the operative word here is "group." Even though one writer would get screen credit, often it was a group effort. One person would write certain scenes, maybe love scenes. Another might write action scenes and yet another polish up the dialogue. There might also be a team of directors, each directing various scenes or different parts of the film. Various film editors would work on the project, as would teams of employees from the music, sound-effects, and costume departments. All of these workers were on staff at the studio. They could not work for any other studio, and they were obligated to follow the directions of the executives and supervisors of their departments.

The actors were also under contract to the studio, and especially at the beginning of their careers, had to do what they were told. Many stars were "groomed" by the studio; at a young age they were "discovered" and the studio would plan their careers and create roles specifically for them.

The producer and other studio executives were often involved in the creative process in a hands-on way. They would make creative decisions that might be in accord with the desire of the director(s), or they might be at odds. The producer's decision was the final word. The producer wielded much more power over creative decisions in those days of the studio system than they do today. In contemporary times, the director is responsible for delivering a final version of the film that is approved by the producers and/or studio. During the making of the film, the modern director has much more control over creative decisions than the director of the 1930s and '40s did, although his final cut of the film is still subject to approval.

Even though it seems impersonal, many great films were made by this process under the studio system. There were different styles to adhere to in film making: romances, melodramas, epic adventures, etc., and the different creative people learned to adapt to a certain style in order to maintain continuity throughout the film. The music, as well, was produced on an assembly-line basis, and many composers and orchestrators had to learn to adapt to the desired style. This is one of the reasons that so many clichés sprung up in the Hollywood films and music of the 1930s; the different departments had to use them to stay within the boundaries of the required style. For example, they produced soaring violins for the appropriate love scenes, and growling low brass or strings for the bad guys.

Another reason that so many clichés were in use had to do with the sheer volume of films produced—there was hardly time to work out fresh, original, creative ideas within the given time constraints. Finally, there was a prevailing attitude amongst producers that existed then as it does today, which is that "if it works, do it again." In other words, there was a general reluctance to try new things, and a conservative desire to use what was tried and proven both in film making and in music.

The Studio Music Department

Starting in the late 1920s, the studios had music departments that were self-contained so that every stage of the music could be done in-house. They had staffs of composers, orchestrators, songwriters, rehearsal pianists, orchestra musicians, conductors, choreographers, music copyists, proofreaders, music editors (then called "music cutters"), and music executives to oversee the process. These people usually worked under one roof in a music building that contained a music library and a recording studio.

The head of the music department was often a composer or conductor, like Alfred Newman, who headed the music department at Twentieth Century-Fox for many years during the forties and fifties. He also had to be an executive who interacted with the studio executives, producers, directors, accounting departments, recording specialists, costume directors when musicians were on-screen, and actors when they were singing or playing. He had to have a firm grasp of budgets and time schedules, and be an accurate evaluator of the skills, strengths, and weaknesses of the composers and performing musicians in his department.

The music department head would be aware of the production schedule of a film, and would know when it was about to be ready for music. If the film was a top feature, then he might assign one well-known composer to score the project. However, many of the second level, B-films, would be assigned a team of composers. These composers would screen the film with others on the music production staff. Perhaps the director would be there, perhaps not.

After the composers began writing, their sketches would go down the line to the orchestrators, copyists, proofreaders, and finally to the orchestra. If there were songs or dance numbers, there were rehearsal pianists on staff to take care of them. Everyone had his own job; it was all compartmentalized. In actuality, this is very similar in process to modern film-score production, with two major differences. Today there is only one composer on a project, and today everything is contracted outside of the studio. All the above roles and jobs still exist, but it is not in one place under one roof, and it is not controlled by the studio to the same degree of detail.

The deadlines and the pace of this process in the 1930s was frighteningly rapid, even by today's standards. Composer David Raksin began his career as a film composer working with Charlie Chaplin in 1935, and he describes this process:

> On the day when the new film was turned over to the Department for scoring, the staff gathered in our projection room. Present would be [the head of the music department], his assistant ... the composers ... two or three orchestrators, the head of Music Cutting and a couple of his assistants.
>
> By lunch we had "broken the film down" into sequences adjudged to call for music, determined what kinds of thematic material would be required and who would write it. After lunch, while the music cutters prepared the timing sheets that would enable us to

synchronize our music with the film, [the other composers] and I went off to our studios to compose whatever specific material had been assigned to us. We would shortly meet again, with several versions of each theme, to decide which ones in each category would best serve our purposes, which were usually quite clear— though never defined; these themes were Photostatted and each of us got a set of all the material for that film. By that time the timing sheets were ready, so we divided the work into three parts, and each man headed for home to compose his third....

Sometimes there was time to orchestrate one's own sequences, but usually the rush was so great that by the next morning we were already feeding sketches to the orchestrators, and by noon they were delivering pages of score to the copyists. On the morning of the fourth day the recording would begin; the Studio had a fine orchestra under contract, and available on very short notice....

On the fifth day a couple of days of re-recording (dubbing) would commence. After that, there might be a brief respite, and then the process started again ... It was wild, and we all enjoyed it.[4]

Five days to compose, record and dub a film is unbelievably quick. Today, a composer usually takes two to eight weeks to write the music and three to ten days to record it. Once his work is complete, three to four weeks are spent dubbing his music and the other sounds into the film, and soon after that, it is ready to hit the theaters. This means that the film will be released between five and thirteen weeks after the composer first receives the locked picture (see chapter 8).

David Raksin relates another anecdote about studio composing schedules:

We did tremendous amounts of music. For instance, when I composed the score for Forever Amber, *that had about 110 minutes of music—about 100 of those I composed myself. The rest was music of the story's time. Originally I had twelve weeks to do that, but they were messing around with the movie, and by the time they got finished doing that I had eight and a half weeks to do that tremendous amount of music. And I did it!*

The budget and importance of the project would determine quality of the music and the amount of time given to write it. B films were rushed through. If the film had major stars and was high profile, as in *Forever Amber*, there would be one "name" composer who would have more time to write the score. Still, the process that ensued once the score was written remained the same; the music went through the pipeline from composer to orchestrator to music preparation to the studio orchestra.

CHAPTER 4

Musical Styles~1930 to 1950: The Golden Age of Hollywood

Study those who have preceded us: Korngold, Waxman,
Raksin, Steiner. Learn what they did. Learn why. Learn how.
Draw upon their genius, and your own understanding
of the marriage of music and film will deepen.
—David Spear

Between 1930 and 1950, an average of 500 films per year were produced. At this time Americans were attending movies more frequently than at any other time in history. For this reason, this time period is known as the "Golden Age of Hollywood." It was an exciting time to be in the movie business; opportunities were many, and technology and the industry itself were growing to maturity from the infancy of silent pictures, constantly making strides and innovations, both technically and creatively. Film music also grew up during this time, finding its way to a language and a technique that is the foundation for what is heard even today.

The musical film-scoring vocabulary of the 1930s and '40s is still familiar to modern audiences. The release of many of these older films on video and their airing on television has enabled even those of us born after this "golden age" of movies to recognize the lush, orchestral sound of the early film scores. Though this sound can seem "corny" to 1990s ears, if we understand where these composers and film makers were coming from, then we can appreciate their artistic accomplishments.

During the silent film era, the music that was most familiar to audiences and thus was commonly used in films was that of the 18th and 19th century European classical composers, popular songs by composers such as Irving Berlin and George Gershwin, as well as some well-known folk songs. When sound became a part of films in the late 1920s, there arose a great need for accomplished composers who could write scores that would appeal to the contemporary audience, and be dramatically synchronized to enhance the action on-screen. At this time there was an influx of European born composers who came to Hollywood, many of whom were Jewish and were fleeing political upheaval and persecution in Austria, Germany, and Eastern Europe. They had conservatory training from their native lands in composition, conducting, and performance, and therefore were well versed in classical music styles—especially those of the 18th and 19th centuries. They had an in-depth knowledge of the operas of Verdi, Wagner, Strauss, and Puccini, and were intimately familiar with the concert and chamber works of Beethoven, Mozart, Brahms, Schubert, Berlioz, and many others.

Of these émigré composers, several were quick to set a high standard for the Hollywood music community. These included Max Steiner, Erich Korngold, Branislau Kaper, Miklos Rosza, and Franz Waxman. A brief look at the musical achievements of two of these men, both before and during their Hollywood careers, will illustrate how the "sound" of the films during the Golden Age of Hollywood came to be.

Max Steiner (1888 to 1971) wrote over 300 film scores including *King Kong, Gone With the Wind, The Treasure of the Sierra Madre,* and *The Charge of the Light Brigade.* An Austrian immigrant who had written his first operetta at the age of fourteen, Steiner arrived in Hollywood in 1929. He was there as film music grew from infancy into a sophisticated art, and was one of the men that molded its growth. He became known for writing emotional, lyrical themes (as in *Gone With the Wind*), but was versatile and could provide any mood required. He used leitmotifs (themes, specific instruments, or both for a certain character or idea in the story) in many films, an idea borrowed from opera composers, especially Wagner. Most importantly, he was originally a composer of operettas, and so was well versed in the marriage of music and drama. It was this dramatic experience that gave him the sensitivity required to write effective film scores. And it was his training and foundation in 19th century composition that provided the necessary musical vocabulary.

Erich Korngold was also an Austrian refugee who was trained in the Old World conservatory system. But where Steiner's background was in operetta, Korngold's was in grand opera. Korngold was a child prodigy in his hometown of Vienna, and by the time he was fourteen, his praises had been sung by Mahler, Puccini, and Richard Strauss. By the age of nineteen, he had written three operas and was considered to be one of the shining lights of Europe. He was well known, well liked, and well off financially by the time he was in his early twenties. Mostly his career consisted of conducting in various European cities while he continued to compose opera and concert pieces.

In 1934, Korngold was invited to come to Hollywood to arrange Mendelssohn's famous incidental music to *A Midsummer Night's Dream*. Although the producer of the project had probably never heard of Korngold, at that time Hollywood producers scored status points by successfully raiding the artistic world of Europe. So Korngold journeyed to California with his wife and children, and spent several months adapting Mendelssohn's music.

This trip proved successful, and Korngold was intrigued by the possibilities of film music. He was to return to America twice in the next few years, finally coming for good when he realized that the political climate in his native Austria was becoming dangerous for a Jew.

Korngold only scored eighteen films in twelve years, and he worked under the best conditions possible. He had the right to turn down any project, and was given as much time as he needed to write the music. As with Steiner, it was his early training in opera that gave him the ability to come up with appropriate musical solutions for Hollywood films. In addition, the musical vocabulary of his German opera writing and that required by Hollywood films was the same.

There were many other fine composers working in Hollywood during this time, but these two are representative of the ongoing style and trend. The strongest musical influences for them were 19th century late Romantics: Wagner, Brahms, Mahler, Verdi, Puccini, and Strauss. The musical vocabulary of these composers became the most common and fundamental language of the music in early Hollywood films.

Much has been said and written about why this happened. A question often posed is: Why did it take so many years for the more contemporary and modern sounds of Stravinsky, Bartók, Ravel, and Schoenberg to find their way into the dramatic expression of popular films? The answer is twofold. First, the late Romantic period of classical music was the most familiar to the film-going audience. In 1935, they were only 50 years removed from Brahms' *Third Symphony* and many other contemporaneous Romantic works including Wagner's *Parsifal*, Tchaikowski's *Sixth Symphony*, and Strauss's *Till Eulenspiegel*. The melodic thrust, the harmonic structure, and the overall thematic development were musical events that the average film audience could easily grasp. No matter what the dramatic need of a scene, whether it be lyrical or turbulent, it could be expressed musically in a way that was easily understood. This was an important requirement of popular films. They were not aimed at an intellectual or academic audience. They were not even aimed at the most educated audience. They were aimed at the great middle. And although many Hollywood films made philosophical, moral or psychological points in their stories, they were not to be confused with the more "arty" movies of film makers such as Fassbinder.

The background of men like Steiner, Korngold and Waxman made them perfectly suited to accomplish the musical need of the time. Essentially 19th century composers writing in a late 19th century and early 20th century style, they were able to bring quality music to films. They had an excellent grasp of harmony, melodic development, and other compositional techniques such as passacaglia and leitmotif. They understood form and thematic development so that they could spin out a melody when necessary, or fragment it and tease the audience. And perhaps most importantly, they had thorough knowledge of the music dramas, the operas of the 18th and 19th century.

When movies were silent, the composer or player was simply an adjunct to a moving picture. He could amplify an emotion, telegraphing danger or sweetening a love scene. But with sound films where the actors were talking, then the role of the music changed significantly. The music had to interact with the dialogue of the actors and find a way to create the right mood, and at the same time stay out of the way of the voices. It needed to express and mirror the emotion of the actors as well as sometimes bring these emotions to a ringing conclusion. The music needed to develop as the story developed and move the plot along. The experience of the European composers in writing opera made them ideally suited to this task.

One listen to (or attendance at) a Wagner, Verdi, or Puccini opera would illuminate this point dramatically. The use of music from start to finish, the thinning out of the orchestra during recitative (dialogue), the grand crescendos and emotional outbursts at high points of the drama, and the use of leitmotif in opera are no different in concept from the marriage of music and film during the early days of Hollywood.

In opera, sometimes the same musical idea or phrase might keep returning to reinforce the audience's understanding and response to an idea or emotion in the film. Max Steiner's score to *Gone With the Wind* did just this. There were seven different motives or themes representing different characters or situations, and they return periodically throughout the film. Korngold's score to *The Adventures of Robin Hood* (1938) had a theme for the Merry Band, a theme for Marion, one for Robin Hood, and yet another for the Sheriff of Nottingham. (Note that this technique is still used in modern times, but with a more contemporary music language. John Williams' score to *E.T. The Extra-Terrestrial,* and Alan Silvestri's score to *Forrest Gump* are but two examples.)

In addition to thematic organization, as more and more scores were recorded over the years, certain conventions came to be used. This has always been the case and still is today, for it is really prevailing conventions that make up a given style. In the 1930s those conventions were numerous, and sometimes born out of necessity. For though all the composers, even those working on "B" films, were highly skilled, the time crunch they worked under was often outrageously short.

We chuckle today at some of these 1930s conventions, for they seem so dated. But every generation of films has had its musical style. There were love themes with soaring violins often in octaves, brass in fourths and fifths whenever there were Romans, Greeks, or medieval kings, and string sections seemingly ubiquitous throughout a film, providing a warm, rich, and lush blanket upon which both dialogue and acted-out emotions could sit. But in the eyes and ears of the 1930s audience, these conventions were as effective as the mournful quasi-Irish sounds in the score of *Titanic* today.

New Ideas in Music

The 19th century romantic style of Korngold and Steiner was used in films through the 1950s. But during the 1940s, new ideas were introduced slowly. Composers like David Raksin and Bernard Herrmann were expanding the range of possibilities by introducing elements of jazz and contemporary 20th century music. Scores like *Laura* (1944) and *Citizen Kane* (1941) did much to open up the minds and ears of the movie industry to new sounds. For example, Raksin wrote a 12-tone score for *The Man With a Cloak* (1949).

David Raksin:

> Man With a Cloak *had a 12-tone row, the first five notes of which spelled E-D-G-A-R. The R became D♭ so it was still Re. I saw Johnny Green (head of music at MGM) the next day and he said, "Gee that's a remarkable score, what's that crazy god-damned tune you've got there?" And I said, "Johnny, it's a 12-tone row." He was astonished because it sounded so much like a theme and wanted to know why I used a row. I told him it was because in this picture you don't find out until the last 45 seconds or so that the hero, the man in the cloak, is really Edgar Allan Poe.*

> *I had a great time doing what I was doing. Sometimes I was motivated by jazz, sometimes by contemporary music. You would have to be crazy not to feel the enormous effect of the music of Stravinsky. For me it was Stravinsky and Berg. So I just wrote the way I thought I should be writing.*

Raksin also points out that, as film music drew its influences from what musical styles were popular, it also influenced those styles. Contemporary music, or dissonant music that was not accepted by audiences for the concert stage, would be accepted in the appropriate scene of a film. Raksin again:

> *If you have a really violent sequence and you write something that is really dissonant, they wouldn't like to hear that as a [concert] piece of music. But they will accept it if it is the right music for a film sequence.*

New ideas, such as twelve-tone rows and other modern compositional techniques, were slow to gain popularity in film scores. However, producers, directors, and the composers themselves gradually saw the dramatic value of these methods, and musical styles in films began to change.

CHAPTER 5

Musical Styles 1950 to 1975

Putting music in a film is not an arbitrary thing.
There's a form and a shape, an overall
pattern of where you put music in.
—Jerry Goldsmith[1]

In any discussion of artistic and historical styles and eras, it seems to be human nature to want to delineate and mark a specific date, year, or piece that ushers in the new era. But it is never really so cut and dry. Monteverdi did not wake up on the morning of January 1, 1600 and proclaim, "Ah-ha, let us begin the Baroque period of music!" Beethoven knew he was breaking away from the old classical style of Mozart and Haydn, but he was not consciously creating a new musical period called "Romanticism." Most new trends are the result of evolution, drawing upon the old and breaking ground for the new. Film scoring styles are no different. The Romantic style of Steiner, et al, remained prominent for about twenty years, from 1930 to 1950. But there were signs of experimentation, and certain scores written during that time seem to point to the future use of more dissonance, atonality, and eventually popular, jazz, and rock vocabulary in scores.

Remember that by the late 1930s the art of synchronizing music with film was quite new—only ten years old. Although composers, directors and producers were still heavily reliant on conventions that were tried and proven, there was always the occasional innovation that stood aside from the crowd. In 1941, in the midst of the Romantic style of Korngold and Steiner, a film was released that was to break the mold of the time, both visually and aurally. This was *Citizen Kane*, a film by Orson Welles with a score by Bernard Herrmann. Many of the more modern compositional techniques used by Herrmann in this film were not in common use until the 1950s—he was about ten years ahead of the pack. What *Citizen Kane* pointed to was the eventual use of contemporary sounds and textures influenced by Bartók, Stravinsky, Schoenberg, and other 20th century composers. In addition, it presaged the rise of American-born composers in the film industry.

By the early 1950s, there were many conservatory-trained American musicians working for the studios as composers, orchestrators, pianists, songwriters, and arrangers. This included Bernard Herrmann, David Raksin, Alex North, George Antheil, Leonard Rosenman, Elmer Bernstein, André Previn, and Jerry Goldsmith. With a firm grounding in traditional harmony, theory, and counterpoint these men had not only studied the new music of Bartók, Schoenberg and Stravinsky— many of them also had a thorough knowledge of jazz styles.

Although Steiner, Korngold, Waxman, and others of the previous generation were often "genius" composers, they remained, for better or worse, heavily rooted in 19th century music and somewhat uninterested or even opposed to newer musical styles. When asked to comment about contemporary music, Max Steiner said: "I have no criticism. I can't criticize what I don't understand."[2] This comment really points up the difference between the old and new generations of film composers.

One composer working occasionally in films who was a great influence—not only on film music, but on all of classical composition—was Aaron Copland. By the time he scored his first film, *The Heiress*, in 1949, he was a world-renowned composer of ballet, symphonic, and chamber music. He only scored a few other films after that, including *The Red Pony* and *Of Mice and of Men*, but Copland left a large musical impression on all who followed. In fact, it was his ability to convey drama in the music to the ballets *Rodeo* and *Appalachian Spring* that brought him to the attention of Hollywood producers. He brought a new and fresh sensibility in his use of instrumentation and harmony. The instrumental textures in Copland's film scores are softer than the big Romantic scores of the time. He used smaller ensembles and avoided the big, overblown orchestral tuttis found in many films. His use of pandiatonic harmonies, polytonality, and controlled dissonance was imitated by many composers.

Aside from musical development and evolution in films, there were several other factors both in the kinds of films released and in American culture itself that must be taken into account when considering the sound of movie music in the 1950s. Perhaps the most important of these is the arrival of the invention of television. There was also the popularity of "rebel" films—films dealing with youth, rebellion and the darker issues of life including alcoholism and drug addiction. The McCarthy committee of the United States Congress, which instigated and led a witch hunt for Communists in many industries, but especially the entertainment industry, had an impact not only on who worked and who didn't, but also on the content of the films themselves. The rise of jazz—big-band swing and bebop—created a new musical culture, especially amongst the nation's youth. Add to all of these events and trends the birth of rock-and-roll music in the mid-fifties, and the need for new styles in film scoring can be clearly seen.

The Arrival of Television

Beginning in the late 1940s television was readily available to the general public. As the cost of TV sets became more accessible, and as more programming was aired by the networks, more and more people made TV a regular part of their lives. At first, the Hollywood studios looked down on this technology as someone might look askance at an unwanted relative who shows up uninvited for dinner. They refused to release their catalogue of movies to television stations, and did not produce shows for TV. In many cases, the studios hoped and believed television was going to be a passing fad. As we know today, they were quickly proven wrong.

In retrospect, it is not so difficult to see why many Hollywood people had a hard time accepting television. This new form of entertainment arrived only twenty years after the arrival of talkies. The studio system was powerful, smoothly oiled, and very profitable, and many people were very comfortable with it. The "Golden Age" of films was generating millions and millions of dollars in profits from the millions of people that attended movies on a regular basis.

In 1946, an estimated revenue of 1.7 billion dollars was generated by theatrical movies. By 1962, this figure was down to 900 million dollars, just over half the 1946 amount. This was the effect that TV had on the movie business. It threw studios, executives, actors, and all the creative people into turmoil as a new playing field and a new ball game were created.

The period from 1955 to 1970 also saw the demise of the old studio system. Two factors were most important in contributing to this: the advent of television, and a court decision citing antitrust laws that required the studios to break up their chains of self-owned theaters. This was a true "double-whammy." First of all, the popularity of TV meant that many people stayed home and stopped attending movies in the theaters, causing a severe drop in revenues. Secondly, with the loss of the studio-owned theater chains, they lost the automatic distribution of a studio-produced film. Previously, a studio could make a film, and no matter how good or bad it was, release it to as many theaters as they wanted, for as long as they wanted to keep it in circulation. Under the new system, if a film was not accepted publicly, the independent theater owner could withdraw it. In addition, because the audience now had the option of staying home and watching TV, if the film wasn't of fairly high quality, or if it didn't strike a chord in the populace, it would fail in the theaters.

With a real pinch in the flow of cash, the studios could not afford to keep thousands of people under contract. So they had to let go of many employees: actors, directors, musicians, and even producers. In the space of a few short years, the dynamic of producing a film completely changed. Producers became independent, using studios to provide financing, a place to shoot, and a distribution network. No longer could the studio control everything from start to finish, though they could approve or disapprove the final product. But the process itself became removed from studio control. Those involved in the production could move from studio to studio as the projects required. This became the norm for all involved in film production, including the composers.

After a few years of refusing to show films originally released in the theaters on television, the studios finally relented in an attempt to gain at least some profit from the new technology. This gave rise to the TV shows that featured movies from the studio's catalogue, albeit frequently edited for length and content, and often interrupted for commercials. This marked the defeat of the anti-TV forces in Hollywood, and was the first step toward fully mobilizing the extensive studio machinery to include the production of television shows. It was only a short time before the studios were actively involved in producing sit-coms, dramas, and TV movies.

The New Music and the Composers Writing It

There were many composers and many films that are excellent examples of the different kinds of scores written in the 1950s and 1960s. Several are worth mentioning because they broke new ground, or in some other way stand out from the rest.

One of the young composers making a mark on Hollywood was Alex North. Brought from New York to Hollywood by director Elia Kazan, his score to *A Streetcar Named Desire* (1951) was a landmark musical event. For the first time, a raw, edgy, and modern sounding score with many jazz elements was accompanying a popular film. It was not only the use of jazz but also the use of dissonance (influenced by modern classical composers) that gave this score a unique flavor. This opened the floodgates for other composers to incorporate jazz into their scores and a whole new musical style began.

In 1953, Kazan again gave an opportunity to a young composer. Juilliard-trained composer Leonard Rosenman wrote a score to *East of Eden*, starring James Dean. Another dissonant, edgy score accompanying a successful film with a popular star did much for establishing that dissonance as an acceptable sound both in the ears of the audience and the minds and pocketbooks of the producers.

In addition to the darker kinds of films that were being produced, there was also a great deal of activity in producing big epics, often based on biblical stories. These films, like *Ben-Hur, The Ten Commandments, Quo Vadis, El Cid,* and many others, required a more conservative score harkening back to the Romantic approach.

Some composers, such as Elmer Bernstein, had the facility to write a contemporary, edgy score like *The Man with the Golden Arm* and then switch gears and write a Romantic score to an epic or adventure film. Here is Elmer Bernstein speaking about creating the score to *The Ten Commandments* (1955) according to the musical tastes of director Cecil B. DeMille:

> *DeMille was a great Wagner lover. His concept of film scoring was utterly simple and very Wagnerian. Every character had to have a theme or motif. In addition to the characters having themes and leitmotifs, certain philosophical concepts had to have motifs too. God, good, and evil each had to have a theme. The idea was that whenever a particular character was on the screen, his theme had to be present as well. It was all very Wagnerian.*

Because of the leitmotif nature of the score and DeMille's desires, this score was more Romantic than modern in its musical language. That is what was necessary, and yet it didn't prevent Bernstein from being able to create a jazz score to *The Man With the Golden Arm* in the same year.

Another composer to take on scoring several epic films was Miklos Rozsa. A Hungarian-born composer with a doctorate in music, Rozsa had a passion for musicology. For films involving historical subjects, he did extensive research and tried to create a musical sound that was palatable to the average audience, yet based on real historical musical premises, motives, and instruments. His scores to *Ben-Hur, El Cid, Quo Vadis,* and others are large, grand and well thought out. They established a standard to which many composers writing these kinds of scores had to bear up.

Theme Songs and Rock 'n Roll

In every period of movies there has been the issue of the theme song, pop song, or end-title song. From the early days of sound films, producers realized the financial benefits of having a hit song. Not only could they entice more people into the theater to see the film, but they could sell more records (CDs in modern times) and sheet music. And because they owned the copyright to the song, they could collect on performance royalties if the song became a radio hit. This "theme song" craze has never really been a craze; it has always been present, only sometimes the frenzy has been slightly greater than others. Every era has had its hit songs, from the '30s and '40s onward to today and the success of "My Heart Will Go On" from *Titanic*.

A significant wave of theme songs began in the 1950s with the huge popularity of the song, "Do Not Forsake Me, Oh My Darlin'," written by Dimitri Tiomkin and Ned Washington for the movie *High Noon*. However, the popularity of this song doesn't come close to the ongoing success of Henry Mancini's 1961 hit, "Moon River," from the film *A Breakfast at Tiffany's*, starring Audrey Hepburn.

Mancini was another Juilliard-trained composer with a strong jazz background. He had his first major success with the theme for the 1958 TV show, *Peter Gunn*. Then there came "Moon River" followed the next year by "The Days of Wine and Roses" for the film of the same name. He went on to score dozens of films of every dramatic style, but remains best known to the general public for "Moon River," "The Days of Wine and Roses," and the scores to the Peter Sellers comedy series, *The Pink Panther*.

By this time, the early 1960s, producers could not get enough of the theme song. The producer of the film *Dr. Zhivago* was so enthralled with Maurice Jarre's melody to "Lara's Theme" that he basically discarded much of the original score and substituted tracks of the song melody. Later in the 1960s we get "Raindrops Keep Fallin' On My Head" in *Butch Cassidy and the Sundance Kid*, and "Mrs. Robinson" in *The Graduate*.

What these songs did was pave the way for a different use of songs in film. Instead of having the song be sung by a character on screen, or be part of the credits, all of a sudden a pop song, which is seemingly disembodied from the film, became an integral part of the soundtrack. The style evolved where a song was just "dropped in" to the movie soundtrack. Maybe the lyrics were applicable, maybe not. Maybe there was a dramatic reason to have a song, maybe not. For some producers, the only reason to have a song in the film was to hope it became a hit, generated lots of royalties, and caused people to go see the film. And as the popularity of theme songs grew, at least amongst Hollywood producers, more and more films came to rely on songs rather than specifically composed instrumental underscores.

Another factor contributing to this was the rock 'n roll soundtrack. Beginning with the beach movies of the early 1960s, given a mighty push forward by the Beatles films, *A Hard Days Night* and *Help*, and coming to full fruition with the cult classic, *Easy Rider*, films consisting completely of rock songs as underscore became vogue. As the dark, edgy films of the '50s appealed to that audience, these rock 'n roll films of the 1960s were aimed at the ever-expanding audience embracing the values of the "Woodstock generation." They were pertinent and popular. And truly, the use of songs was completely appropriate. How else to express the tone of those times but through the music of popular songs? The Grateful Dead. Simon and Garfunkel. Bob Dylan. Buffalo Springfield. Steppenwolf and The Flying Burrito Brothers were perfect for *Easy Rider*. This was absolutely the right music in the right place for certain films.

The problem that arises when this kind of trend hits is that producers and directors jump on the bandwagon rather blindly. When something new works in one movie, there are always several people doing imitations within a short period of time. So instead of choosing a style of music that serves the dramatic intent of the picture, they choose music that they believe is popular or will sell a lot of records. This was a problem in the 1960s, and it is still a problem today.

This is not to say that instrumental underscore in the 1960s became a lost art. Although some prevailing trends favored rock songs, and even jazzy underscores (*The Pink Panther*, some of the James Bond movies), there were many excellent orchestral-type scores. Elmer Bernstein's score for *To Kill a Mockingbird* is a beautiful example of the marriage of compositional structure and dramatic intent. Many other composers of note were active in keeping alive the orchestral vocabulary, including Jerry Goldsmith, Leonard Rosenman, John Barry, Georges Delerue, Maurice Jarre, and John Williams. The trends became parallel. One kind of movie still used traditional orchestral scores, another used pop and rock songs, another kind used jazz-influenced scores, and yet another used more dissonant and avant-garde twentieth century compositional techniques. The possibilities were expanding even as they were heavily weighted towards songs and jazz music during the 1960s.

CHAPTER 6

1975 to Today

I think music is one of the most effective ways of preparing an audience and reinforcing points that you wish to impose on it. The correct use of music, and this includes the non-use of music, is one of the greatest weapons that the film maker has at his disposal.
—Stanley Kubrick

During the 1960s and into the 1970s, as films incorporated scores of many different styles, audiences became accustomed to the pop/rock sound and modern dissonance instead of 19th-century-influenced orchestral underscore. This paved the way in the subconscious awareness of the public to accept what was coming down the road in the 1980s and '90s: the pop flavored orchestral score. But in the '60s and '70s, perhaps the biggest influence on what producers put in the theaters was television.

Many TV themes and underscores were heavily jazz and rock flavored. In an attempt to modernize the shows and make them different from "stuffy" film scores, the producers incorporated contemporary popular music. Mancini's *Peter Gunn*, Lalo Schifrin's *Mission Impossible*, Neil Hefti's *Batman*, and many others reflected this use of jazz and rock. In addition, twelve-tone and other methods of atonal composition began to be heavily used by television composers. In television, because the schedules and demands of a weekly series meant the composer had to work quickly and efficiently, twelve-tone became a valuable tool for writing tense or suspenseful scenes. Once again, in yet another way, audiences became accustomed to a new musical vocabulary. In the space of just fifteen or twenty years, from about 1950 onward, a whole new world of musical sounds became possible, and many composers took advantage of this.

One score that is representative of the new kinds of textures used by composers in the early 1970s was Jerry Goldsmith's *Chinatown*, starring Jack Nicholson. In this score, Goldsmith used four pianos, two harps, one trumpet, and strings. The pianos were often "prepared," a technique where various objects are put on the strings to change the sound; the piano is intentionally detuned, or the player actually plays the strings inside the piano rather than the keys. This created a uniquely dark and mysterious texture that dovetails beautifully with the rhythm of the film, the way the film is lit, and Jack Nicholson's acting.

In his score to *Patton*, Goldsmith used another unusual technique, that of "sweetening," or adding an instrument after the main music tracks have been recorded. In this case he took a short motif on trumpet and recorded it several different ways with a lot of echo. This little idea was then dropped in wherever needed regardless of the harmonic and metrical consequences. It created a disjointed feeling, reflecting the odd and sometimes otherworldly aspect of the character of General George Patton.

These interesting and unusual devices were becoming more common in the early 1970s. As 19th century harmony, contemporary 20th century techniques, jazz, and rock collided together in the entertainment industry, a myriad of possibilities opened up. Audiences gradually became used to hearing strange dissonances, and even came to associate certain impending events with specific musical sounds. Add to this mix the new technology of multitrack recording (early 1960s), and the possibilities expand even more. The film composer's palette was larger and more varied than ever, but during the 1960s through the early 1970s, orchestral scores, though still used, had fallen somewhat out of favor. It was a succession of two scores—one melodramatic and suspenseful, the other big, dramatic and traditionally Romantic in style, that were to create a resurgence in orchestral scores.

Orchestral Scores Return to Stay

The year 1974 saw the release of the Stephen Spielberg film *Jaws*, which was to become one of the classics of suspense and drama. Spielberg and composer John Williams chose to use a more traditional orchestral sound for *Jaws*, and the success of this decision and the resulting score has often been credited with beginning a resurgence of the use of traditional orchestral sounds and a Romantic, or perhaps neo-Romantic musical vocabulary. However, even though *Jaws* was a milestone in the return of the use of a traditional orchestra, there was yet another John Williams score that made movie music come alive in the ears (and the eyes!) of the audience.

In early 1976, the first trailers (previews attached to other films) for the motion picture *Star Wars* appeared in American theaters. Believe it or not, those audiences laughed and jeered at the trailers, causing great consternation for George Lucas and the studio. However, when the film was released it became one of the all-time most popular films, making huge profits not only from ticket sales, but from ancillary merchandising as well. And many give the exciting score by John Williams a fair share of the credit for the film's success. From the moment the opening scroll gave the story background, and the bold *Star Wars* theme was heard, the audience knew that something special was about to happen.

According to Williams, when he first viewed the work-print, it had a temporary music track cut from the 1916 Gustav Holst piece, *The Planets*. He originally was asked to edit this well-known classical score, re-record it, and fit it to *Star Wars*. However, he convinced the producer and director that he could do something original in that style, and make it fit even better. The result is one we all know today: the wonderful themes for the Rebellion, the dark and ominous Darth Vader theme, Princess Lea's theme, and other fine musical moments are familiar to musicians and non-musicians alike. Using a large symphony orchestra and recording in London with the London Philharmonic, Williams brought back the symphonic score to the ears and eyes of filmgoers.

This was not exactly a return to the Romantic style of Korngold and Steiner. The score to *Star Wars* has many elements of Romantic musical language: lyrical themes, exciting brass tuttis, and delicate woodwind writing, but this new kind of orchestral score was not afraid to incorporate contemporary compositional techniques where necessary. John Williams was schooled at Juilliard and UCLA, and has a thorough knowledge of many different styles of composition, including jazz, 12-tone and atonal techniques. So the score to *Star Wars*, and many scores of Williams and others that followed this lead, fused elements of tonal 19th century writing with whatever textures or effects they wanted to use from the 20th century: Impressionism, jazz, rock, pandiatonicism, 12-tone, even aleatoric, or "chance" music.

None of this was new in film scoring; examples of all these techniques abound through the 1950s, 1960s, and 1970s. But something happened when *Stars Wars* was released that caused a shift in the way orchestras were perceived, in the acceptance by the audience of the music as a dramatic effect, and in the popularity of this music. It was one more milestone in the constantly developing art of film scoring.

In 1982, another Spielberg directed film with a John Williams score took the film-going world by storm. This was *E.T., The Extra-Terrestrial*, a magical film with an enchanting score that was loved by adults and children alike. Indeed, Spielberg has said, "John Williams *is* E.T.," emphasizing how important the music was to the emotional impact of that film. Again, as in *Star Wars*, Williams combined a lyrical, tonal style with elements of 20th century styles. (For examples of this modern influence, check out the scenes where E.T. drinks the beer from the refrigerator, and when the children take E.T. trick-or-treating.)

The popularity of these kinds of scores opened the door for many other composers to follow suit and incorporate any possible sound they wanted. But the film-scoring industry was about to undergo a massive infusion of new sounds and possibilities, and the whole business of film music was to shift yet again as it absorbed the new technologies of synthesizers and the personal computer.

Synthesizers and Computers: A Whole New Ballgame

It is ironic that only a few short years after the resurgence of the orchestral score, the score created entirely, or mostly, using electronic synthesizers became all the rage. Around the late 1970s, synthesizer technology had progressed to where keyboards were affordable. Previously synthesizers had been used in movies, but the ARP and Moog were large, expensive, and cumbersome machines that required a huge amount of expertise to operate. The new technology quickly caught on, and the manufacturers were wise enough to create MIDI, Musical Instrument Digital Interface, a language that allowed synthesizers and computers of any manufacturer to interface or talk to each other.

The score that caught the public's attention, and made every producer in Hollywood want the same thing, was Vangelis's score to the 1981 film, *Chariots of Fire*. This score was entirely electronic, with no acoustic instruments at all. The synthesizer technology at the time was primitive compared to today. All Vangelis had to work with were analog synthesizers, since digital had yet to arrive. There was no sampling, digital editing, or hard-disk recording. The various synthesizer sounds were recorded to a multitrack analog tape machine in Vangelis's home studio.

The impact of this score cannot be overstated. It opened the ears of producers, directors, composers, and the general public to the possibility of using electronic sounds in a lyrical manner. Previously, synthesizer and other electronic sounds like the theremin were used in high intensity dramatic situations and science fiction films. They were usually part of a scary, spooky, or otherworldly musical landscape. Vangelis, in one stroke, showed the world that it could be otherwise.

Not only did this score make a huge impact on the success of the film, but it became a commercial hit, selling millions of records and tapes, and getting serious radio airplay. Of course, many producers jumped on the bandwagon and wanted a similar kind of sound for their films. Since Vangelis clearly could not do them all, it meant that other, more traditionally-minded composers would learn the new technology to one degree or another.

The availability and affordability of synthesizers in the mid-1980s was actually embraced by many composers, both the up-and-coming youngsters and the older generation. What open-minded musician could turn his back on the possibility of adding yet another entirely new dimension of sounds to his palette? Jerry Goldsmith, Maurice Jarre, Elmer Bernstein, and many others began to incorporate electronic sounds into their scores, or even compose scores that were completely electronic. Goldsmith's score to *Hoosiers* and Jarre's score to *Witness* are but two examples of traditionally-trained, established Hollywood composers writing scores that used electronic instruments exclusively. Younger composers like James Horner, Basil Poledouris, and Alan Silvestri began to incorporate synthesizer sounds in scores like *Field of Dreams, Conan the Barbarian,* and *Romancing the Stone.* Of course, some of this was necessary as producers were requesting it, but composers found that electronic instruments could aid them in creating new textures.

The swiftness of the rise of this technology was awesome. In a few short years the industry went from having access to only the most primitive electronic sound generators to having extremely sophisticated digital equipment at its fingertips. One downside of this was that for a period of time, many string, brass, and wind players faced a shortage of work. Although there were still many orchestral sessions in L.A. during this time, there were less than before because synthesizers were taking the place of the live musicians. In addition, many TV producers, influenced by the success of the score to *Miami Vice,* also switched to completely or partially using synthesizers. The whole world of commercial music was shaken up and altered forever by the arrival of synthesizers and computers.

One of the consequences of this new medium was that because of the expertise needed to master the ever-expanding synthesizer and MIDI technology, an entirely new niche and a new kind of film composer was born: the specialist in electronic, synthesizer scores. These composers became experts in synthesizer sounds, sampling, MIDI technology and sequencing (the technique of using computers instead of analog tape to record the synthesizers or samplers). German born Hans Zimmer was one of the first to establish himself in this field, and has had many successful scores using either entirely electronically generated music or a combination of electronic and acoustical sounds. His scores to *Rain Man, Driving Miss Daisy, The Lion King,* and *Beyond Rangoon* are just some examples of his work. Zimmer and his team have been on the cutting edge of developing new technology and creating new sounds with samplers and digital synthesizers.

Because of the affordability and relative ease of use of MIDI equipment, many young composers today are writing quality electronic scores for features, television, cable, and documentaries. This technology has become a necessary skill for film composers.

Even though the synthesizer craze hit hard and made a deep impact—not only on the sound and texture of film scores, but on the recording industry in general—the pendulum always swings back, as we have seen with other styles. In this case, after the initial rush to use electronic instruments a la Vangelis, many directors and producers began to recognize the cold and sometimes false sounding nature of these instruments. It was one thing to use synthesizers or samplers to create a new and unusual texture, or combine them with orchestral instruments, but the scores that used them to replace orchestral instruments tended to sound dry and phony. For example, if a string section or cello solo is playing beneath an action scene or under dialogue, then a really good sample can sometimes fool the audience. But if the same music is in an exposed place where there is little in the soundtrack to compete with it, even an inexperienced listener can often hear that it is electronically generated and not real.

The result of this was that composers began to use electronic instruments more as an adjunct to an orchestra, unless the director specified an electronic score. (Here, I am speaking of feature films. For television, cable, and low-budget films, often the film's music budget would not allow the use of an orchestra, and electronic instruments became a necessity.) In addition, many synthesizer specialists, such as Hans Zimmer, began to write scores that incorporated full orchestras. A middle ground was found, and it continues to this day as producers, directors, and composers continue to strive for appropriate uses of electronic sounds.

Pop Sounds, Jazz, and Rock 'n Roll Composers

For many reasons, the language of rock and pop music has found its way into film scores in general. As we have seen, every style of film music has reflected to some degree the film-going audience. For example, in the '30s and '40s the audience understood 19th-century romanticism, and in the '50s and '60s they resonated with jazz-oriented scores. Today, the range of possibilities is the largest it has ever been.

As pop, rock, and jazz styles became more mainstream through the 1970s, their use in films grew. The influences that rock music brings to the world of film scoring are basically threefold: one, rock rhythms and grooves; two, a certain harmonic vocabulary spanning the traditional blues to progressive pop-, rock-, and jazz-influenced songwriting; and three, pop/rock melodic ideas.

Rock rhythms are the easiest to identify when they are used in film scores. This could be a traditional rhythm section of guitar, keyboard, bass, and drums; a hybrid combination of those instruments; or "world" music beats giving a hipper sound to the score. These kinds of sounds have been used in countless scores. In the 1980s, Hans Zimmer used a "world beat" kind of percussion groove in *Rain Man*, Craig Safan used a hip-hop groove for *Stand and Deliver*, and Alan Silvestri used synthesized drums in a quasi-Latin disco beat for *Romancing the Stone*. In the 1990s, Michael Kamen has used rock grooves in the *Lethal Weapon* series and *The Last Boy Scout*.

Many of the harmonic and melodic ideas used by film composers today draw upon pop melodic and harmonic ideas. This can be heard in the scores of those coming from the record industry as well as those coming from the conservatories. Anyone going into film music today knows that there is a fusion between orchestral styles and pop music. James Horner studied at the Royal Academy of Music in London, and Michael Kamen studied at Juilliard, but they can write a pop hit as well as a traditional sounding score. And this is no different from composers of the previous generation like Henry Mancini who did the same thing.

The one difference that exists today is that a composer can be a success in the film industry, and write orchestral scores without any, or minimal knowledge of the orchestra. This can happen because of two factors: one, orchestrators who assist and prepare a full score from a sketch or a tape, and two, the ease of using synthesizers and MIDI technology. Therefore, a talented rock or jazz musician who has some great creative ideas can realize a score that is beyond the scope of his actual orchestral ability.

In order to understand this trend fully, we must go back a few years. In the 1970s and 1980s yet another wrinkle was added to the film scoring community: the desire by some producers and directors to use well-known rock and jazz musicians to create a score for their films. In retrospect, the validity of this idea can be seen, but it seems to have had mixed success.

The impact of the popular music of the 1960s and 1970s cannot be underestimated. No other generation bought as many records, went to as many concerts, or looked to rock musicians for philosophical, political, and social leadership as did the Baby Boomers coming of age in the '60s and '70s. So it was logical that by the late '70s, the same Baby Boomers who were producing and directing films wanted to use the musicians they considered to be icons. The thinking was that these musicians would speak to the audience through the soundtrack as they did in concert or on records. This was a good idea in theory, but in practice it was dangerous for several reasons.

First, a film score requires the ability to create a musical structure that tells a story and remains harmonically and melodically interesting for about two hours. The average pop song is three or four minutes, and many of these artists do not have the expertise needed to sustain and develop their ideas in the way a film demands. Second, film scores need to have a well thought-out texture of sounds, and the experienced composer will draw upon a wide variety of instrumental possibilities. Most rock and jazz stars, although fine players in their own medium, are only able to execute a much narrower range of sounds and styles. If a film calls for this kind of narrow range, then a rock or jazz artist might be an appropriate choice. Finally, the successful film score comes from a composer knowing that he is a partner to the drama. There is a sensitivity that develops from working with many different pictures and different styles of music. The rock or jazz composer who only knows concert performance and CD recording is at a severe disadvantage when attempting to work in the unfamiliar medium of film.

This is not to say that there cannot be a successful rock or jazz score. It can and has happened. Eric Clapton has made fine contributions to the *Lethal Weapon* series. Ry Cooder has written some interesting scores including *Paris, Texas*. Jazz trumpet player Terence Blanchard has become a proficient composer and orchestrator.

One rock musician composer that has consistently stood out from the rest is Danny Elfman. Formerly with the L.A. band, Oingo Boingo, he began scoring films for director Tim Burton in the late 1980s. With *Pee Wee's Great Adventure, Batman*, and *The Nightmare Before Christmas*, Elfman established himself as someone very creative with melodies and sound textures, who caught the imagination of many. He showed a great ability to capture the mood of the different kinds of films he wrote for and has established a cult-like following amongst musicians and non-musicians alike.

There are many composers coming up in the ranks of pop and rock music that do not orchestrate, and occasionally there are stories of those who cannot even read music. This is a far cry from the Korngolds and Steiners, but it is the state of the industry today. But if a musician can create the right mood, and with the right musical support can appropriately heighten the drama of a film, is it a bad thing that they know nothing about an orchestra? This is an open-ended question that has proponents on both sides.

In addition to the many rock musicians who have limited orchestral skills, there are still those who have training in orchestration and composing. Today's film music is richer than ever. Part of this richness is due to rock and jazz composers who bring their own special kind of sound. Another aspect is the range of possibilities afforded from traditional symphony orchestras to electronic scores, and hybrids and fusions of the two. Today's composer can work in just about any sound medium he wants that will accomplish the director's vision of the film.

Production

PART II

35
OUND

CHAPTER 7

The Film-Making Process

That's the fun part about movie collaboration.
You work intensely with a lot of people who are
different from you and you learn a lot from them.
—*Oliver Stone*[1]

The making of a major motion picture is an incredibly complex, costly, creative, and challenging endeavor. It requires people with all kinds of skills. One look at the credits of a film gives an idea of the wide range of expertise needed to pull it off: writers, painters, truck drivers, electricians, carpenters, cameramen, directors, musicians, special-effects designers and technicians, make-up artists, costume designers, publicists, directors' assistants, production assistants, assistants to the assistants, and on and on the credits roll while the music plays. The beauty of a production is that these seemingly disparate groups of people are all working in an organized way to achieve a common goal: the release of the film.

What the average filmgoer may not realize is that many of these groups operate separately, yet parallel to the whole operation. For example, principle photography (the shooting of the film) might be finishing up on location in New Mexico and at a studio in Los Angeles, while a team of special-effects wizards is beginning to work their computer magic in Northern California, the sound-effects people are working at yet another studio in L.A., and the lonely composer is sitting in his studio behind his home in Beverly Hills staring at the swimming pool waiting for the final version of the film.

Actually, this is both far from the truth and close to the truth. Hopefully, nobody will be wasting their time waiting for a film to be completed before they start writing the music because so many films take longer than originally planned. But the reality of the film-making process is that the *music is the very last thing to be done.* The reason for this is that in order to sync up the music to the action, the composer must wait for the final version, or *locked picture,* also known as a *fine cut.* Before getting into what the composer does, though, let's take a look at the film-making process itself.

Decision Makers

There are several people involved in getting a film off the ground: the producer, director, writer, and possibly the talent (actors). These are the people whose creative, financial, and organizational skills actually drive the production.

The *producer* oversees the financial and organizational aspects of the film. This person supervises the hiring of everyone from director and actors to carpenters and electricians. He makes sure there is a workable schedule and ensures that all elements of the production are running smoothly, from the writing of the script to the feeding of the crew. The producer is responsible for the financial bottom line, and answers to the executives at the movie studio that will release the film.

Producer Darryl Zanuck:

> *People outside of Hollywood and New York don't really have a clear idea of what a producer is or what he does…. Most people think a producer is the person who puts up the money, which is wrong. If you're smart, you never put up the money yourself![2]*

Even without putting up his own money, the responsibility for a producer can be enormous, as budgets for feature films climb higher and higher. To paraphrase one producer, a movie can be made for $50 million dollars and last one or two weeks in the theaters. But a huge skyscraper can be bought for the same amount of money and stand for decades. However, the producer does much more than just raise money. He is the one who must shepherd a project through the maze of production. This involves coordinating all the creative people, the technicians, the marketing experts, and the financial overseers.

Zanuck again:

> *Even with the right people, this isn't the furniture business or the car business. You have a lot of personalities and a lot of egos, so there are many factors at play.*
>
> *It's easy to go astray and very tough to carry the vision through completely every inch of the way, to make it all work. There's economic pressures, there's time pressures, and there are always personality conflicts when you put so many people together. Everyone works for the common cause, but it is an ego-driven business, and there's a lot of pushing and shoving going on.[3]*

The organization of the team is one of the producer's main jobs, and the three main components of that team are the writer, the director, and the actors. However, it is the director who is the most important day-to-day member of the team. Once the shooting begins, the producer often keeps his distance and lets the director achieve his vision for the film.

The *director* is the creative captain of the project. He has the overall vision for what the film will say and look like. He must also be able to communicate that vision to everyone working on the project and be strong enough to hold to that vision as the film makes its journey from script to silver screen. That means coordinating the creative efforts of many people. Director Ron Howard puts it this way:

> *The buck does stop with the director, but there are so many others involved. I think that the sooner we all see the same movie in our heads, the sooner the collaborative process works and the film benefits from the valuable ideas coming from all those different areas of expertise.[4]*

The director approves the script (sometimes writing it himself), and oversees all the design elements of the film including the cinematography (the camera angles, lighting, and overall "look of the film"), costumes, sets, props, hair, and make-up. The director is responsible for "directing" the actors on the set, deciding when a take is the right one, which scenes will be shot in which order, and keeping to the overall shooting schedule and budget. The director oversees the editing of the film after shooting is completed, and presents his version to the producer and studio executives for their approval. Except in the rare case of a director like Steven Spielberg or James Cameron, these higher-ups—the execs and producer—have the right to alter the film in any way they see fit. The director is often powerless to control the final version even though it represents months or even years of work.

The *writer*, or *scriptwriter*, takes a story, an idea, a book or a play and makes it into a *screenplay*, or *script*. This person is responsible for creating a script that fits the director's and producer's desires for the film. This can mean that even if the writer is initially happy with a script, it might not be "finished" because of rewrites requested by the director or producer. The final version of the script that is used in the actual shooting of the film is called the *shooting script*.

The writer is responsible for creating an engaging story, making the characters believable, and writing dialogue that fits the characters and the tone of the film. Every line the actors speak, every scene, every part of the plot is considered and mulled over to make sure it is "just right." The screenplay then becomes a blueprint for the shooting of the film. Many people, including the director, producer, cinematographer, film editor, and the actors can have input on the script, both during the writing stage and during the shooting stage. This input can often make it even better as the collaborative process works its magic.

Sometimes several writers work on a film because a single author can't achieve the vision of the director or producer. On many films, "script doctors" are brought in to polish up either the whole thing, certain scenes, or lines of dialogue. Even with only one writer, a screenplay will go through many revisions before a final version, or shooting script, is ready. This process can take as short as a few weeks, or last as long as several years.

Putting It All Together

How does a film make its way from an idea in someone's head, a book, or a play to a multimillion-dollar production showing in your local theater? Depending on who comes up with the original idea for the movie, the process can unfold in different ways, and the people described above come on board in a different order. There are three basic stages of this process: (1) getting the idea for the film, (2) obtaining financing, and (3) hiring the creative and organizational people to make the idea a reality. Often the process is from the top down; the producer gets an idea, receives a screenplay, or buys the rights to a book and then oversees the process from start to finish. However, there are many different ways the process can happen. Here are two possible alternatives to the scenario where the idea for the film originates with the producer:

> *Scenario #1:* A director has an idea for a film, goes to a producer, and pitches a *treatment* (a short synopsis of the plot) to a producer. The producer agrees to undertake the project and begins arranging for financing. He hires a writer, usually with the director's approval. When the script is finished, the producer and director begin to contact actors for the lead roles. Important production roles, such as the cinematographer, film editor, and casting director are hired at this time. When the script nears completion, a production schedule is created and the rest of the crew is hired.

> *Scenario #2:* An accomplished writer brings the first draft of a screenplay to a well-known director with whom he has an established relationship. The director loves the screenplay and agrees to direct it. The story calls for a strong action-hero type, so together they approach a well-known actor who also loves the idea. Next, this trio of proven professionals—writer, director, and movie star—presents a "package" to a producer. The packaged combination of talent, box-office draw, and exciting story line make the project irresistible, and the producer signs on quickly before they pitch the project elsewhere.

There can be many variations of this process, depending on who has the original idea and who that person's contacts might be. Many times an agent will get involved trying to package together two or more elements: writer and director, actor and director, producer, actor, and writer, etc. In the end, the process can be very political, with who-knows-whom being a big part of it. Sometimes it simply comes down to a matter of availability—an actor or director is just not available at the time this production would require him. And sometimes a project is pushed through by the sheer will of one of the parties involved because they believe in it. This is how the 1998 movie *The Apostle* got made. This film features Robert Duvall as actor, director, producer, and major financial backer. He invested several million of his own dollars because it was a project he believed in, and he wanted to see it get made. This is an example of one person performing several roles, putting his creative stamp on different aspects of the project. But whether it is one person filling multiple roles or many people dividing the roles, the making of a film is a huge, complicated, and enormously exciting process.

The Stages of a Film's Production

There are three stages of a film's production: *preproduction, production*, and *post-production*. Post-production can be divided into two parts: (1) editing and assembling the film, and (2) music, sound effects, and dubbing. Keep in mind that this business is a flexible one. Things are always changing and can happen in a different way or in a different order from what was originally projected. But these three main chronological divisions basically stay the same.

Preproduction is largely the process described in the previous section—the inception, planning, and development of an idea so that it can become an actual film.

Preproduction involves:

- Conceiving the initial idea, or
- Obtaining the rights to a book, play or short story
- Writing the treatment
- Obtaining financing
- Writing the screenplay
- Hiring the principle creative people
- Casting (hiring the actors)
- Scheduling
- Scouting for locations (out-of-studio shooting)
- Hiring the crew

Production is the actual shooting of the movie. This can take weeks or months depending on the scale of the production. It is an exciting time when all the planning starts to become a physical reality. It is also a time when people are under a lot of pressure to meet deadlines, which can sometimes be affected by such diverse circumstances as the weather on the location, an actor's illness, or even a union work-stoppage. Production involves:

- Rehearsing the actors
- Shooting the film, either at the studio or on location
- Screening dailies (the scenes shot earlier that day, or the previous day)
- Special-effects photography/animation (continues into post-production)
- Film editors beginning review of footage and sometimes starting to assemble the film
- Dialogue soundtrack construction, sometimes including ADR (Automatic Dialogue Replacement, explained later in this chapter)

Post-production can be divided into two large segments: editing and assembling the film, and creating the audio tracks consisting of dialogue, sound effects, and music. These tasks take place simultaneously for the first part of post-production; at this time the dialogue, sound effects, and music crews begin their work. However, it is not until the second part of the post-production process, after the editing is complete, that the real intensive production of the music, dialogue, and sound effects begins. This is because the film must be completed in order to synchronize these elements properly. (Note: A film is considered *locked* when the director and the producer have "signed off" on an edited version of the film and consider it completed.)

Digital technology is changing these distinctions. One may now edit the picture, music, sound effects, dialogue, and even visual special-effects at the click of a mouse. Before these computer systems were available, changes in the picture needed to be cut and spliced on a work print of the film; music recording tape had to be cut and spliced; sound-effects could not be edited so easily; and visual special-effects were primitive, if existent at all. Now, with powerful software, even after the film is supposedly "locked" and approved by the studio, the director can easily make minor or even major changes. This has led to many situations where the music is being recorded and the director "remembers" that he took out a few seconds of film and forgot to tell the composer. This creates havoc in the synchronization of music to picture. Unfortunately for composers, this is the way of the film-making world as we enter the 21st century.

Post-Production: Stage 1

Editing is when all the footage from production is assembled into a coherent film. This is done by the *film editor*. Often a director shoots several takes of the same scene, with different camera angles, that need to be put together in a natural way. This means matching shots, facial expressions, body language, and dialogue. Once the actual photography, or shooting, is completed, the film editor sifts through hours of footage and makes sure the story is being told in a coherent way, that there is no extraneous material, and that the cuts all make sense visually. It is a crucial task, because this process determines the overall pacing and dramatic impact of the film.

The editorial phase of post-production includes:

- Assembling the rough cut (the working version of the film). The rough cut eventually becomes a fine cut, or locked picture.
- Music temp track
- Screening for studio execs
- Test screenings
- ADR

From the earliest days of film until the early 1990s, editing a film involved running a work print of the film through a projector over and over again. This projector is known as a Moviola, or flat-bed projector. Using foot-pedals, it allows the editor to go back and forth over a print of the film while synchronized with the dialogue track. The editor then decides where to make the edits, physically cuts pieces of film, and splices them together—hence the expression that a scene or line of dialogue ended up "on the cutting room floor." Once this work print is approved by the director, producer, and studio, a negative is cut and spliced in the exact same way. That negative is sent to the lab and copies are made for the theaters.

The method of film editing that uses Moviolas is rapidly becoming extinct. In today's world of computer technology, almost all editing is done digitally on sophisticated systems such as the Avid. All the various takes are loaded into the computer, and the editor then cuts and pastes as he wishes. This also allows the director to easily view several options of a scene. After the editing is completed and the film is approved, a negative must still be physically edited to go to the lab.

Once the film is edited, it enters the stage involving the composer and the rest of the music crew, as well as the sound-effects crew. The composer does not begin writing music cues until there is a locked picture; changes in the picture would affect the planning and synchronization of the music. The exception to this is if songs are involved to which the actors sing or dance on-screen. Then, the music is usually recorded before shooting begins (prerecorded) so that the final version of the song or arrangement can be played back on the set. In addition to music, post-production is when sound effects are finalized and added.

Post-production involves:

Music	Non-Music
• Locked picture to composer	• Sound effects created
• Spotting session	• Foley
• Timing notes created	• ADR completed
• Music composition	• Special effects completed
• Orchestrations	• Dubbing
• Copying parts	• Answer print (preparation
• Song clearances	of physical film negative)
• Recording of music	• Distribution of film to
• Mixing music	theaters

Most of the technical terms listed above are explained in subsequent chapters of this book. However, some of these activities require a brief explanation here:

Foley is a process that creates sound effects through live recording. This can be as primitive as simulating horses hooves by clapping two coconut halves together, as in the old radio days, or it can be something like breaking windows or other glass to create the sound of a crash. There are many libraries of sound effects available today on CD, but often the sound-effects crew has a certain effect in mind that the CDs don't contain, so they must create it.

ADR, or Automatic Dialogue Replacement, is when the actors go into a studio to redo any lines that were not recorded well or have extraneous noise on the production track. Often, the dialogue that is recorded on the set of a film is muddy, unclear, or tainted by unwanted sounds on the set. This is especially common with shooting on outdoor sets or location, when it is impossible to control noise such as airplanes, lawn mowers, sirens, and other sounds of modern life. In addition, the actor may have garbled the line, the boom operator may not have gotten a good angle, or if wearing a body mike, the actor may have brushed it against an article of clothing. In ADR, the actors go into a studio, listen to and watch their original performance, and redo the line or lines until they are synced up exactly. This is quite common, and is an important part of the audio element of post-production.

The audio tracks are the very last element in the film's production. Once the music, sound effects, and dialogue have been added (the dubbing session), the film is ready to be printed, copied, and duplicated for release. The director sends the negative with the sound tracks to a lab that creates a copy of the film called an *answer print*. The director views this copy and ensures that all the colors were mixed properly at the lab, and that the look of the film is correct. Sometimes this is a one-step process; sometimes the director returns to the lab several times to get it right. Once the answer print is approved, it is ready for distribution.

This is a generalized overview of the film-making process. There are many other tasks that must be accomplished, ranging from financial accounting to building sets to feeding the crew—the list could go on and on.

One thing that cannot be emphasized enough is the pressure that can be placed on the composer because of the fact that he must wait for just about everything else to be finished before starting to write. Films are often behind schedule in production, but the release date cannot change; the composer may have less time to complete the score than originally scheduled. Remember our lonely composer sitting by the pool, waiting for a locked picture? Here is a story about post-production schedules:

Michael Kamen was the composer for the Kevin Costner film, *Robin Hood, Prince of Thieves*—a big-budget production of about $40 to $50 million. A huge amount of money had been spent for advertising, and by early spring, trailers, billboards, and buses around the country were announcing a June 6 release date.

Michael expected to receive the locked picture in March. However, production and editing got way behind schedule, and he did not receive the locked picture until the first week of April. This gave him only six weeks to write *and* record about 120 minutes of music for a 104 piece orchestra. (The last two weeks of May were given over to dubbing, color correction, duplication, and shipping of the film to the theaters.)

Now fortunately Michael was smart, and started working on his thematic material while he was waiting for the final cut, though he couldn't do any actual music cues. He remembered a ballet score he had written years before, and extracted a beautiful theme that became the love theme for the film, as well as the melody for the Bryan Adams song "Everything I Do, I Do It For You." He also worked on some of the action themes, preparing those for the time when he could synchronize them to the locked picture. When the locked picture finally arrived, he was ready and could work quickly and efficiently.

The stages of film production outlined here are not set in stone; this whole process involves a great deal of flexibility. For example, editing could begin during production. If enough footage for the beginning of the film has been shot, while the director is off shooting the ending of the picture, the film editor might assemble the first few minutes. Or parts of the script might be reworked even while the movie is being shot. The process is fluid, and the successful people are those who learn to honor that fluidity, and even harness it to improve the project.

CHAPTER 8

The Composer's Time Frame

*Unfortunately, filming is all against the clock …
it's a constant battle between commerce and creativity.*
—*Ridley Scott*[1]

The amount of time a composer gets to score a film can vary widely. In the previous anecdote there was only six weeks for an enormous amount of music, and although this sounds like an outrageously short amount of time, it is not all that unusual. Anything can happen during production that can cause the late delivery of a film; an actor gets ill and delays shooting, the weather on location won't cooperate, the director decides to make some changes, the studio doesn't like the ending and it has to be reshot. All a composer can do is go with it. Or, if the contract allows, refuse to take on the project if it is delivered later than a certain date.

A typical feature film will have from about 30 minutes of music to over 120 minutes. Each individual piece of music is called a *cue*. Each *cue* can be as short as just a few seconds, or as long as several minutes. A *cue* can be played by an orchestra, or it can be a song coming from a radio on-screen. Every new piece of music, regardless of its origin, is still called a *cue*.

The collection of cues making up all the music in the film is called the *score*. So if someone says, "I liked the *score* to that picture," they are referring to the music from beginning to end. If they say, "I really like that *cue*," they are talking about one isolated piece of music, often for a specific scene.

There is no rule of thumb as to how many minutes of music can be written in a certain amount of time. John Williams has said that he considers a good day to be two minutes of music composed. This means that in order to complete a *Star Wars* or *Indiana Jones* type of action film, with an average of 80 or 90 minutes of music, he needs about eight weeks to complete the writing. (Five-day-a-week schedules are often a luxury for composers; they are much more likely to go six or seven days a week for a few weeks and then take some time off.) A one-hour dramatic TV show such as *X-Files* can require as much as thirty or more minutes to be composed *and* recorded in one week. In addition, whether the music is for full orchestra or sequenced often determines the pace of writing and recording. Every composer has his own speed.

In most cases, the composer's first real involvement with the film is in post-production, after the film is locked. This is when the real composing begins. However, depending on what stage the film was in when he was hired, the composer might have had an earlier involvement. For example, if a certain composer is being considered during preproduction, the director might ask him to read the script and then informally discuss his ideas for the film. Some composers like to see the script in advance, for they like to start thinking about musical possibilities early in the process. Others prefer to wait until the picture is locked, or at least close to completed, because so much of what is composed is suggested by the actual visual images and pacing of the film.

There are also times when a director asks a composer to come to the set and observe the shooting of the film. As with reading the script, some composers are happy to participate in this early stage of making the film, but most prefer to wait until the film is completed before getting involved. This is because the shooting of a picture is a slow, painstaking, and sometimes tedious process where an enormous amount of imagination is required to envision the final product.

There are some instances when the composer gets involved with the film during preproduction or production. This is necessary when the film is a musical where characters sing on-screen (*Yentl, Mary Poppins,* etc.), or when the film contains scenes where the actors are dancing to live musicians or dancing to a song on the soundtrack. When any of these events are happening, the music must be planned in advance. The tempo must be chosen, and the music is prerecorded so that it can be played back on the set. If there are live musicians on-camera (called *sideline musicians*), they must be coordinated to appear to be playing. In modern film making, it is often the *music supervisor* who oversees this process.

The Spotting Session

In most cases, for a dramatic, or non-musical film, the composer's active involvement begins with post-production. First, he receives a locked version of the film. Very soon after receiving this tape, the composer attends the *spotting session*—the meeting between producer, director and composer where they decide how to use music in the film. The major decisions in this meeting are: where the music will begin and end for each cue, what it should sound like, and what role it will play in relation to the drama. Most composers like to view the film before going to the spotting session; it gives them a chance to think about it and get familiar with the film before discussing it with the director.

After the spotting session, the composer is really ready to get to work. The music editor prepares timing notes and the other technical aspects of synchronizing the music to the picture so that the composer can begin writing the music. The composer is acutely aware of the project's deadlines—most importantly, the delivery date for the music, the air date if it is for television, and the release date for a theatrical opening if it is a film. Many events are set in motion once the composer gets working on the film and has these deadlines. This includes hiring the orchestrators, studio musicians, booking the studio, etc. The composer must put himself on a disciplined timeline, or writing schedule, in order to make these deadlines. There can be as many as forty or fifty separate cues in a film, so there is a lot of music to keep track of. In order to complete this kind of output on time, the composer must write a certain amount per day.

The reality of this kind of schedule and the nature of the process of writing music combines to make this a solitary time for the composer despite all the necessary interaction with other members of the production team. Many hours a day must be set aside for writing, and this is something only the composer can accomplish. Through the years, film composers have commented on the lonely nature of their job, for once a project is begun they can be like hermits locked away in their studios for days at a time. However, it is a rewarding job and only this part of it is lonely. Another large aspect of the composer's job is interacting with interesting creative people—musicians, directors, writers, and others.

Different Working Styles

Every composer has a slightly different approach to the process of writing a film score. But there are two distinct styles that, for the purposes of this book, I will call the *traditional approach* and the *non-traditional approach*. In the traditional approach, after the composer spots the film, the music editor makes detailed timing notes. The composer then writes the music, usually with pencil and paper, ultimately generating a sketch that is sent to an orchestrator.

In the non-traditional approach, after the spotting session, the composer knows where each cue begins and ends, but often will not have any timing notes at all. That is because this composer plans to sequence his ideas by playing along with the film. In this method, often a team of people assists the composer. In addition to the music editor, there will be a recording engineer and sometimes a synthesizer expert. If a live orchestra is used, then eventually the sequenced music is sent to an orchestrator, who will create a written score.

Both methods are valid and used in Hollywood today. Some composers use one method exclusively, some use both, depending on the project. The non-traditional method is faster, and often must be used when the schedule is really tight.

An Ideal Schedule

For the purposes of this book, here is a generalized and ideal schedule from the time the composer receives a locked picture to the release of the film. Let's say that this film has 45 minutes of music, and the composer is using the "traditional" method:

Week 1

Composer receives the locked picture. Reviews tape at home. Spotting session with director, producer and music editor. Music editor begins preparing timing notes.

Weeks 2 to 5

Writing begins. Composer gives sketches to orchestrator. Orchestrations go to copyist as they are completed. Music editor finishes timing notes and prepares for synchronization.

Week 6

Recording the music: three to four days, six hours per day of recording. Approximately 18 minutes recorded each day. Mixing the music: two to three full days.

Weeks 7 to 8

Dubbing music with sound effects and dialogue.

Week 9

Film goes to lab for answer prints and color correction.

Week 12

Film delivered to theaters.

As with almost anything in this business, this timeline can morph in different directions. It can get shorter if there are delays in production or picture-editing, or there can even be the luxury of more time if things go smoothly during production, or if the release date gets pushed forward.

Mock-ups

As I have mentioned, there can be an enormous amount of pressure on the composer. There is also the added dimension of the pressure that comes from needing to please the director and producer. For this reason, in the age of MIDI, a composer often plays a sequenced *mock-up* of a cue for the powers-that-be. This is a rough version of the cue recorded with synthesizers and samplers to produce the sounds that eventually will be a real orchestra (unless it is an electronic or synthesizer score, in which case this version will not be so far from the final music). This is a dual-edged sword. On the one hand, it can give the director a good idea of where the composer is going with the cue, and the composer can be assured that the director's vision is being accomplished. The director can offer suggestions and comments, feel involved in the music process, and leave the composer's studio feeling secure that the music is going in the right direction. On the other hand, it can be very uncomfortable to have the director literally standing over one's shoulder making musical suggestions. In addition, on this rough version of the cue, the director might hear only the electronic-sounding synth strings and not-quite-real sounding French horn sample and think it is terrible, not having the musical ability to make the imaginary transfer to real instruments. Because he then focuses on the fake-sounding instruments instead of the actual musical ideas, he can mistakenly think that the cue itself doesn't work when all that is wrong is the use of electronic instruments substituting for real ones. It then becomes the composer's job to explain, or even "pitch" the music he conceived, and convince the director that it will work. Or he must change the cue and go in a different direction in order to please the director. Clear communication, and the ability to listen to a director and incorporate his ideas, is necessary.

Mark Isham illustrates this process, and discusses his experience in showing the director and producers the first version of the musical cues he wrote—the synthesized mock-up—for the movie, *Nell*, starring Jodie Foster:

> As I remember, I wrote a whole bunch of music, and Michael Apted, the director, Jodie Foster, the star and co-producer, and Renée Missel, the other co-producer, were the team that would work with me. They came over to my studio and heard the first version. And they hated it! I honestly don't remember what it was about the first pass, except that I don't think it was mysterious enough. The thing I remember having to get— and it seems sort of obvious now because it really did help to align the movie a lot once I got it—was the sense of mystery. Where? How? Why? Who is this person? What could possibly have transpired to create a life for her like this?

Now Jodie Foster is one of the smartest people I've ever met in my whole life. And part of what makes her so smart is that she is really a good communicator. And Michael Apted is such an elegant gentleman. So in a meeting like that where they say, "We don't like it," it's never a feeling that you've been dealt this crushing blow and that you'll never rise up again. They don't scream and yell, "This is shit! How could you...!" It's not that at all. They have good reasons for why they don't feel it, and suggestions for where they would like it to go.

The balancing act a composer often performs is to write something that he is happy with, that fits the film, and satisfies the director's desires. Sometimes the composer disagrees with the director. Then it becomes a matter of discrimination whether or not to speak up and argue, or go with what is asked for. This will depend on several factors, including the composer's personal relationship with the director, the composer's track record and "clout," and sometimes how badly the composer wants to keep the job.

Alan Silvestri did the music for the 1998 film, *Practical Magic*, starring Sandra Bullock and Nicole Kidman, in just three weeks. He had to rely on experience and instinct in order to accomplish the task:

They [the production team] had a bit of a meltdown and they got in some trouble, scheduling-wise. I had to think long and deep about whether I was going to do this movie. I finally decided that if they could give me the time I felt I needed to accomplish a score, I would do it. It was about 60 minutes of music. I wrote it in 12 days, and recorded the entire score in three days of recording. They were dubbing, transferring, mixing, and printing the films while we were on the scoring stage. It was the deepest schedule hole I've ever seen. There may be projects that have been crazier, but for me, writing the entire score in 12 days, and recording it in three—those were consecutive days—and then the movie was out the following weekend ... that was really crazy.

Although the entire process described in this section is based on the scoring of a full-length, large-budget feature film, the same principles apply to television shows and movies, cable and low-budget films, documentaries, and even student films. The composer does not begin writing until the editing of the movie is complete. There is then a spotting session and the use of music will be determined. (Note that in a TV series, also called *episodic television*, the director is often not involved in the spotting. This is because in TV, once shooting is complete, the director's job is finished. The producer then guides the rest of post-production.) There are still deadlines to make and the film makers still must be pleased with the final product. The scale is different, but the concept remains the same. It is still a collaborative effort. Clear communication and good listening skills are always necessary. Proper organization of one's time is crucial in order to meet deadlines. Time frames change, and sometimes the composer feels like he is in the middle of a swirling storm of deadlines and details. But the music must be written, and the deadlines met.

CHAPTER 9

Spotting

*What you're trying to do is to catch the spirit of a picture.
And that means sometimes you go contrary to what's on the screen,
and sometimes you go with what's on the screen. It's a matter of
instinct; if your instincts are good, it's going to work for you.*
—David Raksin

Of the many elements that go into creating the music for a film, one of the most crucial is spotting. *Spotting* refers to where the music goes and what it will sound like. Frankly, one could have fabulous themes, sparkling orchestration, great players and a terrific creative relationship with the director, but if the music comes in and out at the wrong places, it can ruin a film. If a particular instrument enters in a way that is obtrusive, it can destroy the dramatic impact of a scene. If the overall sound and texture of the music is light and bright, but the film is dark and brooding, clearly that will not work. Psychologically, if the music does not fit like a glove in the way the costumes, lighting, and sets do, the audience gets distracted consciously or subconsciously. Therefore, the music's starts and stops, swells and retreats, and specific instrumentation and textures are carefully crafted to fulfill specific dramatic functions. This cannot be overemphasized. The point of the music is to further the story, to move the drama along, or tell us something about the characters or situation. In order to accomplish this, the music must be placed sensitively. When music is present in the film, it must be there for a reason, or it is probably not necessary.

The beginning composer should understand that effective spotting is a skill that comes with experience, so patience is in order. Many composers just starting out make the familiar mistakes of writing too many cues, over-writing the individual cue (as the Emperor said to Mozart: "Too many notes!"), and starting a cue too strongly (for example, using strings in a thick chord when a gentle unison would be better). Learning when to bring the music right in on a cut, and when you can be early or late, is a skill that comes with experience. In addition, as a composer becomes more experienced after scoring many different kinds of scenes, his insight becomes more finely tuned to what is on the screen and the intentions of the director. There are some general concepts that can guide this process:

1. *You are a partner in mixed media.* In most cues, music accompanies an actor's lines, creates a bridge from scene to scene, or gently helps to enhance the drama in a subtle way. In these scenes, the music is truly in the background. In a few situations, the music gets to stand out on its own—the action scenes, love scenes, and grand vistas of mountains or oceans. And these scenes also require sensitivity to how the music fits dramatically with what has happened and what is about to happen.

2. *Does there need to be music?* One must be absolutely sure that a given scene needs music. This surety can come in the form of a gut feeling, a plot driven need, or the director's request (whether or not you are in agreement). Points to consider include the dramatic needs, as well as what music has come just before or just after the scene in question.

3. *If there is music, what am I trying to say with it?* Asking this question helps keep the composer focused. It forces him to form an intent that gives an overall guideline for the emotional impact of the music. This goes beyond happy, sad, light, dark, etc. Similar questions are: Am I moving the drama forward? Am I expressing this character's thoughts or feelings appropriately? What instruments will accomplish these goals best?

Remembering these points helps keep the music a carefully considered element of the film, not just a composer's creative whim. If the composer is clear on why the music is there and what it is trying to accomplish, then his job is that much easier. The music then becomes a whole organic piece, not just a series of short musical sequences.

Elmer Bernstein speaks about how he begins conceiving music for a film:

I spot a film strictly as a dramatist. I'm not thinking of music at all when I spot a film. I look at a scene and say: Should this scene have music? Why should it have music? If it does have music, what is the music supposed to be doing? That's my process.

After the picture is locked, the composer meets with the director, music editor, and sometimes the producer and film editor. They review the film and discuss where the music will go, what it should sound like, and which dramatic situations to emphasize (or de-emphasize). This is called a *spotting session*. At this meeting the film is discussed scene by scene to determine the need for music, and to discuss what the music should sound like—what style, instruments, and emotions are musically necessary. The music editor takes notes for the composer regarding specific timings of cues and dramatic hits (see chapter 10). This meeting is the time when different approaches should be discussed, e.g., to play through a certain piece of action, to emphasize it, or to foreshadow an event or not. Keep in mind that most directors have no formal musical background and must speak in layman's terms, not musical terms. He might try to sound informed about many different styles of music when the breadth of his knowledge lies somewhere between the Beatles and Puff Daddy. Or he might have been a classical piano major in college and have thorough knowledge of the classical masters as well as current pop styles. The composer must find a way to understand the director's desire and translate his words into musical ideas.

Alan Silvestri has a wonderful relationship with several directors, and understands the pressure the director can feel, and how that pressure affects his relationship with the composer:

You've got to remember what you're doing here. You're working for somebody, and you, the composer, are not going to be the one called on the carpet when the movie was supposed to make $40 million this weekend and it only made $150,000 ... You're probably off on your next movie, but there's somebody out there who's sitting in a chair right now with a bunch of people in suits standing *around him, and he's having a real bad day. That person's called the director! So if you think for a minute that the director is not going to have a whole lot to say about what kind of music goes into their film and how it sounds, you're kidding yourself.*

Spotting is the first step towards completing a successful score. It must be done carefully, sensitively, and with the understanding that the music is a partner with the drama, as the composer is a partner with the director. Sometimes this partnership is smooth with excellent give and take. There can also be considerable friction if the director (or producer) requests a certain style or musical idea that the composer finds objectionable. As mentioned previously, it is in these situations that the composer must decide whether to argue with the director, or to go along with his wishes. (This is often where the "temp track" can be useful. More about this in chapter 10.) Ultimately, the composer's job is twofold in nature: one, he must please those who have hired him, and two, he must do it in such a way that his musical integrity remains intact. Being a film composer involves an enormous amount of flexibility and sensitivity, with a handful of diplomacy thrown in for good measure. One must be a good communicator, and especially have the ability to listen and transfer into musical terms what a director is saying.

When I was scoring the TV series, *Monsters*, each episode had a different director. At one spotting session, the director said he wanted the opening to "float, like the beginning of *Citizen Kane*." Now, anyone who has seen this 1941 movie with that awesome Bernard Herrmann score will remember that the opening music features very low-end woodwinds playing non-functional harmonies. To me, it doesn't float; it actually is very heavy, and I feel "sinks" would be a better term. I had to translate what he was really saying. After looking at the show in question, I realized that the operative description was the director wanting the sound of Herrmann's score in *Citizen Kane*, not to the adjective "float." I wrote something low, dark, and ominous and it was just what he wanted.

Clear communication between composer and director is essential. The director's vision of the film is the most comprehensive, and his abstract ideas for cues may provide keen insight into the type of musical ideas that will make a score succeed. The composer must help these ideas evolve into actual music.

Elmer Bernstein reflects on conceiving the music for *The Rainmaker* as a result of conversations with director Francis Ford Coppola:

> *I have to credit Francis with the bluesy ⁶/₈ idea in a roundabout way. What happened was, when I first got on* The Rainmaker, *Francis wasn't going to have a score as we know a score to be. At first, he was going to go the B.B King route—in other words, real Memphis stuff with some very minor connective things in scoring. But as he began to develop the film itself, he began to feel that he needed to depend more on score. So it was my decision to use the Hammond B3 organ, but it came out of his idea of Memphis ambience. Out of that ambience, I retained the three instruments you hear a great deal of: the Hammond B3, the muted trumpet, and the guitar. But that came out of Francis' original concept.*

> *When I came on* Rainmaker *it was in rough-cut form, and the version I finally recorded to was version #26. It went through some amazing changes. The interesting thing about Francis is that each time he changed the film it was for the better. He wasn't just fooling around, he was just "finding" the film, so to speak.*

The most important element of the *spotting session* is clear communication with the director. Once the composer and director share the same vision for the music, then the composer can get to work writing the score. However, there are still many spotting decisions to be made. The music can begin right on a cut, a few seconds before it, or even right after it. It can start immediately after an important line of dialogue, or it can wait and let that line sink in. It can foreshadow a dangerous situation, or play it more neutrally. There are countless spotting decisions to be made that will affect the drama, and the audience's experience of the story. How these decisions are made will be a combination of the composer's experience, his dramatic sensitivity, and the director's wishes.

CHAPTER 10

The Music Editor

Diplomatic skills. You've got a director sitting next to you, you're in a recording booth, the composer's out there, the music is being recorded, and the director says "What the hell is this music that I'm hearing?" Well, what do you say to that? Good luck! You hope that it's a long music cue so it will give you time to think of how to respond.
—Eric Reasoner, Music Editor

The two people assisting the composer on a daily basis are the orchestrator (see chapter 11) and the *music editor*. The music editor is often an under-recognized member of the production team. He must have excellent music skills, thorough knowledge of various advanced software programs (Auricle, Cue, Digital Performer, and Pro Tools are common), and be a cool, calm, and collected diplomat in the service of both the composer and the director. The music editor is responsible for making spotting notes from the spotting session, creating timing notes, and preparing the film or software for synchronization of the music with the final version of the film.

Music editor Eric Reasoner:

> *As a music editor, the more you know about music the better off you are. However, there are still a lot of music editors that have an instinctive sense—not that they studied music, but they really know and have quick instincts about cutting music. They are also good at dealing with pressure and handling a lot of different kinds of individuals, which is a big, big part of it.*

In today's modern world of film making, most of the music editor's tasks are accomplished using computer software. However, there are still some physical tools and pieces of equipment that are used:

A *reel* is the carousel that the film is loaded onto when it goes through the camera during shooting and through a projector. Every reel used during production and post-production contains about 8 to 12 minutes of film, making about 10 to 14 reels for the average movie. However, when a film is delivered to the theater, every two reels are combined so that the theater receives 5 to 7 reels. The projectionist then makes *reel changes* at the appropriate points. At some of the more modern theaters, they can splice and load the film onto one giant reel, called a *platter*, which turns parallel to the floor, making reel changes unnecessary.

Magnetic sound film, also known as *mag film*, is film that is specially coated with a magnetic substance similar to audiotape. This is the kind of film that is used to record and edit sound to sync to picture. Film is used so that the music, dialogue, sound effects, and picture can run on similar machines, and the motors can be easily synchronized. *Mag film* is being used less and less as digital technology replaces it.

The *optical soundtrack* is the stripe on the edges of a finished film that contains the sound for the movie. Until recently, with the arrival of digital technology, this track was read by a light cell that converted the light-sensitive images into sound. Hence, it is called an optical sound-track. This technology has changed very little from the inception of sound films to the 1990s, and is still used in many theaters today as the digital technology that will replace it is still being implemented. (See Fig. 10.1. 35mm Composite)

SMPTE is the time code that enables different computers, synthesizers, and video machines to talk to each other and synchronize music to video, or music to music. The letters stand for "Society of Motion Picture and Television Engineers," which developed this time code in the sixties.

Temp Tracks

Often, the first real involvement the music editor has in a film is towards the middle of post-production. At this time, as the work-print of the film is solidified, the director asks the music editor to prepare a *temp track*. This is a temporary track of music laid into the work-print

35mm Composite

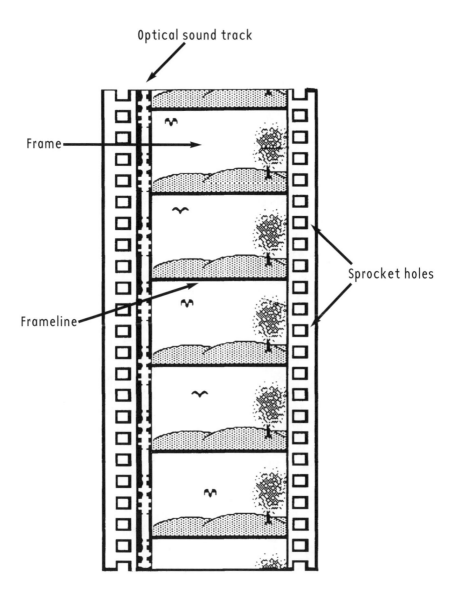

Fig. 10.1. 35mm Composite

of the film in order to give studio executives and test audiences an idea of what the film will be like once the final score is completed. Without any music at all, this work-print can be dry and lifeless, especially in action scenes. So the director gives the music editor some guidelines as to what kind of music to use (if not specific pieces), and the music editor snips and cuts these pieces to fit, not only dramatically, but also rhythmically and harmonically. In the old days, magnetic tape and film had to be spliced in order to accomplish this; today, Pro Tools or other digital audio software is employed. The music for the temp track can come from anywhere—from other soundtracks, from classical, pop, or jazz CDs—anything the music editor can find is fair game. No royalties need to be paid and no sync licenses agreed to because this temporary music will not be used in a version of the film that is shown to the public. It is only used in-house to show the producers, studio executives and test audiences to get their reaction.

Most contemporary films have temp tracks until the final scoring is completed. If one listens closely, often it can be discerned what the temp track was if the composer had to closely imitate it in order to please the director. For example, the temp track for *Titanic* was built from music recorded by the Irish singer Enya. Composer James Horner then had to adapt this kind of flowing, ethereal, New Age style to fit the action. Another good example is the temp track for *Star Wars*. This was Gustav Holst's 1917 classical piece *The Planets*. If the movie is a sequel, it's an easy call. For example, the temp track for *Lethal Weapon IV* was taken from *Lethal Weapon I, II,* and *III.* But no matter what the source of the temp track, music editors must work hard and long to edit a temp track to fit a picture, and they must have command of a huge selection of music from which to choose.

Music editors often use the term *tracking* to describe either the process of creating the temp-track, or to the task of laying-in preexisting music to a finished film. Tracking can refer to the process of creating the temp track for the work print, or to the use of preexisting music in the final version of the film. So, the use of music that is not written by the composer specifically for a scene, where it is taken from another source, is usually called tracking. Eric Reasoner discusses the process of creating temp tracks:

It depends on the relationship between the director, picture editors, and you [the music editor]. You may set up a traditional spotting session where you look at the film and discuss ideas for the temp track. Or you may just screen the film on your own and then converse with the director about styles and things like that, and then just begin searching for music. Sometimes, you have a real wide creative range to pick music that's appropriate, and you can just go your own way.

On The Three Musketeers, *when [music editor] Michael Ryan and I were tracking that film, we had a two or three hour meeting with Steve Herek, the director, where we looked at different parts of the film, talking about style. He had already laid up some music against some scenes as examples, and from that session Michael and I went back to the office and just started searching through tons and tons of existing scores, soundtracks, and CDs, picking out music that fit within those guidelines.*

Spotting Notes

The music editor's next responsibility, after cutting the temp track, is usually to go to the spotting session, take spotting notes, and then prepare the timing notes. *Spotting notes* are a generalized description of where the music begins and ends for each cue. Spotting notes also contain any special instructions discussed between the composer and director for a certain cue like bringing in a theme at a certain point, or hitting a specific piece of action. From the more general spotting notes, the music editor then prepares timing notes, which are very detailed descriptions of each scene with corresponding timings. (See Fig. 10.2. Spotting Notes from *The Simpsons*.)

THE SIMPSONS #5F02 "Treehouse of Horror VIII" · Music Spotting Notes

Page 1

Composer **Alf Clausen** / Music Editor **Chris Ledesma**

9/29/97

CUE #	START	STOP	LENGTH	DESCRIPTION
1M1	01:00:35:17	01:01:04:03	:29	Main Title starts as sword appears; low, change on stabs; play thru title and couch gag to out
1M2	01:01 19:03	01:01:22:14	:03	Open Act 1 - Homega Man - Sci-Fi; tail under Brockman dia
1M3	01:02:12 25	01:02:15:05	:02	Start on cut to military antique store; Homer goes to buy a bomb shelter; tail under next dia.
1M4	01:02:40 11	01:02:44:25	:04	On cut to estab shot of Paris; musette; happy until settle on military compound, then dark on settle; tail under next dia.
1M5	01:02:59 09	01:03:07:28	:09	On cut to Eiffel Tower splitting open; launch missile; ominous and threatening; out on cut to outer space
1M6	01:03:11 08	01:03:23:00	:12	On EOL "What the hell was that?"; through snickering aliens; out on cut to missile headed for earth
1M7	01:03 24:17	01:03:42:10	:18	on cut to missile flying over Springfield; G.P. on comic book guy; resume on POV missile and out on explosion
1M8	01:03:55:14	01:03:59:00	:04	Spooky and creepy on overhead shot of car in traffic; out on cut to back of Homer head leaning out of car
1M9	01:04 20:28	01:04:23:27	03	Sting the push-in on newspaper; out on cut to Homer
1M10	01:04:27:13	01:04:46:21	19	Eerie as Bart ghost appears; thru entire family until Maggie and others are out of frame; then sad as Homer cries; out just before "No, no, no!"
1M11	01:05:02:20	01:05:05:02	02	On cut to estab movie theater; happy Homer; tail on cut to int.
1M12	01:05:23:25	01:05:35:12	12	*SOURCE* -- Homer sings along with a boom box; "War" CD master
1M13	01:05 38:19	01:05 40:10	02	Start on cam settle on mutants; scary/dark; out as Homer shrieks
1M14	01:06 08 19	01:06.28:09	20	As Burns: "And now you must die"; dark and scary; then chase as they run after him; tail on cut to dead chauffeur; thru reveal of coffin and out
1M15	01:06 35 13	01:07 03:13	38	On cut to ext. on car. Car chase; tail on cut to int. house on relieved Homer
1M16	01 07 09 27	01:07 10:14	01	Sting on push-in on mutants; out on cut to reverse angle on Homer
1M17	01 07 22 04	01:07:24:26	03	Start on cut to back of Homer going to hug kids; tail under the mutants: "Awww."
1M18	01 07 56:23	01:08:00:03	03	Sincere Marge as cam pushes in on her during her speech; out to clear "NOW!"

Fig. 10.2. Spotting Notes from The Simpsons.
Used by Permission

Master Cue List

From these spotting notes the music editor creates a *master cue list*, or *music summary*—a list of all the cues and the corresponding places they appear in the film. Eventually, the composer gives every cue a verbal title, like "Billy Splits Quick," or "The Big Kiss." But at this stage, which is before the composer has begun writing, the music editor assigns every cue an alphanumerical designation, like "4M3," which indicates the reel and its location within that reel. The first number is the reel, "M" stands for music, and the last number is a sequential number indicating where that cue is placed in the reel. In this instance, 4M3 means the 4th reel, music cue number 3. Some reels might have several music cues, some might have none. But if a music editor sees 11M2, he knows that piece of music is the second cue in reel eleven.

Note that in television there are variations of this system. Because the shows are divided into "acts," instead of reels, the first number often corresponds to the act number. (An *act* is each segment of the show, divided by commercials.) So 3M2 means Act 3, music cue number 2. And sometimes, in television, the first number refers to the episode number for that particular season, and the second number is simply where the cue falls in the entire show. For example, 14M7 means the seventh cue in the fourteenth show of the year.

The master cue list shows every cue, assigns it an appropriate number, indicates how long it is, and gives the SMPTE time for when it begins. Cues are also called *starts*, meaning that the orchestra has to start a recording for each cue. It is often said, therefore, that the master cue list shows every start. (See Fig. 10.3. Master Cue Sheet from *The Simpsons*.)

Simpsons 5F02
Alf Clausen
Mon 10/6/97 2:00 Pm O'Henry

CUE	CLIX	TIME	TITLE	Vln	Vla	Vc	Bs	1	2	3	4	Hrn	Tpt	Tbn	Tba	Pno	Syn	Harp	Guitar	Drums	Perc	Arr
1m1	9-4	00:28	Halloween VIII	10	3	3	1	R	Ob	BCBC	CB	2	2	2		Syn	Syn	1	·	·	2	AC
1m2	10-1	00:08	The Homega Man	10	3	3	1	AF	Ob	R	R	2	·	2		Syn	Syn	1	·	·	1+El	DH
1m3	12-5	00:07	The Withstandinator·	10	3	3	1	R	Ob	R	Bn	3	2	2		Syn	Syn	1	·	1	2	DH
1m4	9-7	00:05	Cordon Bleu	10	3	3	1	R	Ob	BC	CB	3	·	2		Syn	Syn	1	Gtr	1	1	DH
1m5	16-1	00:09	Rocket In The Pocket	10	3	3	1	R	Ob	Cl	CB	3	2	2		Syn	Syn	1	·	·	2	DH
1m6	21-0	00:12	Kang & Kang	10	3	3	1	·	·	BCBC	CB	3	2	2		Syn	Syn	1	·	·	1	AC
1m7	9-3	00:18	Missile Whistle	10	3	3	1	R	Ob	Cl	Bn	3	2	2		Pro	Syn	1	·	·	2	DH
1m8	13-2	00:08	A Disarming Discourse	10	3	3	1	AF	Ob	R	R	2	·	2		Syn	Syn	1	·	·	1+El	DH
1m9	11-0	00:03	Oh, My Dog Sting	10	3	3	1	R	Ob	Cl	CB	3	2	2		Syn	Syn	1	·	·	2	DH
1m10	15-2	00:19	Just Cos	10	3	3	·	·	EH	·	·	·	·	·		Syn	Syn	1	·	·	2	AC
1m11	11-6	00:07	The Last Man Alive	10	3	3	1	R	Ob	Cl	Bn	3	2	2		Pro	Syn	1	·	·	1	AC
1m13	16-6	00:02	A Mutation Sensation	10	·	·	·	·	·	BCBC	·	·	·	·		Syn	Syn	1	·	·	2	AC
1m14	10-6	00:20	Hearse Castle	10	3	3	1	R	Ob	Cl	Bn	3	2	2		Syn	Syn	1	·	·	·	DH
1m15	9-5	00:28	Cbakie And Dagger	10	3	3	1	R	Ob	Cl	Bn	3	2	2		Syn	Syn	1	·	·	2	AC
1m16	13-4	00:01	Sting Del Mutants	10	3	3	1	R	Ob	Cl	Bn	3	2	2		Pro	·	1	·	·	2	DH
1m17	13-3	00:08	Brings A Tear To Your Eye Socket	10	3	3	1	R	Ob	Cl	Bn	3	·	2		Pro	·	1	·	·	1	DH
1m18	19-4	00:03	Sharing Their Vision - Not	10	3	·	·	AF	·	·	·	2	·	·		·	·	·	·	·	·	DH
1m19	11-3	00:11	That's The Marge I Married	10	3	3	1	R	Ob	Cl	Bn	3	2	2		Pro	Syn	1	·	·	2	AC
2m1	14-3	00:06	Fly vs Fly Theme	10	3	3	1	R	Ob	Cl	CB	3	2	2		Pro	Syn	1	·	·	2	DH
2m3	15-1	00:06	I Must Warn You	10	3	·	·	AF	·	R	·	·	·	·		Syn	Syn	1	·	·	2	DH
2m4	13-6	00:08	The Cat's On His Way Out	10	3	3	1	AF	Ob	Cl	R	2	2	2		Syn	Syn	1	·	·	2	AC
2m5	10-1	00:11	Oh Dog, A New Look	10	3	·	·	·	Ob	·	·	·	·	·		Syn	·	1	·	·	1	DH
2m6	14-0	00:11	A Superfly Fantasy	10	3	3	1	R	Ob	Cl	Bn	3	2	2		Pro	Syn	1	·	·	1+El	DH
2m7	18-4	00:17	Flee, Fly, Flo, Fun	10	3	3	1	R	Ob	Cl	CB	3	2	2		Pro	Syn	1	·	·	2	AC
2m8	10-0	00:05	Big, Fat & Ugly	10	3	3	1	R	Ob	Cl	Bn	2	2	2		Pro	Syn	1	·	·	2	DH
2m9	9-5	00:05	A Little Night Music	10	3	·	·	·	Ob	Cl	·	·	·	·		Syn	·	1	·	·	·	AC
2m10	14-2	00:04	Another Sucker Spidered	10	3	3	1	AF	Ob	BCBC	CB	3	2	2		Syn	Syn	1	·	·	2	DH
2m11	15-7	00:05	Big, Ugly	10	3	3	1	R	Ob	Cl	Bn	3	2	2		Syn	Syn	1	·	·	2	DH
2m12	16-1	00:06	Fly-By Nite Visitor	10	3	·	·	R	Ob	Cl	CB	·	·	·		Syn	·	1	·	·	1	AC
2m13	8-6	00:08	Ew, Gross!	10	3	3	1	AF	Ob	Cl	Bn	3	2	2		Pro	Syn	1	·	·	2	AC
2m14	16-1	00:17	Big Mistake, Flyboy!	10	3	3	1	R	Ob	Cl	Bn	3	2	2		Pro	Syn	1	·	·	2	DH
2m15	17-1	00:12	Don't Trifle With Them	10	3	3	1	R	Ob	Cl	Bn	2	2	2		Pro	Syn	1	·	·	2	AC
3m1	11-4	00:10	Easy Bake Coven Main Title	10	3	3	1	AF	Ob	BCBC	Bn	3	2	2		Pro	Syn	1	·	·	1	DH
3m2	9-5	00:04	The Smoking Lamp is Lit	·	3	·	·	·	Ob	Cl	Bn	3	2	1		Syn	Syn	1	·	·	·	AC
3m3	16-6	00:06	Which Is Witch?	10	3	3	1	R	EH	Cl	CB	3	·	·		Pro	Syn	1	·	·	1+El	DH
3m4	15-5	00:15	Falling Every Witch Way'	10	3	3	1	AF	BH	BCBC	Bn	·	2	2		Syn	Syn	1	·	·	2	AC
3m5	17-3	00:08	Witch Is Which!	10	3	·	·	R	Ob	Cl	Bn	3	·	·		Syn	Syn	1	·	·	1+El	DH
3m6	11-1	00:21	Bats Entertainment	10	3	3	1	AF	EH	Cl	Bn	2	·	·		Pro	Syn	1	·	·	1+El	AC
3m7	12-4	00:09	Frame Spotting	10	3	3	1	AF	BH	BCBC	Bn	·	2	2		Pro	Syn	1	·	·	2	AC
3m8	12-5	00:21	Witch Excitement	10	3	3	1	R	Ob	Cl	Bn	3	2	2		Pro	Syn	1	·	·	2	DH
3m9	13-4	00:01	Crossed-Witch	·	3	·	·	R	Ob	Cl	Bn	3	·	·		Syn	Syn	1	·	·	2	DH
3m10	15-6	00:05	That's Owl, Folks	10	3	3	1	R	Ob	Cl	Bn	3	2	1		Pro	Syn	1	·	·	1	AC
3m11	16-0	00:26	The Story Of Caramel Cod	10	3	3	1	AF	Ob	BCBC	Bn	3	2	2		Syn	Syn	1	·	·	2	AC
3m12	3m12	00:11	Which Witch Is Which?	10	3	3	1	R	Ob	Cl	Bn	3	2	2		Pro	Syn	1	·	·	2	DH
3m13	8-2	00:40		·	·	·	·	R	Ob	·	·	3	2	2		Syn	Syn	1	·	·	2	DH
3m14	10-6	00:03	Gracie Logo	·	·	·	·	·	·	·	·	·	·	·		·	Syn	·	·	·	·	AC

Fig. 10.3. Master Cue Sheet and Orchestra Breakdown from The Simpsons.

Timing Notes

Once the master cue list is done, the music editor makes timing notes for every cue. *Timing notes* (also sometimes called *cue sheets*) are extremely detailed descriptions of every shot, every cut, and every line of dialogue in a scene, with timings to the hundredth of a second. The composer uses these notes to find exact moments to synchronize the music, and also to choose appropriate tempos for the cues. Timing notes are usually prepared on software such as Cue or any word-processing software. (See Fig. 10.4. Timing Notes from *Hearts on Fire*.)

The sequence of the music editor's tasks just described—creating temp tracks, attending the spotting session, music summary, and creating timing notes—are considered the traditional order of events. However, this sequence is changing in today's world as more and more composers begin to digitally sequence their scores by playing along to the video. For these composers, timing notes that describe every single visual event and line of dialogue are not necessary. More common in this situation would be an abbreviated form of timing notes, with a list of any sync points (see chapter 15) the composer wishes to make. A music summary will always be necessary to keep track of the many cues in a score, but it is important to understand that the music editor's job responsibilities change from composer to composer and from director to director.

Syncing and Recording

The next job for the music editor is assisting the composer in synchronizing the music to the film. He prepares click tracks and punches and streamers (see chapter 15, "Syncing the Music to Picture") for the recording session, and makes sure that the music and the picture—either video or film—are locked. Also, at the session, the music editor keeps a log for every take of each cue. If a cue needs to be moved either by a few frames or even by a few seconds, the music editor assists the composer in making the timing changes. This can involve changing tempos, moving bar-lines, or changing the placement of punches and streamers.

In addition, if after the recording session the director asks for significant changes in the music, or wants to place a cue originally

Production: **HEARTS ON FIRE**   Production #: **R#3 Ver.4**   Episode: **Video Date: 4/1/98**
Cue: **3m2** "**DOWNTOWN CHASE**"
Begins at **c3:01:44:17** in Reel/Act 3

ABS. SMPTE #(29):	REL. TIME:		
			Cops FRANK, BILL and JOEY are leaving restaurant. FRANK sees 2 bad guys and:"Hey that's them, hold it!"
c3:01:44:17	0.00		MUSIC STARTS over CLOSE "SHOOTER" (1st bad guy) as he STARTS to RUN
c3:01:44:23	0.20	CUT	CLOSE FRANK and JOEY thru window
c3:01:45:02	0.50		FRANK RUNS
c3:01:45:05	0.60	CUT	CLOSE 2nd bad guy TURNS to RUN
c3:01:45:20	1.10		FRANK CROSSES in FG as bad guy runs away
c3:01:46:02	1.50	CUT	WIDE STREET as BAD GUYS RUN toward CAM
c3:01:47:16	2.97	CUT	MED FRANK RUNS out Restaurant DOORWAY
c3:01:47:27	3.34		OS BILL:"**Hey FRANK!**"
c3:01:48:12	3.84	CUT	MED WIDE STOREFRONT as FRANK RUNS and BILL follows
c3:01:49:09	4.74	CUT	MED CLOSE FRANK as CAM PANS and BILL:"**GET 'EM. HE'S THE SHOOTER**"
c3:01:50:22	6.17	CUT	WIDE STREET as bad guys run down sidewalk
c3:01:51:07	6.67		FRANK into view in BG
c3:01:52:25	8.27		SHOOTER STARTS TOWARD CAM behind VOLVO
c3:01:53:15	8.94	CUT	LONG SHOT STREET as bad guys RUN ACROSS between cars
c3:01:54:24	10.24		FRANK and JOEY START ACROSS as tires SCREACH
c3:01:55:03	10.54	CUT	MED BAD GUYS as they weave thru cars
c3:01:56:02	11.51		CAR SCREACHES as SHOOTER DARTS RIGHT
c3:01:56:10	11.78	CUT	WIDE STREET as FRANK and JOEY run thru cars
c3:01:56:28	12.38		FRANK JUMPS UP ON HOOD of car
c3:01:57:03	12.55	CUT	MED WIDE FRANK FLIPS OVER HOOD as Guys Run in FG
c3:01:57:20	13.11	CUT	MED FRANK lands on street as BILL appears in BG

TOTAL TIME · 13.11

Fig. 10.4. Timing Notes from Hearts on Fire.

slated for an early reel into a later one, it will fall to the music editor to accomplish this task. Although this usually happens at the dubbing stage (see fig. 12.2), sometimes the music editor will move, edit, or rebuild a cue to have it ready for dubbing. This is a time when the music editor's job gets interesting and creative. Taking material meant for one scene and reworking it to fit another requires both technical and musical skill. In addition, this is where the music editor's diplomatic skills come in handy, because at this point he is answering to the director, who may or may not have the ability to communicate musically.

Eric Reasoner:

> Changes occur [at the recording session], and they're subject to tastes of producers or directors—whoever's there running the show. It may be multiple people and that's also frustrating for the composer and any of us that are working to make it right. Basically, you're there to help fix problems. If you're in the booth and the composer's out on the stage, a lot of times you hear things said that would never be said if the composer was in the room, and that's a kind of a nerve-racking experience. So it's basically, figure out if there are problems and figure out what the problems are. If they're simple fixes, like subtracting elements of the music—something that the director doesn't like, you have to find out what they don't like. If it's a sound, a color, or a particular instrument, you can just get rid of it. If it's the whole cue, or how it's structured, then you're really in trouble. The composer will make the musical changes for the orchestra from the podium. But moving bars, and changing the form of the piece creates problems for the synchronization, which is the music editor's department. So you assist the composer by restructuring, whether it's in the computer program or whatever you used to line up the streamers or clicks.

Dubbing

Once the music is recorded, it is mixed to whatever format the film requires—stereo, stereo surround-sound, digital, etc. The music editor then prepares the cues for the final stage, the dubbing. *Dubbing* is when the music, dialogue and sound effects are mixed together for the final version of the film, a process that for an average film takes two to four weeks at the dubbing studio, or dubbing stage.

Until recently, the music editor would prepare reels of mag film with the final music cues that corresponded to reels of picture. Every cue would be placed in order, and if there were a few seconds or minutes of picture in between music cues, the music editor would insert blank film to fill the gaps. The mag film would then run simultaneously with the picture, sound effects, and dialogue at the dubbing stage.

Today, most dubbing is done digitally. The music editor comes to the dubbing stage with a digital file of all the cues, and runs these digital files locked to picture, sound effects, and dialogue via SMPTE time code.

Dubbing happens in two stages. The first is called *pre-dubbing*. At about the same time that the music is being recorded and mixed, the dialogue engineers clean up the dialogue tracks and get them to sound strong and clear, independent of the sound effects and music. (Each voice and each component of a sound effect has its own separate audio "track" that can be controlled independently. Music usually has two to eight tracks depending on the format.) Concurrently, the sound-effects people are doing the same thing in their own studio. One of the reasons pre-dubbing is so important is because of the complexity of some of the tracks; sound effects alone can have over one hundred separate tracks!

When the sound effects, dialogue, and music are all ready (independent of each other), then it is time for the final dubbing sessions when they are all put together. The music editor attends these sessions and assists the dubbing engineers in placing the music at the proper spots. He also has input on the levels and eq of the music.

Also present at the dubbing are the director and sometimes the film editor. This is a critical process because the precise levels of music, dialogue, and sound effects must be found. If one is too loud or soft, it can be distracting or irritating. Also, depending on the format—stereo, stereo surround, digital, etc.—the mix is more or less complex. The director has the final say during this process.

It is at the dubbing session where a composer's music is most likely to be moved around. A director might not really like the cue the way it was designed, and will try a different cue in place of the original. Again, this is his prerogative and it is one that many directors utilize. Many cues from the best composers have been moved around on the dubbing stage. In the movie *Airplane*, during the climactic crash-landing scene, Elmer Bernstein had written a cue with many stops and starts as the picture cut back and forth between the airport gate areas and the plane itself. This was because the humor was in the people waiting, who were running to successively higher gate numbers as the plane came in on its crazy course. Director Jim Abrahams apparently didn't like these stops and starts, so he had the music editor take a low-end ostinato from earlier in the cue and loop it—that is, they repeated the ostinato over and over so there was continuous music throughout the cue instead of the stops and starts Bernstein had written. Incidents like this are not unusual, and the music editor is the one who must accomplish such changes. (The composer does not often attend the dubbing sessions and at this point is usually out of the picture, his job having been completed.)

Eric Reasoner describes the process:

> *It's extremely tedious. You're going back and forth, back and forth, over the same area of sounds with a different focus each time, and if your area of sound isn't of concern at the moment, it's really tedious and you'd like to get out of that room. You may very well spend a 12- or 16-hour day mixing one reel of film— that's a 10-minute segment of film. In action films, when they're really loud, you walk out of there and your ears are just completely fatigued. I can remember going home from the dubbing stage on* Die Hard With A Vengeance *after an action reel. I got up the next morning, and got in the car to go back to the dubbing stage. I started up the car and the radio came on with the volume*

up to 11. I was thinking, oh my god, I was listening at this volume last night when I drove home! It just kind of shows you what your ears and your body can do, shutting down after a bit.

Mark Isham tells how his music editor, Tom Carlson, works at the dubbing stage:

Tom understands the process very well, and he actually looks forward to being the knight in shining armor on the dubbing stage. He's got the patience. He knows how to hang with the guys—the mixers and the whole post-production crew. He's willing to put in those hours, and he's willing to wait until that tenth hour and say, "Can I hear it once with the music up?" And when the director says, "No," he'll just say, "Look, you're missing a chance to be more emotional." He fights the good fight and knows how to do it.

Once the dubbing is completed, there is one more task for the music editor: preparing a finalized list of all the music in the film. This is called a *music clearance sheet*, or *cue sheet*. (Note: cue sheet is a term that has several different uses. Some composers refer to timing notes as cue sheets.) This list is submitted to the appropriate organizations for licensing the music so that royalties can be paid. (Fig. 10.5. Music Cue Sheet from *Die Hard with a Vengeance*.)

After the music clearance list is prepared, the music editor's job is finished. As you have seen, the music editor performs an interesting, important, and unheralded role in the making of a film. In addition, although his musical allegiance and bond may be to the composer, ultimately the music editor answers to the director. An ability to work quickly and accurately under pressure, and also to work with grace under people who are not always kind or gracious, is a must. But the role of music editor is an exciting one that is also crucial to the successful completion of the score and the film itself.

TWENTIETH CENTURY FOX FILM CORPORATION

Music Cue Sheet

(Revised July 1998)

PAGE 1

PRODUCTION: <u>DIE HARD WITH A VENGEANCE</u>   <u>OB27</u>

RELEASE DATE: <u>MAY 1995</u>   <u>WORLDWIDE RIGHTS</u>

1MA
COMPOSITION: TWENTIETH CENTURY FOX TRADEMARK   :21 INSTR BACKGROUND
COMPOSER: ALFRED NEWMAN
PUBLISHER: T C F Music Publishing, Inc. (ASCAP)

1MB
COMPOSITION: CINERGI LOGO   :20 INSTR BACKGROUND
COMPOSER: JERRY GOLDSMITH
PUBLISHER: CINERGI PICTURES ENTERTAINMENT INC. (BMI)

1MC
COMPOSITION: SUMMER IN THE CITY   :49 VOCAL BACKGROUND
COMPOSER: STEVE BOONE/MARK SEBASTIAN/JOHN SEBASTIAN
PUBLISHER: TRIO MUSIC CO. INC./ ALLEY MUSIC, INC. (BMI)

1M1
COMPOSITION: SIMON SAYS FIND MCCLANE   1:21 INSTR BACKGROUND
COMPOSER: MICHAEL KAMEN
PUBLISHER: FOX FILM MUSIC CORP. (BMI)

1MD
COMPOSITION: GIFT RAPPED   :14 INSTR BACKGROUND
COMPOSER: MARK MANGINI
PUBLISHER: T C F MUSIC PUBLISHING, INC. (ASCAP)

1ME
COMPOSITION: GOT IT GOIN ON   :38 VOCAL BACKGROUND
COMPOSER: TED SILBERT/RICHARD BAKER
PUBLISHER: SILBERT MUSIC/HIC-TOWN UNDERGROUND/(ASCAP)

1MF
COMPOSITION: THE FAT OUTRO   :38 VOCAL BACKGROUND
COMPOSER: D. LEE/J. OWENS
PUBLISHER: ZOMBA SONGS INC./BACK SLIDING MUSIC/
                EIGHTY-SECOND SONGS (BMI)

2MA
COMPOSITION: WESTWOOD ON A FRIDAY NIGHT   :13 INSTR BACKGROUND
COMPOSER: MARK MANGINI
PUBLISHER: T C F MUSIC PUBLISHING, INC. (ASCAP)

2MB
COMPOSITION: OFF MINOR   1:29 INSTR BACKGROUND
COMPOSER: THELONIOUS MONK
PUBLISHER: EMBASSY MUSIC CORP. (BMI)

Fig. 10.5. Music Cue Sheet from Die Hard with a Vengeance.
Used by Permission

CHAPTER 11

The Music Team:
Orchestrators and Music Preparation

In today's world, film composing has become a team sport.
—*William Ross*

When writing for a large ensemble of instruments, a full score must be created. This is the version that has one line for every instrument—flutes, oboes, clarinets, French horns, trumpets, violins, etc.—and will be used by the conductor at the recording session. However, making this final score is very time consuming, and it is a job usually given to an orchestrator. So instead of filling in all the notes on a thirty- or forty-line piece of score paper, the composer writes a sketch of the music.

A *sketch* is a condensed version of the cue on 2 to 12 lines of score paper, where a composer lays out the measures and bar lines according to the timings required in a scene. The composer then fills in this sketch to varying degrees of completion. Whether eventually scoring for a full orchestra, a small ensemble, or even when sequencing, a sketch is like a map of the cue. It indicates the timings for each bar and shows the composer where the various dramatic events fall within the boundaries of the music. This sketch can be a simple 2-line piano style version or it can be as many as 10 or 12 staves. It can contain complete information for every melody, counter-melody, chord and even designate individual instruments, as in a John Williams sketch. Or it can be the barest bones, single-line melody with scant harmonic indications, the rest to be filled in by the orchestrator. This sketching process is a great time-saving device for the composer, and allows him to focus on getting the music written for each cue without getting lost in the details of notating the orchestration. It is important to note that many composers, especially the classically trained ones, are excellent orchestrators. Some composers, like Ennio Morricone, insist on having enough time on the film to be able to do their own orchestrations. However, they may still complete a sketch first, and then orchestrate from it. (See Fig. 11.1. Sketch example and finished score.)

In some cases, the sketch itself is not even written down by the composer. This happens when the composer sequences parts of the cue or plays it live to some kind of tape format. In this case, the music needs to be transcribed, written out note-for-note as it is on the tape. Usually this is done by a third person, a *transcriber*, who listens to the cue, writes it out as a sketch, and then passes it on to the orchestrator. For composers who get their ideas by playing along to video, this system works well, for it enables them to work quickly without having to worry about setting notes down on paper.

In today's world of electronics, the sketch can also be generated as MIDI files. These MIDI files are given to an assistant to edit and make sure the printout matches the composer's music accurately. The orchestrator then works from the assistant's edited sketch. This is also known as a MIDI transcription. Some scores are electronic in the entire music preparation process; the composer generates a MIDI file, it is edited, the orchestrator orchestrates on a software program instead of by hand, and parts are generated automatically from the orchestrator's full score. All of these stages are often accomplished via e-mail or the Internet, so no one leaves his home or studio until the recording session.

Orchestrators

Once the composer has completed the sketch, or the transcription is prepared, the next stage in the journey to the recording session is the orchestration. As I mentioned, many film composers are fine orchestrators in their own right. In fact, many of these composers started out in the film-scoring business by orchestrating for established composers. However, many very talented film composers, especially those who come from the ranks of rock, pop, and solo jazz music, are not trained in orchestration and rely on their orchestrators to help them achieve an appropriate sound.

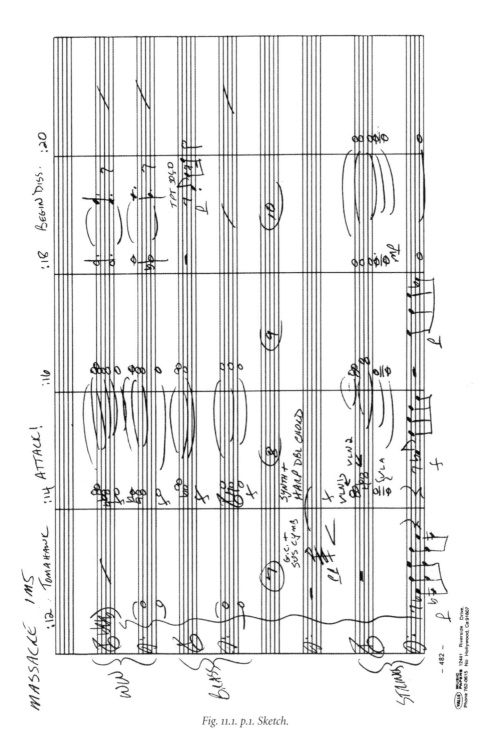

Fig. 11.1. p.1. Sketch.

Fig. 11.1. p.2. Finished score.

William Ross:

> *An orchestrator is a problem solver. Your best skill as an orchestrator is your ability to solve a problem, whether it's musical, psychological, economic—whatever it is. That's the mission: to solve these problems.*

Orchestrators themselves can be from any background in music—classical, jazz, pop, country—but they must have studied composition and orchestration in depth in order to be able to execute what is required of them in a film score. Obviously, a full knowledge of many instruments is required: their high and low ranges, where they sound strong and where they sound weak, which rhythms sound natural and which ones sound awkward, whether there are any troublesome notes, and how they balance, overpower, or blend with other instruments. A thorough knowledge of composition is required since an orchestrator might be required to write a counterline, fill in a harmony, or voice-lead a series of chords.

When the sketch is ready, the composer usually meets with the orchestrator and discusses the cues. Depending on how complete the sketch is, the composer will give instructions as to who will play a certain part, or how loud or dissonant a specific measure might get. The orchestrator then goes home and begins working on the full score. Many orchestrators like to have a video of the cue with a window burn (see chapter 15) as well as the timing notes so that they can know exactly what is happening in the scene and how the music fits. Oftentimes, the composer and orchestrator have an ongoing relationship, faxing sketches to each other and discussing cues over the phone. This saves a great deal of time so the orchestrator does not have to go back and forth to the composer's home or studio. Once the full score is completed, the orchestrator delivers it to the composer to be proofed, and either a messenger brings it to the copyist or the orchestrator sends an electronic file to the copyist.

How much the orchestrator has to add, change, or rewrite depends on the composer and the individual project. Often it is a matter of the orchestrator's ability to determine whether the passage in question should remain as it is on the sketch or whether it should be changed.

William Ross has orchestrated for over 100 films, and is also a composer in his own right. He explains the orchestrator's role:

> *My job as an orchestrator is to assist the composer in getting the job done. Because of today's post-production schedules, it's very difficult for anyone to compose and orchestrate their own music.*

Orchestrators work as independent contractors; they are basically freelance and go wherever their services are needed. The pay scale for an orchestrator is determined by the musicians union (the American Federations of Musicians, or AFM), and is calculated by the number of pages scored (four measures per page) and the number of staves on the page. Depending on the texture and complexity of the cue, this could take a few hours or an entire day. The difficult cues and the easier ones tend to balance each other out in the long run.

One final thought on orchestrators. It is sometimes said that an orchestrator or team of orchestrators has saved a composer. At times this can be true. But the bottom line is that the composer has a vision of the finished music, and even if he sketches only the bare minimum, he is the driving force behind a score. Composers count on the orchestrator's ability to make the music sound good. So if the composer's musical concept is a sound one for the project, then the orchestrator is really just amplifying this concept. If the concept is poor, then no amount of help by the orchestrator can make it succeed.

Music Preparation: Copyists

Once the orchestrator completes the full score it goes to a music preparation office. In the old days of Hollywood, every studio had its own music preparation office. In fact, *all* the music people were under contract and they worked only for that studio. So, the music would go down an in-house assembly line, from composer to orchestrator to music preparation to orchestra, and never leave the studio lot. Nowadays, everything is contracted out to individuals or small companies that have offices in various locations.

When an orchestrated cue arrives at the music preparation office, it is checked off on a master chart. There can be as many as forty or fifty individual cues for a single film, so there is a lot to track. The head of this office assigns one or more copyists to work on each cue. The *copyist* is the person who makes the parts up for the individual instruments. In the past two years (1997 to 1998), most of the copying work has converted from being handwritten to computer software-generated, usually either Finale or Erata. An orchestrator can turn in either a handwritten score, or a score done in one of these programs, and the copyist can prepare and extract the parts for the orchestra.

Once the copyist finishes a part for a cue, say the viola part, he then gives it to a proofreader. The *proofreader* checks the newly copied viola part against the master score for errors. This is to ensure that these errors are not discovered on the scoring stage where they would take costly minutes to fix (time on a scoring stage can cost several hundred dollars per minute). Once the proofreader completes a part or a stack of parts, he gives them to the supervisor of the music preparation office who then goes to the master chart and checks off those parts that are complete.

The next person in line is the music librarian. This is a crucial job. The *music librarian* sees that every musician in the orchestra has the proper music on his music stand at the start of the session. There can be as many as forty or fifty cues being recorded over just a few days. The composer is in communication with the music preparation office to say which cues he wants to record on which days, and to find out which cues are actually ready. The music librarian consults the master chart to make sure the desired cues are completed, takes the music to the scoring stage, and places the music on the stands of the musicians.

By this point in the production process, the film is often behind schedule, and all these music people can be working under enormous time pressure. It is common for the music preparation office to be in full swing from 8:00 a.m. until after midnight, or even all night. All of these people are also musicians, and many of the copyists, proofreaders, and music librarians work their way to orchestrating and composing. These are all union jobs, jobs where the salary is dictated by the American Federation of Musicians, which also covers orchestrators and recording musicians. (Interestingly enough, composers do not have to belong.) Because the union has established good "scales" or rates, these music preparation jobs can be financially rewarding.

Because of the shortened schedules in modern post-production, the composer must rely on his team to get the score from conception to the big screen. This means having reliable people to assist with the myriad details of sequencing, orchestrating, copying, booking musicians, and so forth. The goal is to create a space where the composer can focus on composing, and everyone else does his part to accomplish that.

Fig. 12.1. Scoring Stage. Todd-AO Studios. Studio City, CA.

CHAPTER 12

The Recording Session and Mix

You forget and sometimes you have to pinch yourself and realize, "Oh my goodness, this is amazing!" These are the best players, definitely the best sight-readers in the world. Absolutely the best sight-readers. And, the mistakes-quotient is: there is hardly ever a mistake.
—Lolita Ritmanis

Finally the time has arrived when all the hours of work and preparation become a physical reality. There is nothing like walking onto the scoring stage and seeing dozens of musicians gathered there to play your music. It is the moment every composer waits for.

Present at the session are the composer, conductor (if the composer is not conducting), director, producer, music editor, musicians, recording engineers, and all kinds of assistants and on-lookers. The orchestrators are not required to be there, but often stop by to see how things are going. However, usually an orchestrator, or someone else with score-reading abilities, sits in the control room with the recording engineer and follows the score to check for errors that the conductor might not hear. This person also assists the engineer in determining which instruments are playing when (especially helpful if there is a solo of some kind). The music editor usually sits behind the conductor or in the control room at a table armed with all the timing notes, a copy of the score, and his computer(s).

This is also an exciting and sometimes anxiety-ridden moment for the film makers. They have put months or years of work into producing the film; all the writing, shooting and editing are complete and the music is the final element to be added. Stephen Spielberg has said that a film is "dry and lifeless" without music, and many agree with him. Even though the director and producer may have seen a sequenced mock-up of the cues, there is nothing like the real thing and there is an air of anticipation, even apprehension, as the session begins. The reality is that when a director hands over the film to a composer, he has just lost control of the film for the first time. What the composer decides to do with the music can literally make or break the film. So the moment of truth is the first day of recording.

In the days or weeks before the sessions begin, the composer and music contractor discuss personnel requirements. The *music contractor*, or simply the *contractor*, books the studio, hires the musicians, takes care of all the union paperwork and the payroll for the musicians, and oversees the sessions to make sure everything is on time and happening according to union rules. In their initial conversations, the composer and contractor discuss the numbers of players and the breakdown of the orchestra—how many strings, woodwinds, brass, rhythm section players, etc., are needed. They also discuss any specific musicians the composer requests, and alternates. Some chairs have very specific requirements. For example, a woodwind chair might need someone who can play flute, soprano sax, recorder, and oboe. It is up to the contractor to find the appropriate players.

The music does not have to be recorded in the order it appears in the film, so the composer decides in advance which cues will be recorded in what order, and the music preparation office, as well as the music editor, are informed. There are different methods of beginning a session. Some like to start with something easy to warm up the orchestra, some like to begin with something fairly challenging. Most composers agree that if there is recurring thematic material, it is good for the orchestra to start with a cue where that material is fairly complete—usually the first or second cue—so that the musicians can hear it and recognize any variations or permutations down the line. Often, this is the main-title cue, but it could also come from another place in the movie.

Sometimes a film requires the entire orchestra to play on every cue. However, many times there are smaller groups that play various cues throughout the film, such as strings only, or a small group of strings, guitar, and oboe that are featured in several cues. In this case, the composer records all the cues for the larger group at one time, and then lets most of the players leave while the smaller group records. This is efficient and cost-effective. The larger group is known as the "A" orchestra, the smaller combinations the "B" orchestra, the "C" orchestra, etc.

Because of an agreement with the musicians union, there are certain rules governing the recording session. For feature films, a maximum of nine minutes of music per three-hour session may be recorded. (Sessions are usually booked in three-hour blocks.) For episodic television (series) and TV movies, a maximum of fifteen minutes per three-hour block is allowed. This is so the producers cannot take advantage of the sight-reading abilities of the musicians and record a huge amount of music in a short amount of time. If the session goes into overtime then these formulas are prorated. In addition, there are other regulations, like taking a ten-minute break every hour, a meal break after a certain amount of hours recording, etc. The contractor, who is the liaison to the union, attends the session and assists the composer in keeping track of these rules.

Once the cue is recorded to the composer's satisfaction, he goes into the control room to join the director and producer, and watch a playback of the scene with the music synced to the film. At this point, the director either signs-off on the cue, or asks for changes. Minor changes can be made right on the spot. If a major rewrite is required, the composer puts that cue away to be fixed before the next session, and he proceeds to another cue.

Every once in a while a composer's score is disliked by the director, the producer, or the studio executives. This can create a situation where the score is thrown out and another composer is brought in to redo it. This is embarrassing for the original composer and frustrating, as he has just spent several very intense weeks of his life on the project. It is also costly for the production team; they must still pay the first composer his full fee, they have paid the musicians and the recording studio for their time, and they must then must hire a second composer and pay the music production costs all over again. It is uncomfortable for all involved, yet it has happened to almost every major feature film composer in Hollywood.

One very important thing to keep in mind is that just because a score is thrown out does not mean that the music is bad, or even inappropriate for that film. All it means is that someone with enough power didn't like it. It is entirely possible that this person (director, producer, studio exec) had his own musical concept and could not make the shift to the composer's different, yet dramatically effective, idea. Whenever a score is thrown out, it causes composers to wonder if they are really good enough, or what they did wrong. It is possible, of course, that the score was not what the production team wanted and the composer made a big error in concept even though the music was sound. But it is also possible that the score was thrown out for an irrational reason that has nothing to do with the quality of the music.

Most of the time, the recording session is an exciting and rewarding moment for the composer. Music representing weeks of work is finally heard and its effectiveness evaluated. Flexibility is a key attribute to have at the session, for changes are often requested. Sometimes the director wants a little more dissonance or less musical activity in a cue. Sometimes a cue needs to be lengthened or shortened. Sometimes everyone, including the composer, is in agreement about a certain change, and sometimes the composer disagrees. The bottom line is that the composer needs to be able to make changes quickly without being overly attached to what was already written. Making movies is a team exercise.

Overlaps and Segues

There are some instances when a composer wants to score a scene, and rather than doing the music in one piece, he records two separate cues and edits them together to create one longer, seamless cue. This is called an *overlap* or *segue*. A composer might do this is if the scene is very long, if there is a significant mood or tempo change, or if there are two completely different groups of instruments involved in each cue.

Most composers like to keep each cue under three to four minutes. This is largely due to the recording process. Although the professional musicians that play the top film scores and television shows are incredible sight-readers, they do occasionally make mistakes. It is very time consuming to stop the orchestra, go back to the start of the cue, reset the projection equipment if there are punches and streamers, and go for another take. In addition, at most sessions there is not true "separation" of the different players or sections of the orchestra in terms of multitrack recording. Although every section gets his own track, and soloists also get assigned a track, in the studio itself there is often bleed-through. So a composer or producer must be very careful about accepting a take and trying to "fix it in the mix." For this reason, it is common practice to try to get the best recording of the entire orchestra at once. (With digital editing, it is now easier to edit different takes together, but there is not always time for this.)

So, if a cue becomes too long, then many composers will find a spot to break it up into two or more cues that are recorded separately and edited together. This can be done seamlessly by matching harmonies, finding common tones from one cue to another, or matching instrumentation. The music editor reassembles the parts into one longer piece.

Such segues are planned when the composer writes the score. The composer constructs a segue from one cue to another so that the sonorities match, or don't match, as is necessary.

Mixing and Dubbing

For a major feature film, the orchestra is recorded in 24-track or 48-track analog format, or one of the many digital multitrack formats. This gives the mixdown engineer great flexibility in the final mix. This is necessary because there might actually have to be more than one mix of the music: one for surround-sound digital theatrical playback, one for stereo theatrical playback, and one for the soundtrack CD. Depending on schedules, the composer is not always at the mixing session, often leaving it to a trusted associate.

Because of the tight post-production schedule, the many minutes of underscore must be mixed quickly. In the modern age of automated mixes (where the mixing boards are "smart" and remember fader levels, eq settings and outboard routings), the engineer actually mixes during the recording session itself. That is to say, he sets levels, adjusts

Fig. 12.2. Dubbing Stage. Studio 1, Todd-AO Studios. Hollywood, CA.

eq, and gets a rough version of the mix, so that when the music is finally mixed for real, he has a head start. A good film-score engineer can mix five to ten minutes per day. This is for an orchestra that can have as many as 80 to 100 players! Compare that to the pop-music record mix, which is going very quickly if one or two four-minute songs per day are completed.

Ideally, the same person who engineers the recording session should do the mix. This person is the most familiar with the cues, and thus can move fast. However, sometimes this is not possible. Oftentimes, the schedule is so tight that the music must be mixed as soon as it is recorded. This means that the mixing can overlap the recording. A recording session might begin on Tuesday; on Wednesday, the recording session continues, while Tuesday's tracks are mixed at a second studio.

After the music is mixed to the proper format, it goes to the dubbing stage. This is where the music, sound effects, and dialogue get mixed together for the final soundtrack (see chapter 10).

Reel by reel, scene by scene, line by line, and sometimes crash by crash, the dubbing team mixes, filters, eqs, pans, and generally tweaks the music, sound effects, and dialogue to blend together. Of course, the dialogue is the paramount force here. It always must be heard. But the music and sound effects have important roles as well. The toughest thing is when two sounds happen in the same frequency range. For example, a very high, sustained note in the violins could be cancelled out by the whine of a jet engine. Or a male actor's tender but somewhat throaty declaration of love could be challenged by a lyrical cello line. It is the job of those on the dubbing stage to make all of these things sound like one continuous whole. A sound palette that sounds natural and lets each voice or sound speak where necessary is the ultimate goal.

Dubbing is the next to last stage in the entire film-making process, and it is actually the final stage of the creative process. Nothing can be changed or altered after the dubbing, for the only stage left after this is "color correction"—when the film is processed and the director approves its colors and tints. In many ways, dubbing is the point of no return for the director, for at the various stages of production and post-production, changes can and will be made frequently. During the making of the film, the director makes many decisions, and commits to many paths of action, but the decisions made at the dubbing stage are the final commitment. For this reason, it is a detailed, painstaking process, and the feeling of completion is profound for all.

The Music

CHAPTER 13

Creating the Music

It's like anyone else. If the plumber doesn't take the wrench
out of the bag, he's never going to get that pipe off, right?
Well, if you don't sit down and play something or write
something, you're never going to get it finished.
—Mark Isham

There are times when the most intimidating experience a composer can have is looking at a blank sheet of paper or computer screen. And there are other times when that same blank paper can be something he looks forward to filling with wonderful, exciting ideas. This is the reality of the creative process; there are ups and downs, there are times when the ideas just keep coming, and times when the stream is stone dry. For a composer working in films, there is usually no luxury of waiting until the juices start flowing. Often he must find a way to turn on the faucet himself.

Three Cornerstones of Composition

There are several important, yet simple concepts that can help in actually controlling and sometimes even jump-starting the creative process: first, having a foundation of craft and knowledge of music; second, knowing what you want to say dramatically, emotionally, and psychologically; and, third, knowing your own strengths, weaknesses, and capacity to produce. In the film-scoring business, these are all extremely important. As we have seen in other chapters, because the composer comes in at the end of the film-making process, the pressure to produce in a timely manner is often enormous. So a composer relies on his craft, the intent of what he wants to say, and knowledge of his own capacities to deliver the score on time.

Craft

It is important to have developed your craft so you have as much technique as possible. If you write great romantic melodies, but that is all you do well, then obviously you are rather limited. If you are great at action/adventure films, what will you do if the project you accepted requires some scenes in the style of To Kill A Mockingbird? Will you find someone to ghost it?

The more you know about music, and the more different kinds of music you have analyzed extensively, the more tools you have at your disposal. Your musical vocabulary becomes larger and you can speak in many musical languages. Traditional orchestral, atonal, jazz oriented, or pop-music derived soundtracks will not intimidate you if you are thoroughly familiar with how these styles work.

For many, this is an ongoing life-long process that begins early. For every composer there are variations on the theme of musical learning and development. When you begin a project, if you can draw upon many different kinds of musical expressions, you are much better off. You will know the kinds of harmonies, rhythms, and melodies to write. As you watch a scene, or when you sit down to write, your familiarity with a style may start to suggest possibilities. Or if you are stuck, your knowledge of what it should sound like can bail you out. For example, if you know the director wants a particular scene to be heroic, there are certain rhythmic and melodic devices that you can draw from to create something of your own. On the other hand, if your background is narrow, and you are asked to write something outside of what you know, it can be difficult and time-consuming, if not flat-out impossible, to create something appropriate.

Study requires discipline and curiosity. If you are not interested in a particular style, if it doesn't make you sit up and take notice, curl your ears, or give you goose-bumps, then study that style as an academic exercise. This can be a necessary academic exercise for the aspiring film composer.

Alf Clausen, Emmy-winning composer for *The Simpsons*, strongly believes in the need for musical curiosity and study. He speaks about this issue in relationship to writing songs in different styles:

> *[Students'] questions are always very pointed about "How do you do this, how do you do that, how do you write these styles, etc." My response is to ask, Have you dissected the popular songs of all the eras to find out what makes them work? Have you analyzed them to find out what the chord progressions are, what the melodic tricks are, what chord tones on what chords created a certain sound in a certain era? And can you sit down and write a song in that style because you have spent hundreds of hours dissecting those songs? And they say, "Not yet." Well, I have. I have spent thousands of hours dissecting and playing those songs. It's a matter of craft, it's a matter of study.*

Intent and Concept

The intent of your music, or knowing what you want to say, is crucial. There is such a large range of emotion and feeling that can be expressed by music that it often takes a lot of thought, contemplation, and sometimes even prayer to figure out what to do with a particular film or scene. But to start writing without knowing what you want to say is like trying to swim without knowing the strokes; when you get in the water, you would just flail around and desperately try to stay afloat. It is important to take in a whole lot of information: the flow of the drama, the look of the film, and probably most important for the composer, the tempo of the scene. Every film and every scene has its own musical implications, and the composer must know what a film or scene means before beginning to write.

Elmer Bernstein has composed the scores to over 200 films, and is quite familiar with this process:

> *The first thing I do is to spend a week just looking at the film without prejudice. When I say without prejudice, I say to myself, I'm not even going to try to think music during this week. I just want to look at the film until the film talks to me and the film*

tells me things. What I want the film to tell me is what it's about, and that's not always on the surface. What is the film about? What is the function of music going to be in this film? Why are we having music in this film, what's it going to do? So I start with those kinds of thoughts—it's a kind of intellectual process rather than a composing process.

Now, I had a big problem with that in To Kill a Mockingbird, *because if you look at the film without music, all you're looking at is a film with a lot of kids in it. But you're also seeing a lot of adult problems—problems of racism, problems of injustice, death and violence, violence to children. So it took me the longest time to find where the music was going to go, how it was going to go, and what its specific use would be in the film. I determined after a long time—it took me six weeks—that the film is about the adult world seen through the eyes of children. All these problems, what we call adult problems, are seen as the children see them. Which led me to childlike things. For instance, playing the piano one note at a time, music box sounds, harp, bells, things of that sort. So what really got me into the film was the realization— at least, my realization—that it was a film about adult things seen through the eyes of children.*

Taking six weeks, as in *To Kill a Mockingbird*, to think about the approach to a film is a luxury most film composers don't have today. But they usually can take a few days, or perhaps a week, to come up with ideas. Once the concept becomes clear, ideas will often start to flow because the composer has a firm sense of direction.

Knowing Yourself

Dick Grove, a well-known music educator in Los Angeles, used to say, "We all think we're writing music to make money, or to move people. But what we're really doing, if we just take a look, is finding out about ourselves." When we sit down to write music, many things about ourselves come into play: How disciplined am I? How much do I trust my training and ability? How much do I believe in myself? Am I actually enjoying writing music, and having fun? Or is it a chore? Am I following the instructions of the client, or is my ego too big to listen to anyone other than my own infallible creative voice? On the other hand, am I too concerned with what people will think of me to stand up for my opinions, especially if someone asks for something I know is musically a bad idea?

These questions, and others, can come into play every time a composer accepts a gig. At some level in every writer's consciousness, there is an expression of one or more of these questions, whether they have acknowledged it or not. For example, are you the type that procrastinates until the last minute? If so, get a handle on it, for a film with 60 minutes of music won't get written the night before. Do you have a problem taking direction and/or feedback? Lose it, because as soon as you sign the contract, you are somebody's employee. Do you know you can write quickly and appropriately? Nurture that and utilize it. Are you very organized and structured? Stay organized, but don't forget to stay flexible.

When a composer sits down and starts to write, it is essential that he be brutally honest about these questions. He must know how many minutes a day he can produce, how many days there are before the recording session, which cues seem to be suggesting musical ideas, and which cues are tougher. There is very little time for second-guessing and extensive rewriting of any one cue, so confidence in ones technique is crucial. Being clear in ones communication with the director and a willingness to translate the director's requests into music are fundamental to this process.

Developing the Concept for the Score

In speaking with composers, the one thing that comes through again and again is that the most successful scores have a concept that drives the music. Then, once the concept for the whole score is set, each individual cue presents a particular problem to be solved. For example, just because the main concept for a film is big, orchestral, and Romantic doesn't mean that there cannot be a piano solo if the drama calls for it. But that piano solo must still feel like part of the rest of the score. In today's world, almost any musical language is part of the composer's palette, so the choices abound. But keeping to the overall concept keeps the sound focused.

Elliot Goldenthal is an accomplished composer of film scores, ballets, theatre, and concert works. He has found a way of approaching a score that produces a unique sound for each of his projects:

> Before I approach anything, I have a very strong concept of what I want to pull off, whether it works out or not. That might include limiting the choice of pitches or a very clear choice of orchestration. So I don't go into something and just start improvising, I find that if I do that, I just sort of waste my time. I stay away from the piano, away from the computer, away from the pencil. I think about the scene and I say, How can I achieve the dramatic effect that is necessary for the scene and have it still sound fresh? How can I make it sound like you haven't heard that before, you haven't lived that before? Sometimes the answer can be surprisingly simple. In Alien 3, for example, I used a solo piano to underline the scene with the little girl because I thought that having a piano way out in space would remind you of the most domestic of all instruments—it would remind you of home. Just things like that. That's a concept.

Sometimes a composer's concept for a film can be generated from a feeling or an idea that, in itself, is not musical. Many composers are very artistic in the way they look at the world; that is to say, they see the world in terms of emotional responses that eventually get translated into music. Clearly, this is a very valuable way to see things from the standpoint of writing music for the visual medium of film. Cliff Eidelman discusses his conception of the score to *One True Thing*:

> I had this idea of time changing, the changing of seasons. The feeling of wind passing through trees and then leaves blowing off in another direction. This wasn't music yet; it was just a feeling I wanted to add.

I set individual instruments apart from the orchestra, separated into their own isolation booths. Like three cellos in one room, or three violas with two woodwinds in another. They were off in their own rooms and the orchestra was in the center. Now, my concept was that the piano should be the main idea, accompanied by a small orchestra so that it felt intimate, and never too large. An introverted mood.

I also wanted it to feel like wind was carrying the music this way and out that way, creating different perspectives. The music wasn't just coming from the center of the room. It was coming from over here, and it shifted over there, and then it would come back over here.

So, early on, this conceptual approach merged with the themes. When I started producing musical ideas, my concepts worked their way in.

For me, the main thing is always the spine of the story. So, the first thing I do is look for that emotional core—that emotional spine of the story—within the soul of the music itself.

In *Forrest Gump*, Alan Silvestri had to come up with an opening music cue that would embody the whole film. He first discussed the opening shot, of the feather floating down from the sky and almost landing on Forrest, with director Robert Zemeckis:

[Zemeckis] didn't really go into a whole lot of detail, but the gist of what we did talk about was somehow, "This is the start of the movie. This is the start of this whole incredible odyssey we're about to go on." My take on it was … I've got a couple of things to deal with now. One is, I've got physical things to deal with. I've got some events; the feather floats from the blue sky, makes an entrance into this town. It winds up almost landing on somebody's shoulder then at the last moment it's blown off. It's very symbolic, you know, if you're looking at this as something descending upon someone's life, that guy is not chosen right now. Then eventually the feather lands on Forrest; he's the chosen one.

So now we've got some physical things in terms of the image, and we've also got some events that are episodic in a sense. Coming from nowhere, blue sky, into this town, what does it mean? It's just a feather, then it almost lands on somebody, blows off. Now, there's some kind of dramatic context.

So now, what do you do? The invisible aspect of this is that somehow whatever you do also has to essentialize and embody this entire film. Right now. This cannot be "feather music." This cannot be "falling down music." This cannot be "missed opportunity music." This music somehow has to take everything, sentiment wise, that this film is about, and somehow essentialize it and present it. I'm thinking, at this point, if I can find that, I've got the key to this film. This theme will be all over the movie, and there will be a tremendous sense of cohesiveness for the overall tone of this film.

Now of course all of this is going on under the surface because I'm not sitting there making lists and treatises on 1M1. I know I've got to do something here. So I sit down at the piano, and I'm thinking, "This music has to deal with Forrest," and I start doodling at the piano. Literally in 20 minutes it's done! It's childlike, and it's simple, and yet it's not baby-like. It's innocent. It's what I'm feeling from Forrest. I look at this moment, where the feather moves away from this other guy. I make a key change there—an immediate unprepared key change there. We already planned that we're going to bring the orchestra in, with more sense of scope at this point.

That was the mission in Forrest. *It had to be an honest attempt. Musically, as an actor, as a writer, as a cinematographer, don't get cute with this movie, or you'll sink the ship.*

This anecdote embodies many of the principles outlined above with Silvestri's own personality and musical sensibility bringing it to its ultimate destination. He had a clear idea of what he needed to do, and what *not* to do dramatically. And having this understanding, he was able to sit down and create the theme that was just right for this film.

(Ironically, this theme was eventually used in only one other spot in the film: the ending where we see the feather again. Every time he tried to use it elsewhere, it just didn't work.)

One of the joys of film composing is this process of discovering a concept. Unlike writing concert works or pop songs, the film composer is responding to the visual images and the story on the screen. These images and story-lines suggest musical ideas and provide a framework within which the music can fit. Many composers have said that once they find the initial concept, the rest of the score writes itself. The trial and error, the thought, and contemplation often result in the stimulation of the composers imagination. Then he experiences the satisfaction of completing the director's vision of the film in the language of music.

CHAPTER 14

Technical Requirements of the Score

Nobody goes to the movies to listen to the score.
The score is simply assisting them in watching the film.
—Michael Kamen

Once a composer arrives at a concept for the score, he is ready to begin writing individual cues. However, there are many things to consider for each cue: its placement in the film, what kind of scene it is, whether or not there is dialogue, and how much of the story the music should express. These are just some of the many important considerations in structuring the score of a movie.

Perhaps the most important factor here is that a film can be anywhere from a short subject of just a few minutes to a full-length feature of over two hours. Either way, as the story unfolds on screen, the music must continually develop so that it stays interesting. Themes develop, instrumentation develops, and the overall emotional thrust of the music has an arch that matches the arch of the film. In addition, the music can affect the way the film has been put together; it can smooth out cuts, transitions, or dissolves. It can also help the audience understand shifts in location in time or place. Every cue has an impact that the composer and director are considering when placing it in the movie.

The first question that faces the composer is "What is this cue's dramatic function?" For the purposes of this discussion, I divide the various functions of film music into three broad categories: physical functions, psychological functions, and technical functions. As the interviews at the end of this book illustrate, every composer has a different working procedure. They each approach the task of writing a score and coming up with suitable material from a different angle.

Sometimes they intellectually analyze a scene and determine its musical requirements; sometimes they write from instinct. Frequently, some of the functions of the music overlap, or are vague, because every situation is different and can have more than one dramatic implication.

Physical Functions

Music frequently functions in a way that impacts the physical action or location of the scene. This includes:

Setting the location of the film. If a movie takes place in an exotic location, often this setting is reflected in the music. For example, a movie that takes place in Ireland could use Uillean pipes and a pennywhistle. A movie that is set in the Appalachian Mountains of the United States might call for banjos and fiddles. How much this "ethnic" music is incorporated into the score will be a decision made by the composer and the director. They could decide to have the score sound authentic to the location, or simply incorporate one or two elements of the ethnic music into an orchestral score. (See chapter 15 for more on this.)

Setting the time period. If a movie takes place in another historical era, sometimes music of that time will be used. For example, if a film is set in 18th century Europe, a harpsichord can be used to give the audience an immediate association with that time. For movies set in medieval times, there are various ancient instruments like shawm, sackbutt, or psaltery that can be used. Again, as in *setting the location*, the composer may use a lot of these sounds, or just a hint.

Mickey-mousing. When the music mimics every little action on screen, it is called *mickey-mousing*. There is a difference, however between mickey-mousing and simply hitting various sync points. Mickey-mousing is a term reserved for hitting a lot of the action, not just one or two moments. It is often, though not exclusively, used as a comic device.

Intensifying the action. This musical technique is commonly used in action scenes. Chase scenes, fights, intense arguments between characters, and suspenseful moments are all heightened with appropriate music. To intensify the drama, composers might write music that closely follows the action onscreen, and often has many sync points. In this way, music partners with the drama very closely and accentuates what is seen, as opposed to bringing a different emotional element to the scene.

Psychological Functions

Music can assist the psychological and emotional impact of the film in many ways. Sometimes it can be parallel to the drama and say basically the same thing as what is viewed on-screen. At other times, the music can add a new dimension, thought, or idea that is not expressed by dialogue or action. Some of the psychological functions of film music are:

Creating the psychological mood. Every film score must have a "sound" to be successful. If the movie is one that has psychological implications, then the overall mood of the score or any individual scene becomes very important. For example, in *What Dreams May Come,* a film that deals with death and the afterlife, a score was originally composed that was dark and somewhat serious. The production team decided that this approach did not work; it was too dark and needed to be lightened up. So they brought in Michael Kamen to redo the score three weeks before the release of the film.

Michael Kamen:

> *The original score was too serious. This film is about death and dying and it's a very serious film. I was asked to go the other way with it. I felt very close to the subject matter, as I had a real life experience at that time: my wife had just overcome a mortal illness. So I was able to respond to the film with joy and some sense of magic.*

There are countless examples of a change in the music altering the impact of a scene or an entire movie. The composer must continually be aware of the result of any musical moods, or even individual melodies or harmonies.

Revealing the unspoken thoughts and feelings of a character. Often, a director wants the audience to understand something about the char-

143

acter that is either not expressed verbally or not entirely clear from the visual action. The music can help to communicate these things because it can represent another dimension of the character's inner world—his thoughts, feelings and deepest emotions. A good example of this is the movie, *Thunderheart,* starring Val Kilmer. In this film, Kilmer plays an FBI agent sent to investigate a murder on an American Indian reservation. His father was half Indian and part of the plot deals with his character's struggle to understand his own heritage and ancestry. Towards the beginning of the film, when Kilmer's character first arrives in South Dakota, he sees an ancient Indian costume on display. The visual shows him simply staring at the costume, expressionless, but the music is tense and dark, representing his confused frame of mind.

Revealing unseen implications. How many times have we watched the good guy draw his gun and slowly walk down a deserted alley in search of the bad guys? Then the low strings come in with a sustained, swelling note, and we *know* they're out there somewhere! The music can tip us off to what is going to happen, both in a suspenseful way, and in a way that resolves a situation.

Deceiving the audience. In the same way as *revealing unseen implications*, the music can set us up to believe something will happen, but then a different event takes place. Sometimes known as a "reversal," in this case the music can simply be mirroring what we see on screen, or it can add another dimension to a scene that is visually neutral. This is most often used in suspenseful situations.

Technical Functions

The technical functions are when the music aids the overall structure of the film:

Creating continuity from scene to scene. (Also known as "making a transition.") Music can help the viewer make a transition from one scene to another. This is a result of the way the human brain processes information. If we watch a scene that ends, and then we cut to another scene in a different location, obviously the eye is very aware of this change.

Many times an abrupt visual change is appropriate, but sometimes it is desirable to soften this change. Music can help achieve this by beginning in the first scene, and carrying over to the second. In this way, both the eye and the ear are engaged; the eye takes in the abrupt scene change, and the ear hears a continuous piece of music. The total effect is one that is smooth; the music effectively overrides the visual aspect.

Creating continuity of the entire film. By using themes and textures that return throughout the film, the music can create a continuity of sound. These can be leitmotifs, where certain characters, emotions, or places have distinct musical motifs. There might also be one or several themes that appear in various instruments and harmonic settings. Or there could be a certain combination of instruments or sounds that carry through the entire film. By continually developing one or more elements of the music further, such as certain melodies or instrumentation, the composer can create a dramatic build. Here are three examples:

In *Fly Away Home*, Mark Isham uses a small ensemble featuring solo viola during much of the first part of the film. As the story grows and becomes more dramatic, so does the size of the orchestra. However, the same theme appears throughout, played by the different size groups. This creates a unity in the music even though the sonority grows in size.

In *E.T., The Extra-Terrestrial*, John Williams presents fragments of a particular theme throughout the film in various scenes. It is not until the climactic "flying scene" that these fragments come together as a complete musical statement. This is an example of the music developing with the plot. The basic musical idea is similar in several situations, but the audience doesn't hear it as a complete idea until the story line is also complete.

In *Speed*, Mark Mancina uses a combination of several metallic-sounding samples to create an electronic texture. This is used throughout the film as a sound "palette" that mirrors the urgency of the dramatic situation.

Following the Drama

This is the part of writing a film score that separates those who really can from those who would like to. There are many composers who can write excellent music, but not all are sensitive to the film's action or the director's vision. Once the spotting is done, the director has given his input, the placement of themes has been decided, and the deadlines are clear, then all that is left is to choose which notes will sound and who will play them. These choices are inherently subjective. Every composer decides a scene's musical needs according to his own dramatic sensitivity and musical taste. Many choices contribute towards determining the shape and tone of the music in each scene. Remembering that the music is a partner to the drama also helps keep the focus of the music. Some of these choices are:

- Tempo. What is the rhythm of the film editing? How are the individual shots cut together? What is the overall pacing of the movie? Are there musical tempos implied by this?

- Are there many sync points? Just one or two? Or is the music meant to just "wash" over the scene?

- Are there moments that require a musical comment?

- How much is the music telling the story? Or is it more neutral and mood-setting?

- Is there source music in the beginning or end of the cue that needs to be taken into account in terms of key, tempo, etc.?

- What is this cue's placement in relation to the whole dramatic arch of the film?

- Where is this cue's placement in terms of other cues? Are they close in time? Do the keys have to match?

- Should the cue modulate for dramatic or musical reasons?

- Should there be orchestration changes accompanying the drama?

This list can go on, for the composer must answer many questions and make many choices. But this process is not always a conscious one. The more experienced a composer gets, the more his instincts get developed.

Many of the questions above are asked and answered on a subconscious level. However, it is important to look at every film and break down every scene from many angles in order to really make the music fit.

Writing for Dialogue

Writing for a scene with dialogue is one of the trickiest things for a composer. There is no one way to do it, for every situation is different. The approach to writing music under dialogue is determined by any number of factors, including the mood of the scene, the pacing of the scene, the amount of sound effects present, and the importance of the dialogue itself to the plot. And ultimately, the music will probably be dubbed, or mixed in, very low under the actors' lines. This is the natural fate of film music, for it is meant to accompany the action, and only infrequently does it take a starring role.

There are different schools of thought on the use of music under dialogue; some believe that it is good to move the music when the actors pause, and sustain the music when the actors are speaking. This is a technique used by many composers over the years. Some composers always write sustained tones during dialogue—this is another valid technique. However, it is best to consider every situation to be different, having its own musical requirements.

In order to determine the appropriate music for dialogue scenes, there are melodic, harmonic, and orchestrational factors to take into consideration. How active should the melody be? How thick should the chord be? What instruments should play? Here are several questions to consider when writing under dialogue:

What is being said? If the actors are declaring their undying love, or if some important element of the plot is being revealed, then the music must support that mood, and at the same time stay out of the way. One way to do this is to write a very transparent texture that allows the voices to cut through. However, sometimes a rich texture is appropriate; the theme could soar into the stratosphere while the actors are speaking, and the music will be mixed very low underneath the dialogue.

Who is speaking? There are times when a particular register of a certain instrument conflicts with the actor's voice. For example, cello or French horn played between middle C and C an octave below share the same range as most male voices, and might fight for attention with the dialogue. Instruments between G below middle C, and G an octave higher might fight with a woman's speaking voice. However, whether or not such conflicts actually occur depends on the quality of the voice and the way the melody is constructed. The kinds of intervals used, the tempo, and the overall busyness or simplicity of the melody also contribute to the degree of conflict. Large melodic intervals, quicker tempos, syncopated rhythms, and busy melodies tend to draw the audience's attention to the music and away from the dialogue.

What is the pacing of the dialogue? Are the lines spoken quickly, with urgency, or is the actor taking his time? Are there pauses between each line, or do they come rapid-fire, with each line overlapping the previous one? These considerations will help determine how fast the music moves. For example, the composer can accentuate quickly-spoken lines with very active music, or he can provide a cushion for those lines with long sustained tones.

What is the pacing, or tempo, of the film editing? How the film is edited can provide another clue to finding appropriate music under dialogue. For example, as with the pacing of the actors lines, the composer can write music that mirrors a lot of fast cuts, or it can soften those cuts with a melody line of long tones.

Perhaps the most important point to make about writing music for dialogue is that the music should not draw too much attention to itself. Ninety-nine percent of the time, the dialogue reigns. If the music draws too much attention to itself, two things are likely: the cue will be rejected and the composer asked to redo it, or it will be dubbed very low in the mix. The best music under dialogue is that which reflects the dramatic situation, can be heard through the speaking, and allows the voices to be in the foreground without any aural conflict.

The Main Title

The music that is played at the beginning of the movie when the credits are rolling is called the *main title music,* or simply the *main title.* The goal of the main title music is to set the mood and tone of the film. The audience needs to know what kind of story they are about to experience, and the music should tell them. There are several different approaches to this music, which will be determined by the director's vision. If there are simply credits rolling and the names are all that is seen, then the music will probably be featured. Similarly, if the credits are rolling, and we are seeing footage of the location of the film, the music will also be featured. However, if there is dialogue while the credits are rolling, then the music takes a more subservient role; it will not be so much in the foreground, and act more as an underscore.

The main title music is often one of the few places where the composer can "stretch out" a little bit because there are often no dramatic moments to hit, and because the cue is usually about two to four minutes long. This is enough time to make a complete musical statement, especially if the theme has an "A" and "B" section, whereas in many cues during the movie there is not enough time to complete these ideas.

The End Credits

The *end credits* come when the film has ended, and all the people that worked on the film are being named. Often the music in this part of the film is a song, rather than instrumental music based on the underscore. The reason for this is usually pure commerce. Producers hope that because the song is the last thing heard, that it will stick in people's minds and make them want to buy the soundtrack album. This is a logical business decision, but often one that has very strange dramatic implications. It can feel like an intrusion when at the end of a two-hour movie with an orchestral underscore, a pop song with drum set, synthesizers, electric guitar, and electric bass suddenly begins.

However, there are many films that do use orchestral music to accompany the end credits. In this case, the composer usually develops themes presented during the film. Because of the length of the end credits, often five or six minutes, and the fact that the composer is free from dramatic considerations, he can write a piece that is more like a suite. Unfortunately, very few people remain in the theater to hear this music.

Composing with Synths vs. Pencil and Paper

There are two distinct approaches to actually writing the score; one school writes on a synthesizer and sequences the music, the other prefers writing with a pencil and paper. Both methods have adherents who have achieved great success, and there are those who practice both, depending on the kind of score required.

The pencil and paper method has the advantage of giving the composer a slow-motion experience of every note and every chord. There are no "happy accidents" where the hand just seems to find a particular voicing. This method forces the brain to consider every note and its placement because notes need to be specified one at a time. In addition, writing with pencil and paper requires a certain expertise and experience in being able to imagine the music and to hear what it will eventually sound like even though it is just dots and lines on a piece of paper.

The main advantage of using a sequencer is that it can be faster. A composer can play his ideas, or play along to the video, and it is instantly recorded and notated. A transcriber can clean up the output from the sequencer and then give it to an orchestrator. So the composer can really churn out the music in a short amount of time, especially if he has a team of people helping.

For every composer, the reasons for choosing one method over another differ. Some can write in the traditional way if they want to but because of time pressures they use the sequencing method. Other composers are not as trained in music notation, so it is much easier for them to realize their ideas exclusively from a keyboard.

In addition, sometimes the film itself requires a score with strange textures that can best be designed and sampled at a keyboard, or played by unusual instruments that are layered one over the other. This is something that you can hire professional players to do, or learn yourself. Mark Mancina has had great success with pure sampling, sampling in combination with live orchestra, and designing sounds with unusual instruments.

Mark Mancina:

> *I was doing documentaries all through the '80s, and because of the budget, everything was done electronically, with MIDI. With the advent of samples, I could create something that sounded pretty good. It became, for some of the movies that I have done, a real advantage. For a movie like* Speed *it had to be done that way. The concept of that score for me was to take orchestral percussion and replace it with metallic and metal sounding percussion, which I sampled and set up specifically for that score using all sorts of tin cans and things. All of a sudden* Speed *became such a huge hit and a big movie that I kind of fell into the "electronic composer" category because I used rhythm and electronic sounds for that score.*

> *[Now] I'm very tired of MIDI, and I don't like anything in my scores that isn't played live. I don't like that electronic sound. It has worked on some movies that I've done, but I feel it doesn't work in a lot of movies, although now I hear it done a lot.*

As you have seen, there is never only one solution to a creative problem, and every composer has his own viewpoint and method of working. There are many variations on the same theme. When writing a score with many cues, there is a lot to consider. Some composers plan every cue for thematic content and key center. Some create as they go, and their basic musicianship enables them to make a unified musical statement as the movie unfolds. Whether you plan everything out or do it on the fly, understanding how the music functions in any situation is crucial to creating a successful score.

You may be wondering, "Once I've got my dramatic concept, how do I start writing?" Which notes to put on paper, on your sequencer, or on your hard disc recorder is something that cannot be taught, much less talked about in a book. It will be the sum of your musical *and* personal experience—your ability as a player, how much music you have absorbed over the years through listening and study, your musical philosophy, your life experience, and your personal outlook on life. No one can dictate taste and musical choices; that is what gives every composer a unique musical expression. The way to find yours is by doing it—by writing scores, playing gigs, listening, studying, making choices along the way, and learning what works for you.

CHAPTER 15

Syncing the Music to Picture

*Scoring sessions are the greatest thing in making movies
because the film is ... cut by then.... It's the first time
you can sit back and watch the picture come together.[1]*
—Stuart Baird

Like many technologies in today's modern digital world, the methods available to a composer for synchronizing music to picture are expanding. Traditionally, the composer waited to receive timing notes from the music editor before beginning to write individual cues. However, with today's computer technology, it is possible to score an entire film without ever creating any timing notes, and still sync the music to the picture. In fact, this is how many composers work, especially those that write directly into a sequencer. This chapter discusses the various methods of syncing, beginning with the traditional way of using timing notes. First it is necessary to understand some basic mathematical ratios and terminology of film and music:

Frame

A film is actually a strip of thousands of photographs passing through a lens, giving the illusion of movement. Each of these individual "photos" is called a frame.

24 frames per second

The speed that 16- and 35-millimeter film (most feature films) run through the projector.

30 frames per second

The speed that something originally shot in video will run through the VCR (in the United States).

Two to four frames

The amount of error that the human eye can see if the music is out of sync. Remember those old black and white "B" movies where the actors' mouths and the actual words are out of sync? This could be a differential of as little as two frames for the viewer to discern the difference. Converted to seconds, two frames equals $\frac{1}{12}$ or .08 seconds. In terms of time, that is a tiny fraction of a second. But the eye, ear, and brain are fast and can pick up that small of a difference.

Sync point

A place in the action that a composer wants to accent. This can be the end of a line of dialogue, a cut from scene to scene, or a piece of physical action like a fight, a chase, or a kiss. (A sync point is also called a hit, the place where the music "hits" a certain piece of action or a cut.)

No matter which synchronization method is used, the first thing for a composer to do is view the cue several times. The most important thing at this point is to *get a feel for the tempo of the cue*. Often, the on-screen drama suggests certain rhythms, and the way the different shots have been edited together suggests a certain pacing. Sometimes the music goes against action on-screen. For example, there could be a chase scene where the music moves very slowly for a dramatic reason. Whatever the conclusion, the tempo of the music must be established before writing can begin.

Once an approximate tempo is reached, the composer decides where there should be sync points, if any. Reference to the spotting notes and any decisions or requests from the director are noted, and the composer arrives at a general musical concept for the cue. Some cues have no sync points, and the music just "washes" through the action, creating an overall mood or feel. Others, especially action cues, can have many sync points. When the music mimics the action exactly, it is called *mickey-mousing,* coming from the old cartoons when the music followed the action almost beat by beat (this term is used whether it happens in cartoons or not).

The timing of sync points can also be determined from the *window burn*—a rectangular box on the screen of the work print that shows the reel, minutes, seconds, and either hundreths of a second or frame numbers. This is actually a visual representation of the SMPTE time code used to lock up the video equipment to the audio.

Fig. 15.1. Window Burn.

Once the composer determines the sync points, he figures out how to tailor the music so that these sync points come at logical places in the music, often at downbeats.

Then the composer decides which method of synchronization to use—click track, clock, or punches and streamers. If a cue has a lot of sync points, or if the music is fast and rhythmically difficult, then a click track would be appropriate. If the music calls for rubato and expressive passages, then punches and streamers or clock allow that kind of interpretation. If the cue is short, or if there are no sync points that need accurate timing, then the clock would be appropriate.

Punches And Streamers

In the early days of sound films, it was apparent that a technique needed to be developed where the composer/conductor could manipulate the music to synchronize exactly with the film. The first method that was developed was that of *punches and streamers*. It was realized that once the composer decided the exact timing of where he wanted a musical hit, at the recording session that exact frame could be anticipated and the music synchronized to it. The way this worked was that the music editor would literally punch a hole in that particular frame (of the work print, not the negative) so that when the film passed through the projector, that frame would come out as a flash of light instead of a visual image. But that flash, or punch, needed to have a preparation. So a system was developed where the music editor would literally scrape a line (a streamer) on the film for a certain length, usually 3, 4, or 5 feet, which equals 2, 2⅔, and 3⅓ seconds. The conductor would then see a vertical line move across the screen from right to left, ending in a flash of light at the exact frame with which the music should synchronize. (See Fig. 15.2. Punches and Streamers.)

When using punches and streamers, there are often *reference punches*, also known as *flutter punches*. These are punches that show the conductor if he is going too fast or too slow. They are often placed at every bar, or every other bar, as tempo guideposts. Before computers, a music editor would find the frame of film in which a composer wanted to see a flutter punch, and punch a hole in every other frame of a five-frame sequence. The appearance on the screen when these five frames go through the projector is of a "flutter" of light. These reference punches are not meant to be hard and fast sync points; they are simply guideposts telling the conductor to speed up or slow down a bit.

Today, the music editor no longer has to manually punch holes and prepare the actual film; punches and streamers are generated by computer programs such as *Auricle*. This is a great advantage, for in the old

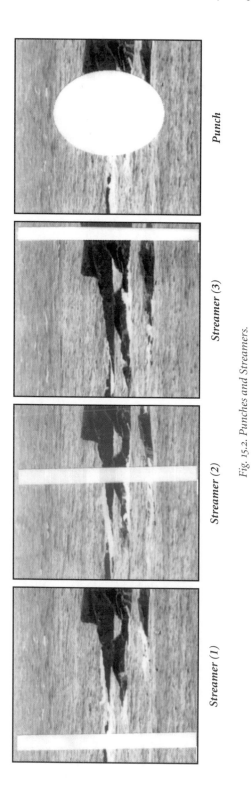

Fig. 15.2. Punches and Streamers.

days, if a change in the music was requested after the punches and streamers were prepared, it could not be done right away, on the spot. The composer and music editor would have to redo the cue, often that night, and record it at another session. With a computer generating punches and streamers, it is possible to make extensive changes on the spot, as long as the composer is able to shift things musically and the music editor is skilled at programming the software.

Using punches and streamers is actually a very accurate method of synchronization, if the conductor is skilled. The advantages of conducting to punches and streamers are that the music can be very flexible and expressive because it is not locked to a metronome, or click track. Also, the conductor sees the film, so he can react to it. The disadvantages are that the technology is not always available, and that if there are a lot of sync points, if the music is fast and difficult rhythmically, or if there are many tempo changes, punches and streamers do not serve the music well.

Click Track

A *click track* provides the tempo the conductor and musicians hear during a recording. Whereas metronome markings are measured in *beats per minute* (BPM), traditionally, film click tracks have been measured in *frames per beat* (FPB). This enables precise synchronization of the music to the film.

Today, computers enable click tracks to be generated in either format, but for many years composers indicated click tempos in their score, marked as pairs of numbers: 24-0, 12-7, 18-3. This has its origins from the early days of film, before the age of computers, when music editors created click tracks by punching holes in loops of film. The hole would pass over the projector's optical sound head and cause a pop, or "click," at a regular interval determined by the length of the loop.

The two numbers represent how many frames, and divisions of the frame, at which the hole would be punched. Since film runs at 24 frames per second, 24-0 FPB indicates a tempo of one beat every 24 frames (one hole punched every 24 frames), or one beat per second (corresponding to a traditional metronome marking of mm=60 BPM). Lower numbers indicate faster tempos. The indication 12-0 FPB means two beats per second, or mm=120. The loop of film was shorter and the punched holes moved through the projector with greater frequency, causing a faster click.

The second click-track number is a very small measurement. Composers and music editors realized early on that smaller increments than one whole frame were necessary, so they used the film's sprocket holes as guides for smaller subdivisions. There are four sprocket holes in each frame of film (see Fig. 10.1.), and a hole could be punched at one of these holes or in between them. This gave eight possible increments of click track tempo for each frame. If a composer wanted a tempo slightly faster than 60 beats per minute, instead of punching a hole every 24 frames for a 24-0 click, he might try 23-7, 23-6, or 23-5.

The human ear can't distinguish measurements that small, and short cues of just a few seconds don't require such precision. However, on cues lasting several minutes, these fractions add up, and the difference can mean hitting or missing an action on-screen at the end of the cue.

There are several mathematical formulas that can be used for finding a click tempo in frames per beat; these were used in the early days of film. Also, *click track books* list the timing on every beat at dozens of possible tempos.

In the 1950s a device called the Urei Digital Metronome was developed. This electronic metronome ended the need for film loops running through a synchronized projector, for it could generate any FPB click tempo electronically with the simple turn of a dial.

Nowadays, computers and sequencers are also used to find and generate click tracks. These easily express tempo markings in FPB and in BPM, which are now also divisible into tiny increments.

A click track is best used when the tempo is constant, when it is very fast, when the music is rhythmically complex, or when there are many sync points to catch. Some cues require a *variable click track*. This is the same as a regular click track, only there are one or more tempo changes. These tempo changes can begin immediately at a new bar line, or can be prepared with warning clicks if the musicians are holding a long note or fermata. There can also be "ramps," or gradual accellerandos or ritardandos in the music. Some composers us very slight variations of click from measure to measure in order to make it sound more "real" and less mechanical. At the recording session, the music editor will have programmed the computer with the proper tempo changes, and monitors this process to ensure that the synchronization is accurate.

Clock

Another method of syncing music to film is the use of a *stopclock*, now simply called a *clock*. In this case, the conductor watches a large analog clock with a sweep hand (basically a large stopwatch about 12 inches in diameter). Using the clock method gives some flexibility in the music, but realistically, it is accurate for sync points only to plus or minus a third of a second. When using the clock, the music editor's job is fairly easy; he just has to know where the music is beginning and ending, and make sure that the conductor is accurate.

Wild

There is one final way of recording a cue, and that is called recording *wild*. This is not when all the musicians go to the studio commissary and party down; it refers to recording without any kind of synchronization reference. A cue is recorded without clicks, punches and streamers, or the use of a clock. The music editor is then responsible for seeing that it is cut into the film at the proper point. This method is often used for very short cues, or cues where changes have been made at the recording studio and the previously prepared synchronization method is no longer valid. If the cue is longer than a few seconds, its success will depend on the skills of the conductor.

There are distinct advantages and disadvantages to each synchronization method:

Punches and streamers are great if the music needs to be free, flexible, or rubato. They are fun to conduct to! They can make your sync points accurate to the desired frame. They can facilitate tempo changes and be effective in any music where there are a lot of holds or fermatas. The disadvantages are they are difficult to use if the music is very fast, rhythmically complex, or has a lot of sync points. The effectiveness of punches and streamers depends on the ability of the conductor. Computers with software that can generate punches and streamers are not available in some studios.

Click tracks are great if you have a lot of sync points or if your music is fast or rhythmically difficult. They can give you spot-on accuracy in making sync points and can assist the players in staying together when there are difficult rhythmic patterns. A variable click track can give very secure tempo changes. The disadvantage to clicks is that they become robotic with a stiff and unmusical pulse. One way around this stiffness is for the studio to send the click into the headphones of the conductor, but not the musicians. This can improve the feel a bit.

Recording to clock is good for having flexibility in the music. It is a desirable method when punches and streamers are not available. It is good for shorter cues that don't require a lot of drama, like going to commercial in a TV show. The disadvantage is that using the clock is the least accurate of all the methods, so if you have any sync points that need to be dead-on, this method is not preferred. Using the clock is accurate to about one third of a second, or eight frames. Remember the rule of thumb that the human eye/ear connection can determine a differential of two to four frames.

Sequencing

Many composers do not use timing notes in the traditional way; they prefer to just play along with the video on a keyboard until they get an idea that they like. Sometimes they establish a specific click in advance because they know where they want to hit the action. But more often than not, they play without a tempo reference and sequence their ideas. If the sequence is going to be orchestrated and eventually recorded live, it then can fall to a music editor, or a composer's assistant, to construct a click track for the musicians to play along to at the recording session. This can be painstaking, and often results in the use of a variable click because of the natural variations of tempo that occur during live playing of the sequence. Most good sequencing programs allow the composers to "tweak" a sequence and move the tempo around; if the composer is a few frames early or late on a specific hit, that moment can be moved to be more exact. However, if a click is used while the composer is sequencing, that is easiest for the music editor, for it keeps the composer's tempo "honest."

Note that if a sequence is the final music for the project, then all of this is fairly straight-forward. All you must do is correctly edit and align the sequence to the places you want to hit. But if you are using the sequence as a mock-up of the cue, as a sketch, or as a way of generating some initial ideas, and the sequence is going to be orchestrated and then played live, then the process can be complicated. It may require a team of people: music editor, MIDI transcriber, and orchestrator.

Music editor Eric Reasoner describes working with composers who sequence, as well as those who use timing notes to prepare their score:

> There are a couple different modes of working. Some composers play stuff into a keyboard and sequencer while locked to picture. That's one mode of working, and that MIDI file then has to be deciphered. A click has to be laid up against what was played if the composer wasn't listening to a click, which happens a lot of times. They just play to picture, and then you have to figure out a click track so that they hit particular musical events where they want to on the picture.

> The other way is where the composer takes the timing notes that you've provided for them and utilizes that information. They do the math, they figure out how many bars, beats, and clicks. They figure out tempos, and lay out their score based upon that information. Then I see the score later and basically line it up with the picture. "Lining it up" means I create the click track and the

streamers and punches after the score is written, according to what timings I see above what measures, and what instructions are given. And that's relatively simple and fast, because they've taken care of it.

Once you choose your method of synchronization, you are ready to set up the score. Whether putting pencil to paper or sequencing, it is a good idea to lay out the entire score, locate all the sync points, and know whether any meters need to be adjusted, before beginning to write.

In beginning this composing process, several things must happen. First, watch the scene many times. Have a strong idea in your mind of what you want to say with the music. Should it be funny or should it heighten tension? Should it be somewhat neutral, or melodramatic? The mood or the emotion you want to express will suggest a tempo. Remember that the composer's role is to help move the story forward. It is of the utmost importance that you know why the music is in a certain scene, and what it is supposed to accomplish. Then your writing will be focused and appropriate dramatically.

CHAPTER 16

Television

The early television years were indispensable.
That was my learning process.
—Jerry Goldsmith[1]

Music for television is conceptually the same as music for feature films in that it underscores dramatic situations. However, the process of writing music for television, the scope of the music, and the sound of the music itself is often very different. The way television shows are produced leads to a very different use of music. In television, production schedules are tighter, budgets are much smaller, and live ensembles are smaller. There are commercial breaks to consider, and the look and feel of the shows is very different from features. Despite the differences in production, a composer must still write music that is dramatically appropriate and meets the requirements of the production team.

There are several different kinds of television shows and each one has different musical requirements. There are episodic series, TV movies, sports shows, news shows, documentaries, TV magazines, and daytime soap operas; each of these has a different need for music. There are commercials and network logos. Some shows use only synthesizers and samples, some use a live rhythm section, some use a live orchestra. There are those that are hip-hop, light rock, metal, or traditional orchestral in style.

This chapter is concerned with episodic series and TV movies—the shows with dramatic music. An *episodic series* (one that has a new show every week) can be a drama like *E.R. or NYPD Blue*; a comedy like *Seinfeld,* or an animated comedy or dramatic series like *The Simpsons* or *Superman.*

The evolution of an episodic television show is similar to that of a film; the idea must be generated, and a producer and a network must be found. A *pilot* is then made, and usually aired in the late spring or summer. The pilot is a single trial episode that gauges the response of the audience. If the pilot is well received, then the network may agree to a whole season, and the show is on its way.

Today there are only a handful of episodic shows that use a live studio orchestra. Because the budgets are smaller, if an orchestra is used, there are many less players than in the orchestra for a feature film. A typical television studio orchestra for a weekly show ranges from 20 to 35 players. (TV movies might use more.) Compare this to the orchestra used for feature films—usually 50 to 100 players or more. This is fitting because the scope of television is smaller in production value, as well as in the sheer size of the screen and audio speakers.

Schedules

When a show is contracted by a network, it is typically for 22 new episodes a year, running from about late September to May. The rest of the year is filled with reruns or alternative programming such as movies or news specials. (When a weekly show is bumped for a special movie or news show, it is said to be "preempted.") Production of these episodes usually takes place between late July and the end of April, with the period in between, May through July, referred to as "hiatus." It is during this time that production is "down" and many people take vacations. This is also the time when pilots are often produced.

Once a show starts weekly production and the first episode has been edited, the composer starts to work on the underscore. From this point on, the schedules are very demanding, for the turn-around is fast. Since new episodes are aired every week, the composer has very little time to write the music; every week a new episode rolls down the post-production assembly line and lands at his front door, ready for scoring.

An important production difference between films and television is that in television the director's role is somewhat diminished. Once the shooting is completed, the director's job is often finished. In television, the director is not involved in post-production, so the person that the composer communicates with is usually the producer or assistant producer.

Once receiving the final work-print of the show, the composer may have to spot, compose, and record anywhere from 10 to 30 minutes of music in a matter of days. And this is not a one-shot deal; he could be on a schedule that requires that much music every week, or every other week. If the composer is writing for a live orchestra, then this schedule gets even more compressed, for the music preparation pipeline of orchestrating and copying parts needs some time. If the composer is sequencing and doing the music electronically, then this kind of schedule is a little easier, but still grueling. In fact, some shows have multiple composers who rotate episodes every two or three weeks. When really in a jam, a composer will sometimes call a colleague to ghostwrite some of the music. This is when the main composer gets the screen credit, but others help by writing one or more cues. (Note: ghostwriting also occurs in features.)

Composer Shirley Walker mostly uses live musicians. She describes working under the pressure associated with a weekly series:

> *The problem with a weekly show is that at a certain point it catches up with you because the schedule is crazy; every week you're turning out a show. Now, it doesn't go like that over the whole season because they plan hiatuses and preemptions and things like that. But inevitably you're going to have a three- or four-week span that hits you several times during the course of the 22 episodes where every week you have to be finishing a show. So you might start out on your first episode, and you've got three weeks, and then your second one you might have two weeks, and then pretty soon the weight of that whole thing is a snowball effect that starts really pounding you and pushing you from behind until every week you have to have finish anywhere from 25 to 45 minutes of music.*

For *X-Files*, Mark Snow composes all of the music electronically, only occasionally bringing in a live musician to his home studio. He usually has 20 to 30 minutes of music in every episode. In addition to scoring *X-Files*, he also writes for *Millennium*, which requires another 20 to 30 minutes per week. This enormous amount of music is possible only because the music is done electronically:

> For X-Files *I get about a week, seven days, but if I have to crunch it, I can do it in three days. If I get the episode on a Monday, I can have it ready for a Friday, which is when the producers come over to the house, listen to the music with the picture, and make their comments.*
>
> *The way I can do the two shows at once is because they usually, for some lucky reason, come at different times. Let's say they're done in the same week, I'd have three days on one, three days on another; it's doable. I'm used to the shows, I know the sounds and the textures and it's not about starting from scratch and walking around the house for days thinking, coming up with a theme or a palette of sounds. It's pretty easy.*
>
> *I can go much faster than if I had to record with a TV orchestra. That would absolutely be out of the question. What I'd have to do then is have someone do a takedown, or send MIDI files to the copyists, have them copy the parts, assemble the orchestra, go to the session. It would just be impossible.*

Alf Clausen does the music for *The Simpsons* with a live studio orchestra of about 35 players. His typical schedule is like this:

> *When we're on a week-to-week schedule, what I will normally do is spot an episode on Friday afternoon. The music editor will prepare my timing notes on Saturday and Sunday and then I'll start writing, usually Monday morning if it's a normal episode of 30 cues or less. If it's more than that, I'll sometimes start on Sunday to get a jump on things and then I'll put in probably four long days—Monday, Tuesday, Wednesday, Thursday— maybe nine in the morning until 11:30 or midnight every day. Then we spot the next week's episode Friday afternoon, and on Friday night starting at seven I'll record the cues that I've composed*

during the past week. We usually have anywhere from a three to a three-and-a-half hour recording session to do those 30 cues. Every week is different on The Simpsons, *as you know. It really is dependent on whether it's straight underscore type of recording that I have to do or if I have to record vocals and do orchestral sweeteners of songs that I've written and already recorded. So it's never a dull moment.*

Main Titles

The beginning part of the show where the opening credits are shown is called the *main title*, a term that is borrowed from feature films. The music for this opening is also called the main title by the music production team—a shortening of the phrase "main title music." For the television main title, the composer usually writes some kind of theme, or catchy music with a distinct *hook*. ("Hook" is a pop-song term that refers to the one most memorable lyric, melodic phrase, or part of the arrangement.) Actually, the composer of the main title is often different from the composer of the underscore on the weekly episodes. This is true especially if the main title music is a song with lyrics.

For television, main titles are short—typically anywhere from 45 to 90 seconds—as opposed to feature films, where they can be three or four minutes long. In this amount of time, a strong statement about the show must be made that hopefully will be memorable. It is not enough time to develop a musical idea; any ideas presented should be concise and easily accessible to the audience.

Act-In/Act-Out

Every segment of a television show or TV movie, from commercial break to commercial break, is called an *act*. An act can be anywhere from 20 minutes long (the first act of a TV movie) to as short as five or six minutes. Often a composer is required to write a short cue, called an *act-in* or *act-out*, that brings us into the show after a commercial, or takes us out to a commercial. In the early days of TV, these transitions were used all the time. Today they are not automatic; their use depends on the show and the dramatic situation. Sometimes the theme for the show is used, sometimes new musical material is introduced. An act-in or act-out can be as short as a few seconds, or it can be an extended cue. The important thing is that the act-in or act-out reflect the nature of the show and the story line.

Related to the act-in and act-out are the use of short bridges or transitions. A *bridge* is a music cue, usually of just a few seconds, that connects the story when it moves to another location or forward in time. This usually involves a cut or a dissolve to a new scene. Again, this is more typical of older dramatic shows, but is still used today in many comedies as well as dramas. The slap bass in *Seinfeld* is a typical use of music for both a bridge as well as act-in and act-out.

There are dozens of TV shows every week that use music, while there are fewer theatrical movies. There is a lot of opportunity for composers in television, and many top-notch composers are currently writing for television. There are also many composers now writing exclusively for features who got their start in television, including Jerry Goldsmith, John Williams, and Alan Silvestri. In addition, television can sometimes be more lucrative for composers than feature films because the royalty payments compound when a show is aired and then goes into reruns. If a composer has shows airing on network TV, reruns on local stations and cable, the royalties add up quickly. (See chapter 22 for an in-depth discussion of royalties.)

Some of the most popular shows on television are animated series, such as *The Simpsons, Batman, Superman, Rug Rats,* and *Teletubbies.* Although many of the compositional and scoring techniques are the same for animation as for live action television, there are also many differences. Such considerations are discussed in chapter 18, "Animation."

CHAPTER 17

Ethnic and Period Music

Motion picture art is different. It is realistic and factual. It not only tries to capture the spirit of bygone eras, but it also tries to make believe that it projects before the eyes of the spectator the real thing.
—*Miklos Rozsa*[1]

Los Angeles is the entertainment capital of the world. And because so many films are produced there, or in New York, their locale is often set in these places. However, every year there are also countless films where the story, or part of the story, takes place in other locations. These can be exotic and unusual locations anywhere on the planet, such as Nepal, Congo, or backwoods Montana. Or they can be large urban centers of the United States or Europe. Some of these locations have music that is instantly associated with them, some do not, and the use of music to suggest a locale will be different from composer to composer, and director to director. The task is finding and creating music that helps reflect the feeling of the location while being effective dramatically.

In addition, sometimes there is the need to create a score for a period film that takes place in historical Europe or America. This presents its own set of problems, but the basic question, how to reflect the time period while being appropriate dramatically, remains the same.

This discussion necessarily takes place from an ethnocentric viewpoint. In the world of film making, we are often dealing with a situation where Hollywood is looking out at the rest of the world. The philosophy is, "Everybody else is different, and those of us here in Los Angeles are the norm." This is actually true for any culture or country—we see the world through our own prescription glasses. Therefore, for the purposes of this book, I refer to "ethnic music" as that which is not Western Classical or popular music. So with apologies to readers from anywhere other than the United States, or Los Angeles in particular, let's look at how to approach "ethnic music," as well as music that describes a different European or American era.

Ethnic Music

Hollywood's approach to ethnic music has changed over the years. This is largely due to changes in film making itself, and to the shrinking "global village"—the fact that all corners of the planet are closer together due to ease of travel and the information technology that connects us.

Films have become much more "real" over the past decades. In the old films, killing was often an off-screen event, and blood was minimized. Cowboys wore fancy, fringed costumes and carried pearl-handled Colt 45s; they were always clean looking and freshly shaved. Today's cowboys are likely as not to be grungy, slightly ragged-looking and dirty, and if they kill someone, the blood flows bright red and freely. Probably this is closer to what it was really like. We not only see more "real" costumes, blood, gore, and violence in modern films, we also see more real emotions as well as special effects. Many films of past decades look dated to us; the younger generations often snicker at the "old" films. So the question becomes: Does the music also need to reflect a realism, and if so, to what degree?

This question has been answered in many different ways over the years, and part of the answer lies in the development of popular music. As popular music has become more sophisticated, the ears of its audience have developed in parallel. In the 1930s and '40s the audience was musically sophisticated when it came to Wagner, Brahms, Puccini, Duke Ellington, or Tommy Dorsey, but they were naive when it came to the music of other cultures. Today we have become more familiar with the many kinds of music heard in other countries; our global village shares resources, ideas, and technology. The composer must take more care in the way a country is represented musically.

There is also a psychological dimension of this process. We associate certain instruments with certain cultures, depending on our own experience. A mandolin played a specific way is definitely Italy;

Flamenco style guitar can only be Spain. A banjo is the mountains or the Old South of the United States. But what about accordion, which is used in many countries? Or pan flute, which can be associated with Eastern Europe or South America? The composer must take care when designing a score with certain sounds that it is really suggesting the place he intends. There is no way to please everyone because different people have different musical associations. However, one way to make sure the music is accurate is to do research.

Research

When writing for a film that requires ethnic music, composers often do research. This can be done in many ways. It can be as simple as buying some CDs, or it can be as complex as spending time in a music library and corresponding with experts all over the world. The important thing is that the composer become familiar enough with the style of the music that he can create it in a way that is convincing dramatically. Oftentimes, he will just use one element of it, like a particular instrument blended in with an orchestra, or a scale derived from that culture. An ensemble of musicians from that country or culture can be used as a separate scoring entity, or it can be blended with the orchestra.

John Williams does this in the film, *Far and Away*, which follows the journey of an Irish couple from Ireland to the United States in the 1890s. Williams uses two Irish-derived melodies as the main themes; they are first heard in the main title, one played on pennywhistle, the other on pan flute. Both are accompanied by a symphonic orchestra. The effect is to achieve a "flavor" of the Irish location and characters, but not actually to be traditional Irish music. However, he also has scenes that are scored exclusively by The Chieftains, one of Ireland's premier groups that performs traditional Irish music. The Chieftains are often not accompanied by the orchestra, but because of the Irish nature of the orchestral sections, there is still continuity between the various kinds of textures.

One composer known for his love of musicology and investigating the music of other cultures was Miklos Rozsa. During the 1940s, '50s, and '60s, Rozsa wrote many scores, such as *El Cid, Ben-Hur, Quo Vadis*, and

Ivanhoe, where he researched the music of the time and place, and incorporated it into his score. He was meticulous and immersed himself into the study of the music of the culture. For example, for the score to *El Cid*, he journeyed to Spain and studied with authorities on medieval Spanish and Moorish music. For *Quo Vadis*, he did a thorough investigation of Roman music and instruments.

Unfortunately, because of post-production schedules, composers today rarely have time for such efforts. However, research can be a valuable tool in enhancing the kinds of sounds and textures available to the composer. The deeper one gets into the music of another culture, the more it can be reflected in the original music for a film. Sometimes hours and hours can be spent researching, studying, and listening to the music of another culture, but very little specific music from that place is used in the score. But after this process, no matter how much ethnic music is used, the composer has an understanding, sometimes on a subconscious level, of the music he studied, which then comes through in his own music.

Cliff Eidelman speaks of the value of researching the music before beginning to write *Triumph of the Spirit,* a powerful 1989 film about Greek Jews in a Nazi concentration camp:

> *I went to the UCLA musicology department and I started listening to recordings of Sephardic Jewish folk music. Primarily pre-war music from Greece and Spain. As it turned out, a lot of what I was hearing was stuff that felt very second nature to me. I really connected to the kinds of feelings that were in that music. They were using mandolins, mandolas, a lot of tambourines, guitars, and drums. There was a certain raw feeling to it, but it was very warm.*
>
> *Then I read the script and started coming up with ideas. I wanted to incorporate some of those Eastern instruments into a Western orchestral setting. I took the liberty of adding an Indian instrument, the tamboura, which isn't a Sephardic Jewish instrument, but I liked the droning quality and I thought it was a nice color. Then I discovered quickly that the language they*

were speaking was Ladino, or at least a big part of what they were speaking was Ladino, which is a combination of Spanish and Hebrew and is essentially extinct today. When I realized I wanted to use a choir, I chose Ladino as the language for the text. In addition to that, I didn't want to use preexisting poems, I wanted to have poems written that were really more specific to the emotional context of what was going on in those scenes. I found a cantor who knew Ladino really well, and he was also a very good poet. I described the emotion, and he wrote poetry based on it. He translated the poems into Ladino, and that became the text for the score.

This story illustrates the kinds of research a composer can do in order to draw upon ethnic musical influences. Notice that Eidelman did not attempt to recreate the music of the Greek Jews; he simply tried to capture the feeling, even to the point of using an archaic language to represent the emotions of the film. Also, just for color, he used a tamboura, which has nothing to do with European Jews. This shows the creative license one can take. It is also interesting that no one outside a few people involved in the film would know that the language being sung was Ladino. But Eidelman and the director felt that the emotional content of this language would somehow transmit part of the experience of the people portrayed in the film. This is a subtle idea, yet one with a specific, if subconscious intent. Many composers and film makers rely on such subtleties to help complete the story.

Sometimes composers use ethnic instruments but inadvertently imply a different culture from the one in the film. This can happen for several reasons, not the least of which is the subjective nature of the audience's musical associations. An example of a film that reflects the exotic location, but perhaps inadvertently implies yet a second or even third different culture, is *Beyond Rangoon*. In this film Hans Zimmer uses a sampled ethnic sound reminiscent of Balinese gamelan, but also reflects instruments in the culture of Burma (now known as Myanmar), where the movie takes place. However, over the top of the texture that is glued together by this gamelan sound is a high wooden-flute sound. Many people who have heard this sound immediately associate it with Ireland, because the high flute sounds Irish in nature to them. However, upon hearing the music and seeing the picture, they concede that it works, that with the visuals of the Burmese countryside and rivers the ethnic association with Southeast Asia comes together, "Irish" flavor or not. This shows the power of combining the sound with images. When the music is isolated, one impression is conveyed. When it is married to the picture, a whole different set of associations can be conjured.

This illustrates the difficulty of writing ethnic music for a mass audience. It can be constructed in many different ways depending on the creative directions of the composer and the director, and it can be interpreted differently depending on the audience. The composer needs to have firmly in his mind how "real" the ethnic music needs to be. Does it need to be like source music, i.e., very real? Or can it just imply the culture? Sometimes the budget of the project determines how real the music gets. Bill Ross used ethnic music in *The Amazing Panda Adventure*, as well as on the television series *MacGyver*:

> The Amazing Panda Adventure *was set in China. [Director] Chris Cane wasn't sure what he wanted, so after thinking about it, I came up with the idea for this mellow Western approach with a kind of Chinese vibe. I did what I could to educate myself about some of the Chinese instruments, and wove them throughout with the Western-style orchestra. There were four cues where I wrote Chinese music as source music.*
>
> *In* MacGyver, *we used some ethnic instruments, but we didn't research them. There was no time and no budget to focus it in any more than a very general way. After a while it came down to large geographical distinctions—East or West, Europe, etc.—and a small group of corresponding instruments. The fortunate thing for a film—like* The Amazing Panda Adventure—*as opposed to television, is that you can afford to have the recording environment and the musicians to do what's necessary.*

Having the budget to do what is necessary is paramount. Hiring extra musicians who play specialized instruments can be expensive. Sometimes composers must make do with samples. But either way, the creative decision is to decide how much of the ethnic flavor is wanted. Most of the time, composers choose to incorporate ethnic instruments with the full palette of orchestral sounds available. This seems to be a solution that is pleasing to the ear of the modern audience, dramatically satisfying, and suggests psychological associations with certain cultures. It can mean simply adding one instrument like panpipes or koto, or a hint of a particular scale, or it can mean using a whole ensemble of ethnic musicians. A combination of research, good dramatic discrimination, and clear communications with the director usually provides the answer.

Period Western Music

Writing music for a film that takes place in historical Europe or America has always presented a problem for scoring. The question here is similar to the question regarding ethnic scoring: should the music reflect the time period? And the answer is also similar: it depends on the vision of the director and composer. More often than not, that vision is a combination of older, period sounds, and contemporary orchestra. The reason for this is the same as with ethnic music: audiences can most easily identify with a contemporary orchestra, yet a certain amount of realism is sometimes appropriate. An excellent example of this is *Anne of the Thousand Days*, with a score by Georges Delerue. In this score, shawms and other period instruments are blended with the orchestra.

Often, in both period and ethnic scores, realism can be achieved through the use of source music. Source music and underscore can often be combined and blended together to make a dramatically and musically satisfying effect. For example, in *Shakespeare in Love,* there are several instances where we hear 16th century source music, and then the underscore played by a modern orchestra actually grows out of the source music, eventually taking over. In *Shining Through*, a film about undercover spying in World War II, there is a scene at a party where the Glenn Miller arrangement of "Moonlight Serenade" is playing. Composer Michael Kamen effectively extends this '40s song by segueing to the underscore with a love theme that is thoroughly modern in sonority. These examples work because we accept the source music as representing the time period, and the orchestra as representing the dramatic situation.

Another example of a score that uses both period music as well as contemporary music as underscore is *Dangerous Liaisons*. In this film, which takes place amongst the aristocracy in 18th century Paris, George Fenton has constructed two distinct musical ideas that serve the drama well. In the main title, the first thing heard is a contemporary orchestra playing a very dramatic, tense and restless theme with a modern musical vocabulary. Then it segues to a harpsichord and a smaller Baroque sounding orchestra. These two contrasting sonorities provide ample material throughout the film; one reminds us of the time and place, the other is used in the more melodramatic moments.

The important concept in scoring ethnic or period films is to have a clear idea of how much of that music is necessary. This often depends on the director's vision, such as Francis Ford Coppola with *The Rainmaker* (see chapter 9). These situations call for the composer to find a solution that suggests time and place, and addresses dramatic needs.

This kind of scoring highlights what is essentially the psychology of combining music and visuals. Because the music addresses both visual and dramatic situations, the audience's attention is split. Their eyes must take in the picture, their ears take in the music. Composers are actually addressing this phenomenon every time they write a cue for any kind of film. The audience is having an experience on several sensory levels as well as several emotional levels. Music is just one part of this, although a big part. In films that use ethnic or period scores, we ask the audience to accept that we are not trying to create "authentic" music of the time or place, but simply add to the color of what they are already seeing. It is more important to be "real" in a visual sense; the music can *imply* the "reality" and still be accepted.

CHAPTER 18

Animation

The art of writing for animation is in keeping the music musical,
while hitting what needs to be hit without sounding choppy.
—Richard Stone

There are currently several different kinds of animated films and television shows. There are old-style cartoons, such as *Animaniacs* or *Tiny Toons,* dramatic action-hero animations such as *Batman* or *Superman,* and comedies such as *The Simpsons, South Park, Rug Rats,* and *Teletubbies.* There is also the feature film animated musical such as *Pocahontas, Mulan,* or *Quest for Camelot.* The way the music is handled depends on the project's style, as well as the creative vision of the production team.

Note that films with real actors are referred to as *live-action films,* in order to distinguish them from *animation,* where the characters are drawn.

The Early Days of Animation

As discussed previously, film music styles were very different in the first decades of talkies from what they are today. In the 1930s, the music was likely to hit many pieces of action and comment on almost every emotion the actors showed. When the first cartoons came out, the musical approach was the same, though taken to an extreme. Almost every movement, whether the characters were falling in love or having a knock-down-drag-out fight, was reflected in the music. The term *mickey-mousing* refers to this style where the music mimics every little thing, as in the early Mickey Mouse cartoons.

Two of the most successful composers for cartoons in the early days of film were Scott Bradley, who did most of the *Tom and Jerry* cartoons, and Carl Stalling of Warner Bros. These men set the standard for the industry. At first, cartoon music was a thrown-together jumble of snatches of different melodies taken from other sources. Both Stalling and Bradley decided that that something different could be done. Bradley describes his thinking:

> It seemed to me that almost anybody could collect a lot of nursery jingles and fast-moving tunes, throw them together along with slide whistles and various noise makers and call that a cartoon score, but that didn't satisfy me and, I felt sure, wouldn't really satisfy the public. So I set about to work out musical scores that would add significance to the picture, that would be musically sound and would be entertaining.[1]

So Bradley and Stalling went about finding a way to accompany the cartoons that was musical, interesting, and had integrity. The dilemma facing them (and composers today) was the sheer number of hits—as many as 30 or 40 in a 30-second cue—coupled with the fact that the action of the cartoons was irregular, in terms of musical beats. Somehow, a way had to be found to make the music *seem* regular. Mixed meters were a way to make musical accents come out on downbeats, yet cartoons had so many places where the music needed to hit the action that it was impossible to have every hit on a downbeat. One solution was the creation of a melody line that stretched over an entire sequence, and the hits in the music would be mostly in the accompaniment to the melodic line. This was more elegant than simply stringing together bits of folksongs, nursery tunes, and arias, which tended to sound quite choppy.

In addition to mickey-mousing everything in the early cartoons, and despite the desire to achieve a more musical solution than simply linking familiar melodies, it became a convention to parody familiar pieces of music in a humorous way. This is probably a logical extension of the way well-known tunes were used during the silent film era. For example, sunrise became the "Morning Mood" from Grieg's *Peer Gynt*, and if a character was drunk, something like "How Dry I Am" or "Little Brown Jug" would play. Many classical and popular pieces were quoted or parodied. To score these moments, composers still used the old silent-film fake books of Rapée or Becce, since these books provided dozens of excerpts of many different kinds of melodies. Books like these are still used as a reference by composers today.

The process for the composer in the early days of cartoons was different from today. Today, the composer receives a rough-cut of the film, the music editor creates timing notes, and the composer writes from the timing notes and the rough-cut. In the early days of animation, the composer often would not even see the film before the music was recorded. After a spotting session with the director, the composer would receive a "detail sheet," also called an "exposure sheet." (Note that the nomenclature varied from studio to studio.) Richard Stone describes the *exposure sheet*, as it was called at Warner Bros.:

> These sheets laid out the action on paper and were a sort of mini-storyboard. The director would decide, for instance, how fast a character was walking, and would have this very elaborate sheet saying, "Daffy is walking across the street taking a step every eight frames." This information would be copied onto the exposure sheet giving Stalling a description of all the action and the frame measurements of all the action. That is what he wrote to.

Once the composer had the "frame measurement," it was just a matter of math to figure out the rhythm and timings of these moments. The *exposure sheet* also had music staves below these verbal descriptions so the composer could fill in the sketched music.

Occasionally the composer would receive a "pencil reel" or a "storyboard" of the film. A *pencil reel* is a black and white rough-cut with line drawings as opposed to complete animation. This would be viewed by the composer on a Moviola. A *storyboard* is a series of boxes on a page, like a comic book, that sums up the story and the action and includes timings for each box.

Pencil reels, now called *pencil tests*, and storyboards are still used today. Animators often use line drawings in live-action films to roughly draw a sequence that ultimately gets computer-generated special effects. Storyboards are used during preproduction in animation, commercials, and occasionally in features.

The composers of the early cartoons were remarkable and often unappreciated. They had fine music skills in composition, orchestration, and conducting, and they were often self-taught. They had an innate sense of drama and what was needed in a film. And, of course, they had a great sense of humor.

Today's animations, except for many of those produced at Warner Bros., are very different. Let's look at the different kinds of contemporary animation one by one.

Warner Bros. Cartoons: The Old Style

In a world of modern computerized animation and musical trends that encompass Aaron Copland and Snoop Doggie Dogg, Warner Bros. has continued to use the musical style originally developed by Carl Stalling in the 1930s. Cartoon series like *Tiny Toons, Animaniacs,* and *The Sylvester & Tweety Mysteries* all use devices that were popular in the '30s, '40s and '50s: traditionally-based orchestras, mickey-mousing action to the smallest detail, and quotes from well-known songs and classical pieces. Creating this kind of show is demanding because the music is constant and there are so many hits. Richard Stone is the supervising composer of most of these Warner Bros. cartoons, and he describes the process:

> *It's like anything else. We still sit with the producer and have a spotting session. In our case, the music is wall to wall; the decisions are not where the music starts and stops, as in a feature film or a live-action television show. In our shows the music never stops. So the question at the spotting session is always about musical style, and what specific things we're going to hit— how loudly and with what instrumentation. We might talk about which public domain tunes we will use....*

What we do is an outgrowth of Carl Stalling's style, trying to stay in sync with as many things on screen as we can. Characters walking across the screen with pizzicato celli and a bassoon, if a boulder falls on somebody it will have a piano glissando on it, the xylophone eye-blink, and all the rest of those clichés. We also try to do musical puns with folk songs—PD tunes that we can use. We quote from the classical literature all the time.

A team of composers works on these shows; typically they rotate and do one show every two weeks. William Ross describes being one of several composers working on episodes for *Tiny Toons:*

They were about as hard as anything you want to do. It's like working inside this little tiny box because of the number of hits. Music has seams, let's say, and so the number of seams you have to do in cartoons is a lot. As a composer, I find that most of my time is spent making the seams seamless. Once I get a texture I like, it's easy to continue it for five, six, seven minutes. But every time I have to transition that texture to another one, it takes a lot of thought.

Tiny Toons *takes that to a whole new level. In the course of a few seconds, you may have ten hits. I know that sounds ridiculous, but there are lots and lots of hits, things you need to address where the music has to do something in these few seconds. So I would have a 30-second cue that had 40 things I had to hit. I tried to limit the number.*

It was difficult for any of the composers to take on an entire episode and finish it by themselves. It was essentially 19 minutes of music that had to be done in a week or two. It wasn't for the faint of heart. People would be on the floor trying to figure out how to get through this 19 minutes of music. Those that had arranging experience and could manipulate melodies seemed to fair well. I got to where I could do two minutes a day.

This honest assessment of the difficulty of writing for an old-style cartoon makes one appreciate the work of Stalling and Bradley even more. That they could crank out enormous amounts of music that worked effectively with the picture, day-in and day-out, shows the high degree of skill they had.

Animated Dramas: Action Heroes

Another type of animation that is very popular is the cartoon or animated drama with an action hero like *Superman* or *Batman*. These television shows or feature films are scored like regular live-action shows. The music does not mickey-mouse every move on screen; rather, it simply tries to support and enhance the visual action.

For animated dramas, the composer receives a work print of the show, and works exactly as he would for a live action show. There is a spotting session, timing notes if needed, and either a synthesized score or live orchestra. Whereas a series like *Tiny Toons* features wall-to-wall music, in an animated drama there is usually less music; it comes in and out as needed.

Animated Dramas: Comedies

One of the most difficult things to decide in any film, live action or animated, is when to be musically funny and when to be musically serious. In the *Tiny Toons* or *Animaniacs* type of show, the choice is obvious: the music must be as goofy as the drama. However, there are many comedies where it is much more effective to have the music be more serious or neutral, and let the comedy routines speak for themselves. *The Simpsons* is a great example of a show where the music does not mimic every piece of action; it simply comments where necessary. Composer Alf Clausen explains the concept:

> *Matt Groening [the producer and creator of* The Simpsons*] and company told me in our first meeting that "It's not a cartoon, it's a drama where the characters are drawn." And when in doubt, he said, score it like a drama, not like a cartoon, not to mickey-mouse everything. Matt was the one who made the request for the acoustic orchestra. He said, "I hate electronics, I think they cheapen the sound. I want the real orchestra."*

I have an old friend that came up with the phrase, "You can't vaudeville Vaudeville." That has also served me really well on The Simpsons. *The producers keep saying, "We don't want the music to comment on the scene. We don't want the music itself to be funny." I'm always in agreement with that; we kind of joke in some of the spotting sessions about how the more serious I can play the music, according to the way the emotion is laid out, the more we pull the audience in and make them think that the situation is real. Then "boom," all of a sudden the gag comes and it becomes twice as funny than it would have if I had tried to set up something leading up to the fact that there was going to be a gag.*

Musicals and Songs

Musicals, whether animated or live action, are extremely complex endeavors, from a production standpoint. The composer of the songs is involved during preproduction and writes the songs based on a script and conversations with the production team. There is a lot of back and forth between the songwriter and the production team regarding the musical feel and the lyrical content of the songs. This can be an efficient process or it can be drawn out, because in preproduction, people feel less pressured and take their time getting the music just how they want it. Finally, after everyone—the producer, director, songwriter—has agreed and signed off on them, the songs are recorded. The animators take the final recording of the song and synchronize the singing and movements of the animated characters. Finally, months, or even years later, when there is a locked version of the film, the underscore is written by either the same composer as the songs or by someone different. David Newman did the underscore to *Anastasia*, and talks about his experience from the composer's perspective:

I used all material from the songs because I thought that would be the right artistic choice for the movie. That's what my dad (Alfred Newman) would do with all those musicals, with all those Rodgers and Hammerstein musicals. I really liked that in shows like Carousel *and* The King and I. *He interwove the score right with the song, and then right out from the song back into the score. I approached* Anastasia *like that, just like it was a tra-*

ditional film. Steve Flaherty and Lynn Ahrens did the songs long before I began the underscore. Taking their themes and developing them in dramatic ways made the movie seem really unified.

Alf Clausen writes both underscore and the songs for *The Simpsons*. His process for these songs is exactly the same as if it were a feature film musical and not a half-hour television series. The songs need to be recorded before the animation is begun, months before the show aired. The process is very complex whenever music is done like this during preproduction, and requires a lot of planning:

The procedure is that normally I am given the script pages that have a lyric already written by one of the writers on staff. Then I'll have a conference with the writer and the producers about what they feel the thrust of the mood of the piece should be, and what the intent should be.

Then, once I've composed the song, I write out the rhythm-section parts, we do a demo of the song, and record the rhythm-section track first. If the song is going to be recorded by cast voices, then I'll record scratch vocals, which are thrown away eventually. They're just used for demo purposes so that we can make cassettes for all the cast members in order to learn the material before they go into the voice-record session. If the songs are not going to be sung by the cast members, and we're going to use our own vocalists, then normally we'll keep the vocals that we've recorded all the way to the end of the process.

The animators then animate to those tracks that are given to them with the rhythm section, the cast voices, and the click track. Nine months later, when the show is finished at the animation house, it comes back to us and hopefully they've left the songs alone and I don't have to do any major surgery.

So when I score the underscore cues for that particular episode, I'll also sweeten the song tracks that have come back, which means that I replace the rhythm section track with an orchestral track so it sounds as if the orchestra is accompanying the voices in the finished piece. So, there also needs to be new orchestrations written.

The composer's task in a musical is to weave songs and underscore together. When the music is continuous throughout the film, key relationships become very important from one cue to another, and between songs and underscore. There also must be a sonic unity between the songs and underscore. In addition, sometimes the animated story is about animals who need to be given human qualities, as in many of the Disney pictures. Mark Mancina produced many of the songs for *The Lion King*, and wrote the underscore—in addition to producing the songs written by Phil Collins—for *Tarzan*:

> *When you do an animated movie, it's hard because you're not only scoring the same way you score a normal movie, but you're having to bring a certain sense of realness and humanness to characters that are animated.*

Mancina also discusses the need for good collaboration with other musicians, as well as constant awareness of the flow between underscore and songs:

> *Key relationships between songs and underscore are tremendously important, especially in a movie where the music doesn't stop. Basically, in* Tarzan, *the music never stops. There needs to be continuity between the songs and the underscore. I don't like going to a movie, and when the song starts, I yawn, or I start going, "Oh God, here comes the song." I hate that. So does Phil (Collins). One of the ways we achieved a unity between the two elements was by me playing on his songs, and by him playing drums on some of my cues. That way the score and the songs can sound very similar. Not only the key relationships, but also the sonic relationships between cues.*

In addition to collaborating with other musicians, the process also involves collaboration with the production team. Because music is driving animated films, there is a whole team of people, from the director to the head of the studio, that gives input to the composer and songwriters. Mancina describes this:

> *There's not just one guy that comes in and listens to what I do; there's a group of guys. There's the director, the producer, the executive producer of music, the VP of theatrical, Michael Eisner, Joe Roth, the Chairman of the Board. All of 'em. They're all going to hear it! They're all going to have their own opinions on every note of the music, every frame of film—and they're all going to have something to say about it. Five of them might think it's the best cue they've ever heard me write, and three of them might say "I don't like it, and it's gonna have to be changed."*

Animation can be an interesting, fun, and grueling scoring assignment. There is the opportunity to have fun with the music, as well as write serious underscore. Depending on the project, the composer can use traditional instruments or electronic sounds. The creative scope is wide, and though the process is difficult at times, animation can be among the most inspiring and fun genres of film scoring.

CHAPTER 19

Songs, Soundtracks, and Source Music

If everyone on the movie, from the studio execs all the way down, is in sync and agrees we need a hit song for this movie, then it is a totally great situation because then everyone is shooting for the same goal. But that's never the case and I don't believe that will ever be the case. Even if it is, everyone's vision of what that hit song will be is going to be totally different.
—*Jeff Carson*

Many films use music besides the instrumental underscore. In addition to the kind of composed score that has been discussed so far, film scores frequently include songs. In musicals, as well as some dramatic films, the actors sing on-camera. Often there is *source music*, music that comes from a source on-screen that the actors can hear—a radio, stereo, live band, or someone singing or playing an instrument. A song can be used in place of instrumental underscore to heighten or comment on the dramatic action. For example, in the last scenes of *Michael Collins*, when Sinead O'Connor sings, "He Walked Through the Fair," the picture alternates between Michael Collins driving to what is ultimately his assassination and his fiancée trying on her wedding gown. This creates a poignant bridge between the two characters in their different locations. When the music for a film is mostly, if not completely, comprised of songs instead of underscore, as in *Pulp Fiction, Jerry McGuire,* or *The Big Chill,* it is called a *song score,* or *compilation score.*

There are several ways a song can end up in a film. If an established song is used in a new movie, the producer must obtain the right to use it, either in its original form, or by having a new version, or *cover,* recorded. Alternatively, the producer might commission a new song to be written for the film. Of course, if the movie is a musical, then several songs must be commissioned.

The composer's participation in a score that contains songs will vary from project to project. He may be involved in composing the songs, or he may only compose the underscore. For musicals, the songwriter might also write the underscore, as Alan Menken has done for many Disney films. If the songs are used as source music, then the composer is usually not involved, except when they are instrumentals and can be recorded at the same session as the underscore.

Regardless of whether or not the same composer is used for the underscore and the songs, there are always dramatic considerations to keep in mind when choosing or writing songs for a motion picture. Hopefully, the song will enhance the drama in some way, if it is used in place of underscore. But the hard reality of the entertainment business is that there is always a pull-and-tug between creative considerations and those of commerce and profit, and this duality has a large influence on the use of songs in a film. This chapter discusses the many aspects of using songs in movies and the process that lands a song in the film—from the featured songs in musicals to the more subtle and less memorable, but still dramatically important, songs used as source music.

Commissioned Songs

Many times a producer or director wants a song, or songs, to be written specifically for the film. The obvious case for this is a musical, where there are many songs that are essential to the plot. Another possibility is when a producer wants an individual song either for the main title or end credits, or for an important point in the film. Either way, there may be a music supervisor assigned to the project who assists the composer in facilitating the recording of the songs. The director is usually the decision-maker of what music appears in the film, including both songs and underscore. The director (sometimes the producer) is also involved in the process at the approval level, wanting to make sure the songs are appropriate both musically and lyrically.

Once it is determined that a commissioned song is required, a songwriter or songwriting team views a work print of the film. If the song is to be used in a particular scene, they watch that scene over and over.

They then come up with a tune and lyrics that specifically reflect the content of the film. If the composer of the score is also the composer of the song, the thematic material of the song will often be woven into the underscore. The song may use musical material written by the underscore composer (especially if the underscore composer and songwriter are the same person), or it may be a separate musical statement. The song may be used only in the main title or end-credits, or it could be featured as a dramatic statement in the body of the film. "How Do You Keep the Music Playing," from *Best Friends*, is organic to the score of the picture; Michel Legrand uses the theme in his underscore as well as in the song itself. Lyricist Alan Bergman (who writes as a team with his wife, Marilyn) describes the evolution of "How Do You Keep the Music Playing?":

> *This film has two people involved in a relationship. The woman overcomes the man's resistance to marry, and they go back East to meet their respective families. The visits don't go well, and by the time the honeymoon is over, the marriage is almost over. There is a sequence in which they are on a people-mover in the airport, separated and not talking to each other. It was a marvelous sequence for us [as songwriters] because there are no sound effects or dialogue. Here was an opportunity to find a new way to say, "How do you keep romance alive?"*

> *After viewing the entire film several times, we watched this scene over and over again. Then we said to [composer] Michel Legrand, "What if the first line of the song is 'How do you keep the music playing?'" And he said, "I like that." He wrote the whole melody from that line. We then wrote the rest of the lyrics to that melody.*

When writing a new song and tailoring it for a certain movie, writers try to reflect either a single dramatic or emotional moment of the film, or to make a statement about the entire film. In a situation like the one above, it is as close to putting words in the characters' mouths as possible without having them actually sing. This use of a song greatly enhances the story by reflecting exactly what the characters are feeling. In *Up Close and Personal*, the song, "Because You Loved Me," by Diane

Warren was commissioned for that film and used in the end credits. Even though it is not used dramatically in any scenes in the film, the song reflects the feelings of the film's main character, and articulates the emotional thrust of the film.

Sometimes a film maker uses songs containing lyrics that are close to what needs to be expressed, but are not exactly right on. There are many instances where songs are used because the title of the song fits the film, or part of the lyrics fit the film, but the rest does not. A good example of this is *The Big Chill*. This film's opening sequence is a montage where some old college buddies living in different cities find out that one of their old gang has committed suicide. Playing through this montage of several minutes is the original recording of Marvin Gaye singing "I Heard It Through the Grapevine." On the surface, these words fit the scene nicely, for we are seeing all the pals getting the news over the phone. However, these lyrics: *"I bet you're wondering how I knew, 'bout your plans to make me blue ..."* don't really fit the story; they are about a heart-broken guy singing to his girl. The only line that is really relevant is the title line, and this is one reason the song is in the film. Another reason is that it is a song many people know and love, so using it in a film preys upon the audience's familiarity with it—the feeling of nostalgia.

Musicals

Musicals are the ultimate genre where songs are tailored to fit a film. They must be, because the characters are singing them. The words must reflect the story and the music must fit with the overall musical style of the film. The process of writing songs for a musical, whether animated or live action, can be different from that for dramatic-action films. In a dramatic film the songwriters might not be involved until post-production; they probably do not see a script, and develop their ideas from a work print. However, for a musical, the songwriters are involved at an earlier stage. They read the script and discuss with the director where the songs shall go, what the feeling of a song should be, and what the lyric content will be. This is necessary because the songs must be completed before production begins. Then they write the songs, make demos for the production team to hear, make any requested changes, and make a final recording. The final recording is then played back on the set so that the actor(s) can lip-sync accurately. (It is called a *prerecord* when the music is recorded prior to shooting so it can be played back on the set.) This entire process, from writing to release of the film, can take anywhere from one to three years. Note that because all of the recording must be completed before the shooting of a scene, often the songs will be completed as long as a year before the release of the movie.

In writing a score for a musical, songwriters are usually involved with the screenwriters. Alan Bergman talks about the process of creating the music for *Yentl* with songwriting partners Marilyn Bergman and Michel Legrand, as well as Barbra Streisand—producer, director, and star of the film:

> *We agreed that this was a wonderful book for a musical. From the moment Yentl puts on the clothes of a boy and begins the masquerade, she cannot express to anyone her true feelings as a woman. This inner monologue was a perfect opportunity for music.*

> *So, first we spotted where the songs should be. Then we started writing. Michel is a dramatist; the best composers are dramatists. For one song, we said to him, "Yentl's father has just passed away. This is the first time she's been away from her village. It's a dark night in a forest and she is alone. In a way, she's pleading with her father." Michel wrote the melody that expressed in musical terms what our thoughts were for this song, and we wrote "Papa, Can You Hear Me."*

> *When he writes, or when anybody writes the music first, which we prefer, there are words on the tips of those notes and we have to find them. It's a search.*

Exploring, being a dramatist, finding just the right words to go with a character and a story are the jobs of the songwriter in a musical. These are the songs that are featured and are often the reason the audience goes to see the film.

Source Music

There are many, many instances of songs that are not featured and that are part of the background of the actual scene. *Source music* is any music that appears to be coming from a "source" on screen. Said another way, it is any music the actors in the scene can hear. Car radios, home stereos, bands in a nightclub, street musicians, and actors humming in the shower are all examples of source music. Source music can be familiar songs by known artists, songs by new artists, or music written by the composer specifically for the film. Source music can be strictly in the background as part of the aural landscape along with various sound effects, or it can become a strong dramatic statement.

Songs used as source music are usually chosen by the director, often with the assistance of the music supervisor. In the case of instrumental source music, it can be chosen from existing recordings, the composer can write or arrange something, or another composer can be brought in to do the source cues.

Dramatic Use of Source Music

Often, source music is mixed in the film at barely audible levels; it is frequently part of a room's ambient sound, far in the background. However, there are times when source music can play an important dramatic role in the film. The proper choice of songs can create an atmosphere that runs the gamut of dramatic possibilities. Composers often interweave the source music with the underscore in order to add to a dramatic situation.

For example, in *The Pelican Brief*, there is a scene where Julia Roberts leaves a hospital in fear of her life and ventures down a crowded New Orleans street, eventually ending up alone in a hotel room. The first thing we hear is James Horner's underscore consisting of piano and strings as she leaves the hospital. This fades into source cues as she goes down the street in a state of shock. These source cues consist of different kinds of rock or jazz music emanating from each nightclub she passes, and they blend one into the other as she weaves through the partying crowd. Finally, the underscore fades back in while the last piece of source music fades out (called *cross-fading*). This whole sequence has a continuity because of the way the music is structured. The source music reflects the craziness of the New Orleans nightlife, and as each song fades in and out, we experience what the actor is experiencing. The underscore gives the audience the sense of what she is actually feeling—fear, uncertainty, and confusion—helping to make the transition from the hospital to the street, and eventually to the hotel room.

Source Music to Establish Time or Place

In addition to dramatic usage, source music often establishes a time or place. By using source music that is indigenous to a culture, the feeling of that culture is placed in the mind of the audience. The underscore can then also use elements of the cultural music, or it can be a completely different entity.

There are also countless films that have used source music to establish a time in history, such as *Anne of the Thousand Days*, *The Madness of King George*, and *Shakespeare In Love* (see chapter 17).

The Composer and Source Music

The composer may or may not be involved in creating source music. It depends on the kind of underscore being written, and whether or not the composer has the musical background to write what is needed. If the movie needs source music describing a specific culture or time period, the composer must have the research and musical skills to write the appropriate music. If the underscore is closely related to the source music, or uses elements of it, it is best to have the composer also write the source music. However, if the source music is in a style unfamiliar to the composer, he will hire someone else to do those cues. In addition, if there are sequences like the one in *The Pelican Brief* described above, then the composer must at least be aware of the key, instrumentation, style and tempo of the source cues.

Whether or not the composer is involved in the source music also depends on dramatic considerations. Often, songs used as source music are taken from existing recordings and the composer is not part of the selection process. However, there are times when the composer is asked to write a source cue that is not a song, most likely an instrumental of some kind. The composer can utilize the players at the recording session for the underscore to record the source music. This is an efficient way to create source music without getting clearances and having extra recording sessions. In addition, if the composer writes the source music, then the theme for the film can be worked into it, as Alan Silvestri did during the fiesta scene in *Romancing the Stone.*

People often wonder why they don't remember hearing many of the songs on the CD soundtrack in the movie. The answer is, they probably did hear those songs, but they were source cues played for only a few seconds at a very low volume under dialogue. However, many record companies are quite content to have their artist's songs in the film as source cues, as long as they also appear on the soundtrack album. Soundtrack albums are now one of the biggest financial considerations in making a film.

Soundtrack Albums

At one point during the summer of 1998, three of the top five best-selling albums were movie soundtracks. And for the whole year of 1998, twenty-two of Billboard's top 200 albums were also soundtracks. The top selling album of 1998 was the soundtrack to *Titanic*, which grossed $26 million in sales for that year alone and spawned two subsequent *Titanic* soundtracks—one with more songs, and another with James Horner's underscore. During that same year, soundtrack album sales rose by an amazing 36 percent.[1]

With these kinds of numbers, it is no wonder that producers are all hopping on the soundtrack bandwagon, hoping to generate both profit and publicity for their films through the use of songs. This is not a new phenomenon, although the current sales numbers and profit levels are higher than ever. As discussed in chapter 5, from the earliest days of talkies, producers have used songs in films. In today's filmmaking world, this process is not so easy as simply commissioning a songwriter to create a tune for the film; there are many different elements to take into consideration. In an age where the record companies and film studios are often owned by the same conglomerates, there are several dimensions to the game. Financial considerations, not the creative ones, are often the overriding factors in making a soundtrack. Michael Greene, president of the National Academy of Arts and Sciences, which produces the Grammy awards, discusses this trend:

> *The connection between soundtracks and films has never been more vibrant. Not only have there been more soundtracks issued, but you have to back up and remember some of the reasons why—not the least of which is that many of the film companies are also the owners of the music companies. So they've found a good way to cross-promotionalize the music and films to everybody's advantage.*[2]

There are many films where the use of songs in the film is fabulous, entertaining, and totally appropriate. However, there are many that shoehorn songs into the film in order to get the song on the soundtrack album. The problem is that this often ignores the wishes of the film's creative team: the director, writer, editor, and composer. The people that win most often in the soundtrack game are the record companies, artists, and film producers. The lament frequently heard from those in the creative parts of the film industry is that the "suits," or businessmen, are making decisions that have nothing to do with the quality of the movie—only with the ability to "cross-promotionalize" and increase profits. Truth be told, this is a complaint that has echoed throughout the history of Hollywood, only at no time has it been so loud or futile. Film making is essentially a commercial enterprise, and with the kinds of profits that can be made, there is much motivation to exploit this burgeoning soundtrack market and little motivation to give creative considerations more weight. As music supervisor Jeff Carson says, "How do you make a hit movie *and* a hit soundtrack, and make them work together at the same time?" It is not easy. It can be done, and yet the mystery is that no one really knows which soundtracks will take off and which will be duds.

There are many different paths a particular song can take to find its way into a film. It can be commissioned by the producer; it can be requested by the director; it can be suggested by the film editor, music editor, or composer; or it can be part of the catalogue of the publishing company that the movie studio happens to own. The film could use the original performance, or record a new version. In all these instances, sync licenses need to be issued, clearances obtained, and royalty deals hammered out. If there are to be recording sessions for a song, someone must produce and oversee them. There are also budgets to adhere to. All of these elements are part of the complex process of bringing a song to a film, a process that is usually managed by the music supervisor.

Music Supervisor

The *music supervisor* is a role that has developed since the late 1970s into what we know today. It is a hybrid of many aspects of the music scoring business. Although there has often been someone with the title "music supervisor" since the earliest days of sound films, the tasks that today's music supervisor fulfills are vastly different from those of his counterpart fifty years ago.

The main job of the music supervisor is to oversee the process of placing songs in a film. These can be songs that are eventually used on the soundtrack album, or songs that are used strictly for source music. The music supervisor communicates with the composer, but does not oversee the composing of the underscore. Also, it is important to know that there are essentially two types of music supervisors: those that simply organize the choosing and clearance of the songs, and those that are musically trained and can produce a recording session as well.

The tasks that a music supervisor fulfills are as follows:

Creating and monitoring budgets. Since the music supervisor is often doing some of the actual business negotiations on behalf of the producer, he usually assists in creating a music budget for the film. This can involve budgeting only for the use of songs, if that is what the score is, and can also include overseeing the finances of recording the underscore and hiring the composer. It is also the music supervisor's job to oversee the day-to-day budgets in the recording studio during production of any songs.

Helping to pick the songs. This is often the largest part of the music supervisor's job. Which songs are chosen depends on many factors, including the budget, the director's wishes, the producer's wishes, instructions from the executives at the movie studio, which artists and publishers agree to allow use of their songs, and which artists are available for recording. It can be a difficult and politically complicated labyrinth to negotiate.

Getting clearance for songs. Before a song is used in a movie, permission must be obtained. First, the publisher must grant *sync rights*, the right to synchronize the song with the movie. If the producer or director wants to use the original version of a song, then a second permission must be granted by the owner of the original master-recording—usually the record company. The music supervisor either handles the negotiations for these clearances himself, or hires a music clearance company to do that work.

Record producing. No matter whether it is an old song being rere-corded or a song commissioned for the film, the music supervisor often produces the recording session. This job is often done by the film composer if he wrote or co-wrote the song, and sometimes an outside record producer is contracted. But even then, the music supervisor makes sure these sessions go smoothly and stay on budget. Whether old songs are re-recorded or not depends on how much money the record company wants for the use of the original master. Sometimes it is cheaper to use the master; sometimes it is cheaper to redo it.

Recommending the composer. Because the music supervisor is often involved in the project at an early date, often he is asked to recommend a composer he considers appropriate for the film, and who fits the budget.

Overseeing the temp track. Often the music supervisor is part of the team, with the music editor and director, that chooses the music and builds the temp track.

Overseeing music performed on camera. If there is a scene where the actors are singing or dancing, the music supervisor will be present to ensure that everything is going well. This means making sure the playback is correct and that the lip-syncing is accurate.

As mentioned above, helping to pick the songs for the film is a large part of the music supervisor's job. Although the process can sometimes go fairly smoothly, many, many problems can arise in the clearing of publishing rights, as well as clearing the use of original masters. In addition, there are often many different voices trying to influence the song selection process. Producers and directors often request specific songs; some are reasonable requests, some are out of the range of their budget, and some will not be released by the artist, record company, or publisher. There is the screenwriter, who may have written the idea for a specific song into the script. Then there is the movie studio, which might own a certain record company, and they want to promote its artists. The film editor, who has worked with the film for several months, has his own ideas. And there are even the spouses of these people that can get into the act, because *everyone* has an opinion about music and songs! This situation is familiar to music supervisor, Daniel Carlin:

> *It's not just picking any song that will work. Anybody that listens to the radio can do that. We've got to have a budget. We've got to think about a soundtrack deal, we've got to think about the politics. For example, say I go in and I put this great Mariah Carey song into a scene. What if the budget is $300,000 for 30 songs and I have just spent $100,000 of the budget? Because the director falls in love with it and will not have it any other way, that does not do anybody any good. Now everybody is fighting. The director is fighting with the studio, and somebody goes, "Who is the jerk that put this Mariah Carey song in there in the first place?" I don't what to be the guy who raises his hand.*

The music supervisor is often caught in the crossfire of these situations because he is the one handling the songs. And it often comes back to the idea that movie making is a balance, and not always a delicate one, between creativity and commerce. When so many different powers are trying to influence the use of songs, it can get diplomatically difficult for the music supervisor.

Jeff Carson:

> *Music supervision is kind of like trying to thread five needles at once, or hit five bulls-eyes all at once. It's very difficult to hit five bulls-eyes all at once. You're trying to accommodate the movie with the right music, you're trying to please the director, the producer, the studio executives, the studio's music department. Everybody.*

There is no one rule, or guide, for how much a song will cost. If it is going to be the title of the movie, obviously the owner of the copyright will ask for more money. If it is a well-known song by a well-known artist, then that will cost more than an unknown song by an up-and-coming artist. Daniel Carlin creates a hypothetical example of the kinds of negotiations that take place:

> *There is no law or rule about this stuff. You go to the publisher with hat in hand, and you say, "Here's our movie, here's our budget, and here's how much money we have to spend. Can you help us out?" And it depends. I mean if it's a one-hundred-million-dollar movie, they're not going to give you the song for eight thousand. But if you make a three-million-dollar movie, and you can them tell it's a labor of love for everybody, then they might say: "Here's what I'll do for you, I'll make a deal if you use five of our songs, and I'll give them to you for $6,500 each." And that way they get paid not only what I pay them for the songs, but then, when it goes on television, they get those residuals. Then it gets released overseas and gets more residuals. So they make up a package deal. The volume helps them, and it helps me too. And it also means that I'm not going to put in a competing singer. I'm gonna have five of their songs, and it makes everybody's life easier.*

As you can see, there are countless ways that songs can be used in a film, and many different motives for using them. The balance between creative and financial considerations is a tricky one that everyone in the film-making business experiences. Unfortunately, everyone involved rarely shares the same vision for the music, especially when there are songs involved. Because royalties and sales profits generated from songs and soundtrack albums are enormous, there are many interested people other than the film makers who try to sway the choices. The director might want it one way, the producer another, the movie studio a third, and an interested record company a fourth. There are often two conflicting goals in the choosing of what kind of music to have: the creative choice, based on the director's vision for the film; and the commercial choice, which is based on what will make the most money, both in soundtrack album sales and in helping to promote the popularity of the film. The music supervisor guides the process of choosing songs, whether they are intended for a soundtrack album or not. And hopefully he is able to guide the process towards serving the drama as well as serving the financial bottom line.

The
Business of
Film Scoring

PART IV

CHAPTER 20

Making the Deal:
Agents, Attorneys, and Contracts

When we need a lawyer to navigate through the complexities
of modern life, we want one who doesn't "miss a beat."
—*Don Campbell*[1]

Many musicians seem to want to avoid discussing the business aspect of film scoring. They would prefer to be *artistes* who can live in lofty heights above the humdrum, mundane world of money-changing hands. Some are simply scared at having to actually deal with making money doing music. But every artist, every creative person who works for himself, is also in business. Because of the free-lance nature of our work, *we are in business for ourselves* and must learn to handle our financial affairs, deal with contracts, conduct ourselves in negotiations, and make the best deals possible. Many young composers have the impression that they will somehow get a gig writing music for films, be compensated handsomely for their music, and then someone else will handle the money. Unfortunately, this is far from the truth. Many composers have made a very good living writing film music for TV, cable, and documentaries and never have had an agent. Some are lucky enough to have an efficient and honest agent, but who oversees the composer's transactions with the agent? Ultimately, it comes down to every musician having control and being knowledgeable about his own business.

There are several key factors in controlling one's own business and one's own financial destiny. The first, as I mentioned, is knowledge. The more you know about your fee structure, royalties, budgets, expense accounts, taxes, and day-to-day expenses, the more informed are the decisions you make. This can be terribly dry stuff, but it is a part of a composer's livelihood.

Another key factor is organization. Keep a file for all those receipts. When you come home from the music store with a new piece of equipment or book, file that receipt right away under "expenses." Paperwork can be a drag, but if you don't do it, it can come back to haunt you. Keep another file for all your royalty statements, another for tax papers, completed copyright forms, correspondence, etc. In addition, keep your phone numbers organized and don't throw any out! You never know when you will need that duduk player again, even though it has been five years since he played on your session.

Agents and Attorneys

A third key factor in keeping your business affairs in order is to have competent and honest people assist you. These are the attorneys, agents, and financial advisors who have expertise in specific areas.

Many film composers have agents who help the composer obtain jobs, and provide career management. The agent negotiates deals and sees that the terms of a contract are honored. An agent has thorough knowledge of projects in various stages of production, and contacts the producer or director to pitch one of his composers for a project. He constantly networks with people in every facet of the entertainment business, always looking for opportunities for his clients.

Agent David May of the Zomba Group:

> What we depend on for our work is, number one, our relationships. This includes the music people out at the studios, the major production companies, and the major music supervisors. We are constantly calling them and they are constantly calling us about what they have on their plate and what they are looking for and who we have that might fit the bill. It's our business to be providing them with constant information about our clients, and also to suggest appropriate candidates wherever we can.
>
> You want to find out when projects are occurring, when they are going to be looking for a composer, who the key people are that will be influencing that decision, whether you are going through

a music producer or music supervisor or directly to the direc-
tor—just who do you deal with. So, at the appropriate time we
can make the calls we need to make to that person, and get our
people in there. And then, the next step—once we have some
kind of entry, when we know what kind of person they are look-
ing for and what kind of budget they have—we put together
music or credits, whatever we can put together to hopefully make
them interested in our client.

Most agents have a roster of composers, so the trick for the composer
is to find the agent that works best for him. There is no way that an
agent can give his full attention to one composer 100% of the time. For
the agent, it is a constant juggling act that also involves an intuitive
sense as to which of his clients to pitch for a job. So the composer must
also be aggressive in searching out work, and then let the agent handle
negotiations once the job is offered.

In 1991, composer Cliff Eidelman had already successfully scored several feature films including *Triumph of the Spirit* and *Crazy People*. He
knew that a new *Star Trek* movie was in production, and decided he
wanted a shot at it. Without the help of his agent he had a meeting
with the director, read the script, and thoroughly notated places he
thought music would happen. He also did a sequenced mock-up of
several possible cues. His persistence, interest, and willingness to go
the extra mile paid off and he got the job, leaving the particulars of the
contract to his agent.

Agents welcome this kind of aggressive job seeking by a composer; it
makes their job easier. But the good agent will always be looking out
for your best interest. Also, the agent must be someone you can trust
and count on to be honest and up-front with you.

David May:

It's a partnership between an agent and a composer. The theory
is that if both of us are doing everything we can, and communicat-
ing as frequently as we can, then we're going to stand a much,
much better chance in moving a composer's career forward.

For new composers, it is difficult to get an agent. There is a catch-22: you must have done some work before they will take you on. And then, you are at the low end of the food chain, so to speak. It behooves the composer to pursue his own contacts and gigs as much as possible. When the gigs start coming in, this will get the agent's attention.

Attorneys

Perhaps the most important and most lampooned of all career advisors is the attorney. All shark jokes aside, a good attorney's advice (or an attorney's good advice) is invaluable. For a film score, after the agent negotiates the deal, the attorney reviews the terms of the contract. He may negotiate through your agent, or negotiate directly with movie producers. He also may make deals with publishers and record companies, and will often give career guidance. Your attorney will know exactly how much money you are making, how much you are paying in taxes and how much that new house just cost. Because of this, you need to find an attorney you can trust—someone who you feel is looking out for your best interest. One important thing to remember is *that you are paying this person.* For your hard-earned money, the attorney is performing the services mentioned above. If you don't like the way he conducts himself or his business, you can walk away and find someone else. Many people forget this and feel bound to one lawyer forever. The services of a lawyer are expensive and necessary, but you are the one doing the buying!

Despite all the negative stories we hear about attorneys and agents, there are many good ones out there. In our culture, bad news and negativity get the headlines. Yes, there are many attorneys and agents who are low-lifes, and there are some who get tempted by self-serving fortune, but there are also many who are honest and trustworthy. Use your instinct to find someone who works well for you.

One final note about agents and attorneys: any deal they strike with a producer, publisher, or other executive *must be approved and signed by you.* And that brings us full circle. In order to know that you are making the best decision for yourself, and sometimes for your family, you must be informed and have a good grasp of the issues and items in your contract. Let the attorney and agent give you advice, but don't let them run your life.

Contracts

For a film composer, the financial bottom line is not just the fee received for writing a score, but also the royalties that can be generated for many years after the film is originally released. There are royalties for when the film is shown on TV or when the music from the film is played on the radio or in concert halls. There are royalties generated for music included on a soundtrack album. There are also additional royalties if the film is shown in foreign countries, either in theaters or on TV. If the composer writes or co-writes a song that is included in the film, it can generate another whole branch of the income river. One film score can generate royalties equal to several times the composer's original fee for writing the score. (Royalties are discussed in detail in chapter 22.)

How does this work? Where does all this money come from? Who keeps track of it? Before any music is written, before any money is generated, the composer signs a contract with the producer that specifies the services the composer will provide and the compensation the producer will pay. The terms of this contract coupled with the popularity of the film and its ability to generate royalty income determines how much the composer will make and where the money comes from.

After the composer is offered the gig, then either a *deal memo* or a *short-form contract* is drawn up. The deal memo summarizes the terms the composer and production office have agreed upon, and is the binding legal agreement until the final contract is completed by the attorneys. A short form contract is a little more detailed than the deal memo, but not as detailed as the final contract.

Agent David May:

> *Once we have verbal terms for whatever creative deal we finally come up with, I will typically generate a deal memo. If it's a*

studio, sometimes they will generate it, and different studios have different policies. Sony does a short form agreement first—they don't do deal memos—followed by a long form (contract). Others go straight to a long form, but I want to make sure that there is something on paper as quickly after the verbal agreement has been transacted as possible. Memories can be hazy, and it also is common for weeks, if not months, to go by between making a deal and actually getting a contract. So I don't want to be at that stage arguing with an attorney saying, "No, wait a second, your client agreed to half the publishing." And the attorney is saying, "Well, I don't have anything in my notes there."

Based on the deal memo, attorneys draw up a final *long-form contract*. Where the deal memo is a summary of the terms agreed upon, the final contract is a complex legal document. However, every composer should understand the basic items that are covered. There are many clauses in the film composer's contract that must be addressed and approved. Some of the important ones are:

- How much is the fee?

- How will the fee be paid?

- Is it a "package" or "all-in" deal?

- The length of time for composing the score

- Screen credit

- Advertising credit

- Copyright ownership

- Transportation and miscellaneous expenses

- Royalties for other use of the music (other than the film)

- Suspensions/terminations/defaults

- Royalty fees for underscore on soundtrack albums

- Royalties from video sales

- Exclusivity of the composer

Some of these items are fairly straightforward. *Screen credit* refers to how your name appears on-screen and where it is placed in the credits. Before the costume designer, after the cinematographer? Should it read:

Music by
Richard Davis

Or do you want the full treatment:

Music composed, conducted, and orchestrated by
Richard Mark Davis

Advertising credit is similar, referring to where and how your name is placed in newspaper, magazine, and billboard ads.

Transportation and expenses is for going out of town to record or do research. Will they fly you first class or coach? Will they pay for your spouse? How much per-diem? Many composers think this item is unnecessary, as they do all their work in Los Angeles or New York. But with many sessions happening outside of these cities for various reasons, this item needs to be negotiated up-front, and not left to see if it is actually needed.

Exclusivity of the composer means that the composer will not work on other projects during the time that he is committed to the one indicated in the contract. This is a protection for the producer to insure that they get your full attention. Composers are freelance and are always juggling schedules and projects, and the producer is investing a lot of money in your coming through for him. So it makes sense from the producers standpoint that you are working exclusively for him during the specified time. Another variation of this clause is *"non-exclusive, but first priority."* This means that the composer may work on other projects at the same time, but must give the other party of the contract first priority.

It is worth adding at this point that I believe in putting everything in writing, even when dealing with friends. There is nothing like a written agreement in the form of a contract or deal memo to prevent misunderstandings down the line. It is actually a protection for both parties in the event that one person has a different interpretation of what was agreed upon several months before. Or in a worst-case scenario, if one party tries to deliberately misrepresent or distort the agreement, a written contract can settle the dispute. Gentleman's agreements are lovely, altruistic, and philosophically desirable—we all want to believe that our business partners are honorable. But in reality, verbal agreements sealed on a handshake can be somewhat quaint if not just plain bad business. If ever someone actually tries to avoid signing a written contract or a deal memo with you, walk out the door as fast as possible! This is a sure indication of a person who knows they cannot or will not honor the terms of your verbal agreement and just wants to take you for a ride.

The contract is a supremely important document. It is your security that certain terms have been agreed to by both sides. It must be clear, complete, and fully understandable by an unrelated third person (another attorney, etc.)

Two of the most important issues in the film composer's contract are the composer's fee, and package deals. There are several dimensions to both these items, and they require in-depth discussion.

Composer Fees

The first payment the composer receives on a film is the first installment of his composing fee. When we refer to a fee in this sense, it means that the producer is paying the composer for writing the music. If the composer accepts a straight fee, as opposed to a "package deal," then he is not responsible for any music production costs, e.g., studio time, orchestrators, musicians, etc. Fees for a feature film can cover a wide range, from about $25,000 for a low-budget film and a relatively unknown composer, to over $700,000 for a "name" composer on a big-budget feature. For TV, cable TV, documentaries, and cartoons, fees are less and depend on the total budget of the project.

Note: It used to be the rule of thumb that the complete music budget, including composer, musicians, music editors, recording studio, etc., would be a certain percentage of the film's overall budget, often in the range of 1.5 to 3%. If the film's total budget was $50 million, the music budget would be between $500,000 and $1.5 million. However, that practice is no longer in use. Some movie budgets are as high as $200 million, and music costs have not risen proportionately.

There are several ways the composer's fee can be paid. Often the fee is paid in three parts: the first when the spotting is completed and the composer begins writing, the second at the beginning of recording the music, and the third at the completion of the dubbing session. Sometimes a specific number of weeks are written in the contract, like *"the composer shall commence services on the spotting date of the picture and will complete the score within 12 consecutive weeks from that date."* Sometimes the completion date is tied into the post-production schedule. Other contracts give a specific month, day, and year by which the composer shall deliver the finished (recorded) score. If the composer is needed beyond the set time frame in the contract, there is another clause that provides additional compensation.

Package Deals

One of the newest wrinkles of the past decade, and most important factors in determining fees, fee payment schedules, and music delivery dates, is the *package deal*. Also known as the *all-in deal*, this is when the composer agrees to accept a certain amount of money in return for getting the music produced and recorded. Many low-budget films, cable and television films, and episodic television shows work this way. As opposed to receiving a fee for composing the music with the producer paying for all production-related costs, in the package deal, the composer is responsible for these costs with some possible exceptions.

Since the biggest cost outside of the composer's fee is hiring the musicians and recording studio, when a composer accepts a package deal, they are often planning on producing most, if not all of the music electronically. Many high profile composers now accept deals like this. For example, Mark Snow's music for the *X-Files* TV series is produced in his home studio with the occasional live musician (that *he* must pay). James Horner and Mark Isham are but two prominent composers who have recently done feature films as package deals. Many other composers with extensive electronic set-ups are happy to accept a package deal for they know how fast they can work, and what is financially viable for them.

The danger to the composer in a package deal is that if he miscalculates, the recording session, or other related costs, may escalate beyond his original budget. Then the composer can be responsible for paying the extra costs out-of-pocket in order to deliver the final music. However, there are often exclusions to what the composer is responsible for, and these vary from deal to deal. In lower-budget deals, the composer tends to be responsible for more of the music production costs than in major feature films. Some of these exclusions for which the feature film producer is normally responsible are:

- Music editing costs
- Licensing of songs if not written by the composer
- Dolby and noise-reduction system costs
- Mag stock and transfer
- Reuse, new use, and other payments to union musicians
- Rescoring for creative reasons not due to the fault or omission of the composer

The final item on this list is extremely important. It protects the composer from directors or producers that make arbitrary, capricious, and frequent changes in the film, or ask for many changes in the music. Often a specific number of minutes of music will be agreed upon as a ceiling, and if this number is exceeded, the composer is entitled to extra fees.

The advantage to the composer of a package deal is that if he works quickly and enjoys working with synthesizers and samplers, a good profit can be made. And don't forget all those royalties coming down the road. The disadvantage is that the pressure of music production and the music budget is on the composer's shoulders. The reality of the film scoring business today is that in many instances, if a composer does not agree to the package deal, they will not get the job. The producer will simply find someone who will agree.

Mark Isham speaks about package deals:

A real important point for newcomers to understand is, because you're a newcomer you're probably going to get package-dealed from the beginning these days. It's very rare to just walk in and have someone say, "Here's a fee and we'll pay any costs you have." That's not going to happen unless you have a champion who says, "Look, I really want you to score this and I'll take care of it. Don't worry about a thing."

The important thing to remember is that everything is negotiable. You can negotiate for gross points. You can negotiate for album points. You can negotiate for publishing. You can negotiate for how many musicians you guarantee to employ. Every aspect of a package deal is negotiable. And make sure you do your homework, because if you miscalculate, and you agree contractually to supply 20 strings for 40 minutes of music, you better know what that's going to cost you. And you better do things like go to the director and say, "I will accept this on the terms that you sign off on everything that I play for you in demo form." Sometimes the director is sitting on the scoring stage and says, "What if this were faster?" Then you're looking at writing more music, changing your tempo, and somehow getting new music on the stand while the musicians are waiting for you. That could eat up your profit right there. So it's very crucial that you have a good line of communication with your director. Even if you can't get it in writing that they'll sign-off on the mock-ups, at least, man-to-man, get them to agree that this is a package deal, and you're going to try to help each other.

Agent and attorney David May also speaks to the package deal issue:

The package needs more definition and it needs to be more limited [than a "straight fee" deal]. Otherwise the composer can lose *his shirt. What we'll do then is define what the package includes, and what it doesn't. What I try to do is limit it to certain number of minutes of music, limit to a certain number of live players, so if we agree to a package of $65,000 but for that there is no more than 35 minutes of music, no more than ten live musicians. We try to limit it in every way possible so that they realize that if they want more than that, then they've got to pay more than the package amount. I really talk to the composer to make sure, before we agree to it, that the composer does a rough budget to make sure he can make what he wants to make. I'm always telling composers, you are in fact entitled to make a living at this.... But things happen, you want this, the director wants that, and that $30,000 profit ends up being whittled down to $17,000. I'm trying to avoid that.*

Package deals need to be approached with care and planning. Everything must be in writing, and communication with the director/production office must be clear. The best package-deal situation is when you are planning to produce most, if not all, of the music in your home studio. As soon as you venture into the world of studios, engineers, and live musicians, you are leaving yourself open to cost overruns for which you may or may not be protected contractually. But the package deal is a way of life, especially for low-budget features, episodic television, and television movies. Learn how to budget a package deal so you can make a reasonable amount of money when you get the opportunity.

CHAPTER 21

Publishing and Copyrights

*One of the first lessons I learned in this business is you don't have
the luxury of being a tortured artist. Go get a gig in the tortured
artist venue. Hollywood has no time for that. It isn't allowed.*
—*Mark Isham*

Publishing and copyrights is an area of the film composing business
that is crucial to the composer's financial well being. *Most of the
time, for feature films and television, film composers do not own their
music due to a clause in their contract called "a work made for hire."*
However, this is not always the case, and how your music is published,
who owns the copyright, and in what proportions that ownership is
divided between writer and publisher determines how much money in
royalties you see down the road in the months and years to come after
a film has been released. Royalties are discussed in depth in chapter 22,
so first let's talk about what makes a work *published*, and what it means
to have that work *copyrighted*.

What is a Copyright?

Copyright refers to the ownership of a creative work—in this case
music. (It could also be a book, a poem, a photograph, an artwork,
etc.) It sounds somewhat circular, but copyright means "the right to
copy," or the right to reproduce a certain work. The person who owns
the copyright owns the rights to that work. Therefore, the person who
owns the copyright controls how it will be published—that is, offered
for sale to the public.

The history of copyright laws in the United States is a complex subject.
Simply put, in the earliest days of the nation, laws were enacted that
gave authors and publishers exclusive ownership of their creative

works and protected them from theft of those works. In this century there have been three significant copyright laws enacted: in 1909, 1976, and in 1998.

The first copyright law in this century is the Copyright Act of 1909. This act set the length of the original copyright at twenty-eight years with a copyright renewal making the potential life of the copyright protection fifty-six years. After that fifty-six-year period, the work would enter the public domain (become PD) and no royalties would be paid to the copyright owners for use of the work. So, if someone wrote a song in 1910 and filed the renewal form in 1938, in 1966 the copyright would have expired and that song would enter the public domain. *Public domain* means that there is no ownership of a copyright, so anyone who wants to can reproduce or use the work in any way because there is no one to whom royalties must be paid. Older songs, folk songs with no known author, and classical music written before the earlier part of the century are examples of works in the public domain.

By the 1950s, this law had become outmoded and Congress began to look at ways to change it. It took until 1976 to enact a new law: the 1976 Copyright Revision Act. This law made the duration of the original copyright to be the life of the author plus fifty years. So, the copyright stayed in effect for fifty years after the composer or writer died.

The current law is this: In 1998, the U.S. Congress amended the Copyright Revision Act of 1976 to make the length of copyright protection *life plus seventy years.* This means that if a composer created a work in 1998 and lives to the year 2025, the copyright will continue to be in effect for his heirs or estate until the year 2095, a total of ninety-seven years. If the same composer creates a work in the year 2024, and passes away in 2025, the length of the copyright is only seventy-one years. This new law (beginning with the 1976 Revision act) is very beneficial for composers (and all artists) for it guarantees that as long as the creator is alive, his work will be protected by the copyright. Many composers outlived the previous fifty-six years protection of the 1909 law and saw their works enter the public domain while they were still alive. And some suffered the loss of copyright by forgetting to file the renewal forms, thus seeing the work enter the public domain after only twenty-eight years. This newest law insures the heirs or estate of the composer seventy years of copyright protection and potential income, whereas under the previous laws that protection was usually much shorter. And it also brings the United States into line with similar protection offered in European countries.

What is a "Published" Work?

The legal definition of *publishing* according to United States copyright law is "*the distribution of copies or phonorecords of a work to the public by sale or other transfer of ownership, or by rental, lease, or lending.*" In addition, a published work is one in which there has been "*an offering to distribute copies or phonorecords to a group of persons for purposes of further distribution, public performance, or public display.*"

A work is considered to be published if it is offered for sale to the public. If a composer writes an incredible heart-stopping symphonic poem but leaves it on a shelf in his studio for years, that work is not considered to be published. However, if copies of the same work are printed and consequently offered for sale in a classical music store, that work is considered published. If a band makes a CD and just gives it away to friends, that work is not published. If the same CD is offered for sale at gigs and the local music store, that music is then considered to be published. When a film is released in theaters or shown on TV, that music is also considered to be published. (Note that in all the above examples, the works are protected by copyright whether or not they are published. More on this below.)

Once a work is published, royalties can be collected from performances of the work and from sales of recordings, sheet music, and songbooks. These royalties are divided into two portions: half goes to the publisher who is the owner of the copyright, and half goes to the writer (composer). In some cases the publisher and the writer are the same person, in some cases they are different. In addition, both the publishers' and the writers' portions can be divided into smaller parts if there are co-writers or co-publishers.

When a work is considered published, by natural implication, that work has a publisher. A publisher can be an individual, such as a film composer or songwriter, who is self-publishing their own catalogue of works, or it can be a large corporation with hundreds or even thousands of titles to oversee. The duties of the publisher are to register the copyright, oversee the financial administration of a work, collect royalties, negotiate new uses, and make sure that there is no infringement on the copyright.

Registering a Copyright

Registering a copyright is very easy. This is done through the United States Copyright Office, a branch of the Library of Congress in Washington, D.C. You can obtain forms from them over the phone or Internet; the one that applies to film scores and songs is called *Form PA*, for "Performing Arts." You simply fill out the form and send in a copy of the work with the $20 registration fee. This copy can be in the form of a tape, CD, video, or a handwritten or printed manuscript. After a period of about three weeks to three months, you will receive a copy of your completed form with a stamped seal of the U.S. Copyright Office indicating completed registration and full copyright protection. However, your protection begins on the day your form is received by the Copyright Office, as long as it is filled out correctly.

Copyright Protection

The questions are often raised: Should I bother to register my work? Is there any benefit to me in doing the paperwork and paying the fee? and, Am I not protected as soon as I create the work? The answers are yes, yes, and yes. But first, an explanation of how copyright protection works.

Whether or not a work is protected by copyright has to do with a term used by the writers of the law. This is where they refer to a work being *fixed*. This means that the work is set down, or fixed in some kind of tangible, physical form, like writing it down on paper or recording it. Here is the copyright law of 1976 defining what is fixed:

A work is "fixed" in a tangible medium of expression when its embodiment in a copy or phonorecord, by or under the authority of the author, is sufficiently permanent or stable to permit it to be perceived, reproduced, or otherwise communicated for a period of more than transitory duration. A work consisting of sounds, images, or both, that are being transmitted, is "fixed" for purposes of this title if a fixation of the work is being made simultaneously with its transmission.

As soon as you begin to put the musical idea on tape or on paper it is considered to be fixed, and protected by copyright law. No registration needs to take place; no forms need to be filled out. If you are writing the work over a period of time, whether it is days, weeks, or years, the protection is in effect as you work. In addition, the last sentence of this excerpt of the law says that if an uncopyrighted work is transmitted or broadcast over TV or radio, and the author of the song has given permission for a recording of the initial broadcast, that work is considered to be "fixed" and protected by the copyright law.

This is actually the answer to the question above: Am I not protected as soon as I create the work? The answer is that you are protected in a technical and legal sense. However, strange things happen in a world of laws, attorneys, and courtrooms. If you created a work in the privacy of your home, the burden of proof as to when that work was created is on you. Unless you have witnesses, you could be hard-pressed to convince a judge or jury of the truth your story. If you are ever involved in a copyright infringement suit, you will want to have the most foolproof evidence of the origination of the copyright. This would be the stamped registration form you received from the Copyright Office. You would be kicking yourself if you lost a lawsuit you should have won because you did not want to pay a $20 fee and take ten minutes filling out the copyright registration form several years before.

One thing to remember is that as a film composer you often do not own the copyright—the producer of the film owns it (see *work made for hire* at the end of this chapter). In this case, the producer has the copyright registration form filled out and returned to him. However, on some projects you will retain the ownership of the copyright and will have to go through the registration process yourself. Either way, it is good to know the procedures.

The Rights of the Copyright Owner

What exactly does it mean to own a copyright? To sum it up, the owner of the copyright has the right to reproduce the copyrighted work, to distribute it through "phonorecords," and to perform the work publicly. (*Phonorecords* used to apply to just that—records that go on a turntable; now it legally means anything that reproduces sound. CDs, cassettes, prerecorded MiniDiscs, and any future invention of reproducing sound is covered by this term.) If you own the copyright to a piece of music, you have the exclusive right to decide how to initially reproduce copies of it, where and when the initial performance takes place, and who initially performs it.

Notice how that word "initially" snuck into those last few phrases. This is important since after the work is initially "offered to the public," or published, your ability to control the use of your copyrighted material changes. Remember that a copyrighted work is not necessarily a published work. A work can be under copyright but not yet be published. So if someone wants to use your music on their CD or perform it in public, and your music is copyrighted but not yet published, they need to get your permission. You have the right to decide about the initial performance or reproduction of copies. If your song or film score is yet to be published and another artist wants to record the entire work or a portion of it, they must get your permission first. However, if the work is already published, if you have already recorded and released it on a CD, or if it has been released in the theaters as a film score, then your permission is not necessary as long as they pay you a minimum royalty. This is a royalty paid at a rate established by the Copyright Royalty Tribunal (a five-person panel appointed by the President) called the *minimum statutory rate*. Or you could agree to a lower rate if it suits your interests. For songs, this minimum statutory rate is calculated by the song; currently it is set at 6.95 cents per song per unit sold. So if someone else records one song of yours, and their album sells 1,000,000 units, then the royalty would be $69,500. This is called a *mechanical royalty* that is paid to you by the record company for the privilege of using your music. If the music is instrumental film music, the royalty rate is calculated either by how many minutes in duration the piece is, or sometimes by how many selections appear on the album. For a film composer, this arrangement is one of the important items covered in his contract. (For more about royalties, see chapter 22.)

Copyright Infringement

Another question that often comes up is "What constitutes copyright infringement?" There are two types of copyright infringement: the unauthorized use of a copyrighted work, and the copying of substantial portions of a work.

The unauthorized use of a copyrighted work is the more clear-cut type of infringement. This is when someone records or performs copyrighted material without paying royalties to the owner of the copyright. This can happen if a performer records a copyrighted song, sells thousands of units and doesn't pay the appropriate royalty. Even though the copyright owner does not have to give permission for use of a published song, he must still be notified that the song will be used, and must be paid at least the statutory minimum royalty. In a film score, if a producer uses music from another film or recording but does not obtain a *sync license* (a license that gives permission to use the music and synchronize it to picture), that producer is guilty of copyright infringement; he has violated the copyright owner's exclusive rights.

The copying of substantial portions of a copyrighted work is a more difficult issue to determine. Many composers and songwriters are under the impression that you can copy up to four bars, or some other amount of actual music, before you are in danger of violating the copyright laws. This is a misconception. The copyright law says that you must have music that contains a "substantial similarity" to the copyrighted work before you are guilty of copyright infringement. In addition, the law says that for there to be infringement, the owner of the copyright must show "proof of access." In other words, if you are being accused of copying a substantial portion of a copyrighted work, the owner of the copyright must prove that somehow you had access to hearing the work in question.

For example, if this work has had substantial radio or TV airplay, then it is assumed that you had access to it. You cannot claim that because you do not own a TV, you never heard that sit-com theme song. The same applies for a film score. You cannot claim that you never saw the movie and therefore are not guilty of copyright infringement. If the music is widely disseminated to the public, either in theaters or on the radio or TV, then it is assumed that you had access to it.

On the other hand, say you have written a work that has only been performed locally in your city, Burlington, Vermont. Suppose that a composer based in Los Angeles comes out with a hit movie theme or song that sounds just like your song. In this case, you cannot claim copyright infringement, since you would be hard-pressed to prove that a composer from Los Angeles had access to your song that was only played in a nightclub in Burlington, Vermont. However, if you can prove that the composer in question had recently spent time in Burlington, and even was present at your gig, then you would have a case.

Copyright infringement is an area in which you should pray never to be involved. Be aware if you are subconsciously "borrowing" someone else's music. Try to always be original. These kinds of lawsuits can be messy, lengthy, and expensive. In our litigious society, there are people out there with no case at all who go after those they perceive as having deep pockets, hoping that they will at least get a settlement. This has happened to major performers including the Rolling Stones, the Beach Boys, and Sarah McLachlan. There are also cases where composers do unconsciously copy someone else's music. For example, this happened to George Harrison of the Beatles when he wrote "My Sweet Lord," which was obviously an unintentional rip-off of "He's So Fine" by the Chiffons. He was taken to court where he admitted that he unconsciously used this tune, and had to pay the writers and publisher a substantial settlement.

In songs, infringement could be based on musical or lyrical similarities. In film scores, there is only music. Actually, you often will hear similarities in two or more different scores of the same composer's work. For example, John Williams uses the interval of a fifth as the opening motive for the main themes of *Star Wars (1977)*, *Superman (1979)*, and *E.T. (1982)*. Is this copyright infringement on the part of the latter two scores? The answer is no, because the rest of the music after the opening interval in each of these scores continues on in different melodic, harmonic and rhythmic directions. One could find similar examples in the work of many of the top Hollywood composers, including Jerry Goldsmith, Ennio Morricone, James Horner, and others.

You will hear similarities in themes, harmonies, and instrumentation that run through almost every composer's work. One could dissect Mozart or Beethoven in this way and claim that they repeated themselves. Some self-repetition is bound to happen, since every composer has his own style. When it becomes copyright infringement (stealing from themselves) once again depends on whether the similar parts of the music are considered to have "substantial similarity," and whether or not someone has the desire to file a lawsuit.

What Is a Sync License?

There is an added dimension for film composers that makes its way into this discussion of copyrights and publishing. If a published work is going to be used for a film, television show, television commercial, or radio spot, the person desiring to use the copyrighted and published material must obtain a *sync license* from the publisher. This license allows the person to synchronize the music to their film, TV show, or commercial. Therefore, if you own the copyright to a song or film score and PepsiCo wants to use a portion of it for their next ad campaign, they must obtain a sync license from you allowing them to use the music for a specified amount of time, and for a specified amount of money.

Note that when you agree to write original music for a film, in the contract it will state that you are allowing the producer to use the music for that particular film, the promotion of that film, and purposes related to the marketing of the film. However, *under normal conditions, you will not own the music written for that film—the producer will.* You are still entitled to the writer's share of the royalties, but the producer controls the copyright because the standard agreement between composer and producer is that the composer is creating a "work made for hire."

Work Made for Hire

Work made for hire is yet another dimension for film composers in the complex, yet important area of copyrights and publishing. Many of the above hypothetical examples assume that the composer actually owns the copyright of his work. However, the usual conditions under which a film composer signs a contract and delivers the score is that he is completing a *work made for hire,* or simply, *work for hire.* This legal term describes a work, in this case a film score, that is created as a commission. The composer is hired to write the work by the producer, and while he is writing he is actually considered to be an employee of the producer. Once the work is completed and delivered, it belongs to the producer, who paid for it. The producer then owns the copyright and can decide how the music is to be used, both in the project it was composed for, and in the future. The composer still receives the "writer's share" of the royalties, but cannot control the reuse of the music. (Note: Future reuses are sometimes dependent on the agreement of the composer, depending on the kind of contract that was signed.) This is standard procedure, with some exceptions, in the film-scoring business.

Work for hire applies to both instrumental underscore as well as songs. If a composer is commissioned to write a song for a film (James Horner, "My Heart Will Go On," from *Titanic*; Michael Kamen, "Everything I Do, I Do It For You," from *Robin Hood, Prince of Thieves*), then that song is written as a work for hire. This is different from the song that is already in the composer's catalogue for which the producer must obtain a sync license from the publisher. When a song is written as a work for hire, the producer becomes the publisher.

Many composers have commented on the unfairness of this situation—that a person should spend weeks of his time using his creative talents and training to produce a unique product, only to turn over the ownership and future control of that product to someone else. This is not the case in the classical or concert music scene, where a composer usually retains the copyright ownership. In the film business, the future use of the music and potential royalties are often controlled by a producer who has no artistic interest in the music, only a financial one (sometimes not even that). As one producer's attorney said, "When we buy a score, it's as if we are buying a suit of clothes. If we want to hang it in the closet and just leave it there, that's our business."[1]

In addition to this hard-nosed attitude that the score will never see the light of day after the film is released, there is the possibility that the music will be used in a way that is creatively or morally reprehensible to the composer. To use a crass hypothetical example, a composer who has been a life-long vegetarian and animal-rights activist might not want his music to be used in a McDonalds commercial. And although he might reap tens of thousands of dollars in royalties, he still might not want his music to be used for that purpose. Yet, he may have no say in the matter.

Some composers have achieved a degree of success and enough clout in Hollywood that they can negotiate at least part ownership of their music. Once a composer is in demand, he has some bargaining power. If he is at the top of the field and has some choice over what projects he undertakes, he might be willing to turn down a project because the producer will not share the ownership of the music.

Composers have many horror stories as a result of a producer owning a copyright. Some involve the composer suffering significant loss of income because a producer or studio refuses to give permission for use of the score. Others instances are more benign but equally outrageous in the behavior of the studios. Writer Roy. M. Prendergast relates two such stories:

> *In 1971 composer Lalo Schifrin received a request to conduct the music from one of his films in connection with an appearance at*

a university. He called the studio and asked for a score, but was perfunctorily informed that the music did not belong to him and that if he wanted to play it he would have to rent the music from the studio. Eventually the studio was gracious enough to lend him the music for nothing.

Another well-known film composer, Maurice Jarre, was asked by a major symphony orchestra to conduct his score for Dr. Zhivago. *Incredible as it may sound, when Jarre asked MGM for the score, he was told that it had been destroyed since MGM needed more storage space.*[2]

There is also a historical side to this issue that puts the disagreement between the composers and producers into another perspective. As mentioned earlier, in the early days of the movie studios, all the music at a given studio was done in-house. All the composers, orchestrators, and musicians were under contract to the studio. Under this system, the studio automatically owned any musical creation. Even though the origination of the studio system was in the 1930s, and the dissolution of this system came about in the 1950s, studios and producers today have resisted changing the nature of the ownership of the music. They know a good thing when they see it; a film score can generate thousands—or even millions—of dollars in royalties over several years. In addition, the producer or studio owns all the other creative elements of a film: the script, costumes, sets, etc. To them, the music is just one more "suit of clothes" for the closet.

Work for hire is a tricky subject, and for some it is an uncomfortable working situation. However, it is the reality of the film-scoring business, and all composers have to deal with it, from the newcomer fresh out of music school to the established old-timer.

One instance where a composer might want to try to negotiate out of the work-for-hire clause of his contract and retain the rights to his music is on certain low-budget projects. Occasionally on such projects the composer is offered a very low amount of money to do a package deal. If this is the case, you can attempt to negotiate retaining ownership of the music—or at least sharing the ownership—in exchange for an extremely low fee. In this way, you can make some extra money down the road collecting both writers and publishers royalties, especially if the film is ever shown on television. However, even low-budget producers are often resistant to giving up their ownership of the music.

Also, it is a good idea to attempt to retain ownership of the music if you are scoring a student film. Some universities do not allow this, but some do. Since most student films don't even pay for music production costs, you might as well attempt to keep the copyright ownership and be able to use the music somewhere down the road. The chances of a student film having a long theatrical life are nil, so it is a shame to write some good music that gets lost forever under the work-made-for-hire contract clause.

Keep in mind that you should never push too hard on this issue unless you are willing to walk away from the project if your demands are not met. It is standard procedure throughout the industry for a composer to write the music as a work for hire.

As a composer, I obviously have a bias about this issue. However, it is one of those unpleasant things, like taxes or telephone solicitations at dinner time, that is very difficult to change and is a part of life. Therefore, students and composers who are just starting should accept this arrangement at the beginning of their career as necessary. Once a composer has some degree of success, he is in a position to negotiate for part ownership of the copyright and be able to have more control over the use of his music.

CHAPTER 22

Royalties, or Show Me the Money!

It is a very special gift, this gift of being able to compose for film.
—Michael Gorfaine

When a composer writes a film score for a feature film, he can receive a fee that is anywhere from $25,000 to over $500,000. Either of these amounts is lot of money, but often the real income for the composer comes in the form of royalties. Money can be made for months or years after a film is completed from network and cable TV airings, soundtrack albums, use of the music for commercials, showings of the film overseas in foreign countries, use in a sports video, etc. Writing the score for a TV series especially can generate large amounts of royalties because of the number of episodes and reruns. There is a difference in the amount and the way money is generated between underscore or instrumental background music and the money generated in royalties from songs in a motion picture or television show. Although many modern composers are active in creating both underscore and songs, this chapter focuses on instrumental underscore. But first let's define what kind of royalties there are, where they come from, and who collects and distributes them.

Performance Royalties

There are two kinds of royalties to be collected: performance royalties and mechanical royalties. *Performance royalties* are those that you receive when a work has been performed. This covers some live performances, radio airplay, and television. These performances are monitored by the three performing rights societies in the United States: ASCAP, BMI, and SESAC, or a similar society in every country around the world. The three U.S. performing rights societies are affiliated with counterparts in foreign countries, so that if your music is performed overseas, the foreign society will report your earnings to ASCAP, BMI, or SESAC, who will distribute them to you.

These performing rights societies issue licenses to anyone who uses music in their catalogues. This includes TV and radio stations, restaurants, nightclubs, and Muzak-type companies that produce "elevator music." A yearly fee is paid to the performing rights society for a blanket use of the music in its catalogue. The performing rights society then determines the amount of royalties owed to the various writers and publishers that are its members, and distributes the money in quarterly statements.

Note that a writer can only belong to one of these societies and that his publisher must belong to the same one. Many publishers have several different companies under the same umbrella so that they can work with writers of any performing rights affiliation.

Small Rights And Grand Rights

There are two types of performance royalties: small rights and grand rights. *Small rights*, also called *non-dramatic rights,* are the ones previously mentioned—performances on radio, television, nightclubs, etc. *Grand rights*, or *dramatic performance rights,* are for performances in a dramatic setting—Broadway, ballet, or opera. The performing rights societies do not issue licenses for grand rights and do not monitor this type of performance. So if you write the music to a Broadway show or ballet, then either you or your publisher must negotiate the license for that music directly with the producer.

Most of the time, film scores fall under *small rights*, or non-dramatic rights. If a movie is shown on television (or is a TV show to begin with), or if the music is played on the radio, it is covered by a *small rights* license, and your performance royalties will be collected and distributed by ASCAP, BMI, or SESAC. However, if the same music from a film is adapted for a ballet, then the publisher must arrange for a *grand rights* license.

Royalties from Theatrical Performances of Films

The other thing to be aware of regarding royalty collection is that *in the United States no royalties are paid for the showing of the movie in theaters.* This is a situation that came about in the late 1940s. At that time, ASCAP was the predominant performing rights organization. BMI was just getting started and SESAC had yet to come into existence. In 1947, almost every film composer belonged to ASCAP and was receiving healthy royalties for his scores that were shown in theaters around the country. Every theater paid a yearly amount to ASCAP for the right to use copyrighted music, and ASCAP made quarterly distributions to the composers. However, in 1947, ASCAP tried to raise the fee substantially and the theater owners filed suit. On March 14, 1950, the judge handed down a decision in favor of the theater owners and against ASCAP, declaring that the raising of the fee was illegal. He also took this decision a step further, declaring that it was a violation of antitrust laws for ASCAP to demand *any kind of license* for the theatrical use of motion picture music. This meant that the theaters could show any movie with any music and not have to pay performance royalties at all.

This ruling was a blow to composers and greatly affected their royalty income. Unfortunately, it is still in effect today and is the reason why film composers do not collect royalties from the showing of films in America. However, most other countries do allow the issuing of licenses for theatrical performances, and if an American composer scores the music for a film that is released in theaters overseas, he will collect royalties through the foreign affiliate of his performance rights society.

The distribution of royalties from the performing rights societies is determined by complex formulas. For radio performances, it is based on a *sample survey*. The society takes a sample of radio airplay around the country, adds a multiplier to it, and comes up with a figure representing the total number of performances for that song. Then, the percentage of that song's performances is measured against all the other songs surveyed, the percentage is calculated with the total money received by the society, and the royalty is paid. What this amounts to is that you will receive royalties based on how often the song gets played, how many stations it is played on, and how long it stays on the charts. This can be an enormous amount of money, often as much as $250,000 in the first year alone for the writer of a number-one hit song.

For film composers, royalties from television performances are much more relevant. These are done by a *census survey*, meaning that everything that is performed in a given area, whether it be ABC, CBS, NBC, WB, HBO, TNT, etc., is counted and prorated, and then a royalty is paid. The size of the station, the time of day of the broadcast, and the kind of performance will determine how much the royalty actually will be. Performances on large, urban stations are weighed the heaviest. Prime time slots (7:00 p.m. to 1:00 a.m.) are the best time of day to have performances. The major networks, ABC, CBS, and NBC, still pay the most, with FOX, WB, UPN, and the others trailing behind. (The use of term *networks* can be confusing. Originally, there were only three TV networks: ABC, NBC, and CBS. With the advent of cable, there are now many smaller cable networks attempting to challenge the predominance of the three originals. This is a situation that is in flux, and future years will see the ultimate results. It may soon be anachronistic, but *networks* or *major networks* still generally refers to the original three: ABC, CBS, and NBC.)

Performances on television fall into the following categories, and each category gets paid a royalty at a different rate: visual vocal (songs sung on screen), background vocal, background instrumental, and theme songs. Visual vocals and themes get paid the most, and are paid per performance. That is, they get paid the same whether they were used for 30 seconds or 60 seconds. Background instrumental gets paid the least, and is paid on a *durational basis*, determined by the cue's length.

The way performances are tracked is that the producer or studio submits a summation of all the cues in a particular show or film to the royalty society, noting whether it is instrumental underscore, source music, or the main title to a TV show. This summary is called a *music cue sheet* (see fig. 10.5.). The performance royalty society knows when the show is aired, how many stations aired it, and how the music was used, and it will calculate the appropriate monetary distribution. Prime-time network TV pays the most, main-title theme music pays more than instrumental background music, and source music (songs) pays more than instrumental background music. Commercials have yet another formula, but that is beyond the scope of this book.

A lot of money can be made from hit theme music or background music for a television show. But before taking a look at the possible numbers, let's take a look at mechanical royalties—yet another source of income for the composer.

Mechanical Royalties

Mechanical royalties are those received from the sales of CDs, tapes, sheet music, music books, and sometimes videos. Although mechanical royalties are much more important to songwriters than film composers, they can create a sizeable royalty income for film composers as well. This is especially true in recent times with the explosion of the soundtrack market. Since the unanticipated success of the soundtrack from *Titanic*, the possibility of making major amounts of money in mechanical royalties has increased.

Mechanical royalties came about when, at the turn of this century, before radio, before stereo recordings, before long-playing 33-RPM records, even before 78s, the home music entertainment machines of choice were cylinder records, pianos, and player pianos. At this time, the 1909 Copyright Act was passed guaranteeing the writers and publishers of music a royalty for every record, piano roll, and piece of sheet music sold. Because these records and songs were reproduced on machines, they were called mechanical royalties. At that time, sheet music and piano rolls became the biggest income generators for composers and songwriters, with records running a distant second. As the technology changed over the years, records (of the various kinds), cassette tapes, and now CDs have replaced printed music as the primary source of mechanical royalty income.

There are actually two types of mechanical royalties. In the previous chapter we discussed how someone can perform and record your copyrighted material without receiving your permission as long as your work has been published (distributed or offered for sale to the public). When they do this, they are acting under a *compulsory mechanical license.* This license allows a person or company to use your published material without having to receive your permission, as long as they abide by certain rules, including:

- They agree to notify you within thirty days of making or distributing the work that they are using your copy-righted material,

- They will send you a monthly statement and payment of royalties earned, and

- They will pay the statutory mechanical rate based on the number of units manufactured.

The other kind of mechanical license is a *negotiated mechanical license,* which is very similar to a *compulsory mechanical license,* only it is more flexible. This license is simply referred to as a *mechanical license*—the license that is issued to someone who wants to use your music, and would like more lenient terms from you than those in the compulsory mechanical license. These terms usually involve the receipt of a quarterly statement instead of a monthly one, an agreed-upon lower rate than the statutory minimum, and the payment of royalties on units sold, as opposed to units actually manufactured. For film composers, the nego-tiated mechanical license is usually the one in effect.

Mechanical royalties are administered by the record companies, which keep track of how many units are sold and pay accordingly. For film composers who are not songwriters, until the late 1990s this was a significant, but not a huge, amount of money, for soundtrack albums traditionally sold small amounts compared to hit pop albums. However, as the soundtrack craze has taken off in recent years, enor-mous amounts of CDs are being sold that include not only songs, but also instrumental music from the film. This means more royalties for the composer of the score. Before this recent time, soundtracks that consisted of only the instrumental music from the film would sell 50,000 to 100,000 units at best. Now ten times that many can be sold from a mediocre film that does so-so at the box office.

Usually the film composer's contract specifies a dollar amount per album sold as his mechanical royalty. This is because film cues are not like songs; they can be much longer in duration, especially after the music editor is finished editing. This editing can involve cutting as many as fifteen short cues together to make eight or ten long selections for the CD. Remember, mechanical royalties for songs are based on the statutory minimum, 6.95 cents per song, or even lower if you negotiate a different rate. Therefore, if the film composer goes by that rate, for 10 selections on a CD that is actually a compilation of 15 or 20 cues, he will receive only 69.5 cents for every CD sold.

A typical amount of mechanical royalties for a film composer is usually between seventy-five cents and one dollar per unit if the album consists entirely of excerpts from the instrumental score. In addition, if the composer is also given credit as the producer of the album, another 5% of the retail price (seventy-five cents) per unit will be paid in producer's royalties.

Real Dollars: Show Me the Money!!!

Here is the nitty-gritty of royalties, and after reading this section you might be wetting your lips anticipating your pot of gold at the end of the royalty rainbow. Note that performance royalties are the main source of royalty income for film composers, so they take up the bulk of this discussion.

To sum up the previous section, when your music is aired on the radio or played on TV you are often going to receive royalties. If your music is played on television, either on network (ABC, NBC, or CBS) or cable, then you also will receive performance royalties. The amount of these television royalties depends on the length of the music, whether it is aired on network (more money) or cable (less money), what time of day the show is aired, and how the music is used.

Let's look at some of the possible numbers in performance royalties. The rates that each performance royalty society pays are comparable, although they all have slightly different formulas for computing the rate. Currently, for background instrumental music on prime-time network television, the performance royalty rate is about $180 to $200 per minute. That means if you do twenty minutes of music for a show that is aired on ABC, CBS, or NBC between 7 p.m. and 1 a.m., you will receive between $3600 to $4000 in royalties. If you do twenty-two shows in a year, that is at least $79,200 a year in royalties. (Keep in mind that this is the writer's share; the producer is receiving an identical check for the publisher's share because you have created a work made for hire.) This is in addition to the fee you were already paid for composing the music.

After the initial twenty-two airings, many of those episodes will be shown during the summer rerun season. For this airing you will also receive the prime-time royalty rate. A few years down the road, the producer will syndicate the show to local and cable stations, and you will continue to collect royalties, though at a lower rate. The initial, or first year of the syndicated airing, is paid at one rate, while subsequent airings, or *strip syndication* (when the show is aired every day on various stations) royalties are paid at yet another rate.

If you have written the theme for this show, then that music is calculated at yet a different rate. For each performance of the theme, you will receive about $750, and since the theme is usually played at both the beginning and the end of the show, you will receive $1500 for each show. So for a season of twenty-two episodes, your performance royalty for the theme will be $33,000. Add to that any airing of the show in re-reruns and the money keeps growing.

Here is a sample list of the *approximate* royalty formulas in the spring of 1999. Remember that these numbers change frequently, depending on many factors at the performing rights societies. These figures are for prime time television.

Background Instrumental

• ABC, CBS, NBC	$180 to $200 per minute
• FOX, WB, UPN	$100 to $120 per minute
• HBO	$7 per minute
• USA, TNT	$10 to $12 per minute
• Syndicated local TV	$1 to $40 per minute (depending on the size of the station)

Themes

• ABC, CBS, NBC	$250 per airing (regardless of length), for the first 14 weeks, $600 to $700 thereafter

Featured performance (visual vocal)

• ABC, CBS, NBC	$1500 per airing (regardless of length)
• FOX	$750 per airing (regardless of length)

A glance at this (incomplete) list reveals that it is most desirable to have your music played on the networks. They pay the most in licensing fees, so they generate the most weight in calculating royalty payments.

Also, note that some cable stations, such as HBO, have a terrible royalty rate. This situation is being addressed by all three performance royalty societies.

Finally, it is obvious from this list that if you have a song or a theme performed in a television show, you get far more royalties than for background instrumental music. And if your theme is used in a background instrumental cue, then you get a part of the royalties from that cue, even if it is written by someone else. This happens frequently, and affects many composers' royalties because often the composer doing the week-to-week episodes is different from the one who wrote the theme.

Examples

Let's take a look at some hypothetical examples for feature films and television that take into account performance royalties from several possible sources, mechanical royalties from sales of CDs and tapes, and the composer's fee. Note that I am leaving out possible future revenue from commercials and other reuses. Also note that I am starting at the top and working my way down. That is, the first examples are for major feature films, next are network episodic television shows, and finally, network movies-of-the-week. And please make one final mental note that the following scenarios are hypothetical, although entirely possible.

Possible Scenario #1:

Let's take a look at some of the possible numbers for music in a feature film. Let's assume the film has 60 minutes of music, is a money-maker with big stars, but not a blockbuster hit. It is shown on cable six months after the theatrical release, and network TV one year later:

• Composer's fee	$250,000
• U.S. cable television (HBO), multiple broadcasts (60 minutes x $7 per minute x 50 showings)	$ 21,000
• Network broadcast, prime time (60 minutes x $180 per minute)	$ 10,800
• Foreign theatrical and other foreign performances (1st year)	$150,000
• U.S. and foreign local television performances (5 years)	$ 50,000
• CD and tape sales (100,000 units x 75 cents per unit)	$ 75,000
	$556,800

Now keep in mind that this scenario excludes many possible future royalties such as more television performances, possible use in commercials, or even use in other films. In addition, a film can earn as much as $250,000 in performance royalties for the composer over many years of TV airings.

Possible Scenario #2:

Here is how the money—fees and royalties—can add up for music in a
network, prime-time TV series. Let's assume there are twenty minutes
of music in each of twenty-two episodes, with each episode broadcast
twice (the initial airing and reruns) on prime-time network over the
course of one year:

- Composer's fee, twenty-two episodes:
  $7500 X 22 $165,000
- First year, U.S. network prime time,
  initial airing, and summer reruns:
  44 shows x 20 minutes x $180 per minute $158,400
- Main title theme royalties:
  44 shows x $1500 $ 66,000
- First year, foreign television performances
  (1 year) $ 30,000
- First year syndication $ 50,000
- Strip syndication (1 year) $ 40,000
- CD and tape sales $ 10,000
                                          $519,400

You might have noticed that the TV series composer is making more
money in this particular instance than the film composer. In real life
this might be true, but there are several big differences. First of all, the
TV composer is working steadily, maybe even six days a week for
twenty-two weeks, whereas the film composer will probably spend
four to twelve weeks on a feature film, and can score three or four films
a year if he is really busy. In addition, there are creative benefits for the
film composer. The budget for music on a film will be substantially
higher, so the film composer is often writing for a large orchestra. And in
many films, the acting, directing and overall production value is higher,
making the composer's job creatively more interesting.

Possible Scenario #3

Network TV Movie:

• Composers fee (or profit after package deal production costs):	$20,000
• Prime time airing of film at 45 minutes x $180	$ 8,100
• Foreign television performance:	$10,000
• Re-airing on cable network:	$ 1,000
	$ 39,100

Once we leave the area of feature films and episodic television, the numbers drop significantly. As you can see from the chart earlier in this chapter, when you have a film on HBO or local television, the royalties are paltry in comparison to other networks. So, it is important to get as much money as possible in the form of a fee. This is not to say HBO movies are not worth scoring. They can still be a good source of income, as well as a step towards bigger and better things.

Performance royalties are the film composer's great friend. They can provide steady income during slow times, and can add up to substantial amounts from all the different possible sources. In addition, the composer does almost no administrative work; the performing rights society takes care of it all. The only thing a composer must do is make sure that the cue sheets are filed properly with the performing rights society. Even that task is administered by the production office of the film; all the composer has to do is review the summary of cues.

The more work you do, the more you build up a catalogue, the more money will flow to you in the form of performance royalties. Shows or movies that you did ten years ago can still generate foreign or syndicated performances, so the more of these shows you have, the more income is generated. It can be like an annuity for retirement.

CHAPTER 23

Out in the Real World

The most important thing is a love for films,
and a fascination, a desire, a love, and feel for music.
—Mark Snow

There comes a point when a dream can become a reality. The musician who has dreamt about working as a film composer is ready to live that dream when he has the appropriate composition and orchestration skills, has mastered dramatic synchronization, knows some basic sequencing, and above all, is ready to start making money writing music for movies. The questions are: How to get started? Where is the work? What materials are needed? Who should I call? Am I good enough? On and on these questions go, with many variations on these themes.

There is no one answer, there is no one best route to film composing success and stardom. Every successful composer has a different story to tell. They all involve some combination of hard work, persistence, preparation, and sheer luck. Maybe the 347th door you knock on will be the one. You never know when a director will hear your New Age album and decide that your music is perfect for his film. You could knock on every door in Hollywood, Beverly Hills, and Century City for years, only to get into a fender-bender with a director who is looking for a composer. Maybe your charm and good looks will open many doors, even if your writing skills are minimal. So the best thing a composer can do is write a lot, get better at writing, be prepared, and be persistent.

There are hundreds of aspiring film composers living in Los Angeles right now, hoping to catch that big break. So how can you hope to compete? It is part luck, and part self-effort. Mark Snow puts the perseverance angle well:

You knock on every door and you're merciless, you keep persever-ing like crazy and pray, and 1 out of 10 guys who come to town make it. I don't know, maybe 1 out of 100. Maybe 1 out of 4.

And Mark Isham talks about luck:

I never set out to be a film composer. I just happened to write music and other people said, "God, this would be great for film." And then somebody actually said, "I want you to do it for a film." And all of a sudden I had another career.

There are many ways to get started in the film-composing business. You can move to Los Angeles and try to swim with the big boys. Or you can go to a smaller town, get some smaller projects, and gain expe-rience and credibility. Either way, there are two things that must happen while you are getting started: first, you need to be actively involved in making or writing music on a regular basis, and second, you need to have your act together in terms of presenting yourself and your music. Take the time to organize your materials in a professional way. Remember that this is a business based on person-to-person rela-tionships, and your demo, résumé, or bio could be the first step of this relationship. Create a logo and a company name, get stationery and business cards, make sure your answering machine is warm and wel-coming—not goofy sounding. When you go to meetings, be well dressed, arrive on time, and be confident. In short, create an aura about yourself that says to a producer or director, "This person has his act together, and I'd like to work with him."

Demos

The first thing you must have is a professionally recorded audio demo with a variety of your music on it. This is commonly submitted on either cassette tape or CD. In either format, choose cues that are recorded and played well. Remember that non-musicians might hear an out-of-tune trumpet but not know what is wrong and think it is something inherent in the music. Then it becomes your fault, and in their mind you do not write good music. Or they could hear a poor quality recording of an ingenious piece, and not be able to hear through the bad sound.

Also, choose pieces that are film-like in nature. Cues from film projects you have already worked on are best. Excerpts from classical concert pieces are not recommended because they do not usually sound like film music, especially chamber groups. A chamber group is always a chamber group, and is a very specific sound in the ears of most people. Some films use chamber groups, but not many.

Songs are not considered film scores. Do not submit songs on a film-scoring demo except: (1) If you know the project is looking for songs, and (2) The songs submitted are in addition to other music you are submitting.

If you are sending in a demo for a specific project, as opposed to a more general demo, then choose cues that you think are in the ballpark of what the director is seeking. After you have presented these kinds of cues, then you might add one or two that show another side of what you can do.

Composers have gone to various lengths to make great demos. Some have hired small orchestras to the tune of several thousand dollars in order to make the best presentation. There are demo orchestras that you can pay by the hour in Los Angeles and in Europe. The key is to make it sound as good as possible. This is the audio representation of who you are musically, so you must make it shine.

Cassettes

Generally, if you are making a cassette demo, it should be about seven to ten minutes long with excerpts from various cues you have done. Remember that you are showing a sample of your work, and you want to include as many different type of cues as possible. Therefore, edit and keep it short! If a director or producer is interested, then he will ask for more material down the line, but make the first presentation short and sweet. Try to include as much material as possible that is thematic in nature, as opposed to cues that are more like underscore and less melodic. Cues with catchy thematic material are generally more interesting than cues that were originally conceived as underscore. Make the space between selections brief, and as smooth as possible. Try to create the master on ProTools or similar software. Editing on a home cassette dubbing deck is not recommended as it creates audible and annoying pops and clicks between selections, and there is usually no way to fade in and out.

A way to show more than one aspect of your skills is to use both sides of the tape. For example, Side A could be "Orchestral Film Cues," and Side B could be "Songs." Or side B could be "Electronic Music Cues."

Purchase cassettes in bulk with no printed labels already on them. Make the labels for the individual cassettes and design the J-cards (the cards that go in the cassette box) on the computer, or have a cassette duplication house print them for you. A logo of your name or company can look impressive, but if you don't have one, any nice font will do. DO NOT submit demos with cassettes bought at a record store with your contact info and the titles of the selections hand-printed. This would make you seem unprofessional when compared to the many tapes that have laser-printed labels.

Finally, make sure your contact information—phone number, address, or e-mail—is on every cassette and every J-card. This way, if those items get separated, the person at the other end will always know where to find you.

CDs

With the technology becoming more affordable and more user friendly, homemade CDs are now often submitted as demos. Many of the same guidelines apply to CDs as cassettes: choose well-recorded material, a wide variety, etc. But with CDs there is no need to make excerpts of your cues. Because of the ease of browsing through the different selections, it is acceptable to include complete cues on a CD. If you are submitting material for a specific project and want to show another side of what you do musically, include additional music after the project-specific material. As with cassettes, keep the material as thematic as possible. But note that cues that sound like underscore are acceptable on the CD demo because they can show a different dimension of your music, and the listener can easily forward through them if he is not interested in hearing the entire cut.

As with cassettes, make all the printed material look professional and eye-pleasing, and include your contact information on a sheet inserted in the jewel case as well as on the CD itself.

Video Reels

Some producers request video reels to show that you not only can write good music, but that you can write appropriate music for dramatic situations. For this reel you might select cues that are different from the ones on a cassette or CD. Cues on the video reel should be your efforts that have really shone as a partner to the drama, which might be different from the cues with the biggest, most impressive musical ideas. In this case, the guideline of finding thematic material doesn't apply; just choose the cues that *look* the best. Make it 10 to 15 minutes long with a variety of styles.

With a video reel, it is customary to begin with a "card" of your name, and your contact information. Visually slate each new cue with a card. The card should say the name of the cue, the project it was from, and any other brief, pertinent information such as the director, studio, TV network, or year of release.

As with cassettes and CDs, make the presentation professional. Have all the contact information on the video itself, and on the box. Print the labels, do not hand-write them.

If you are just getting started and have yet to score any films, there is still a way to produce a video reel. With today's technology, it is fairly easy to rescore a scene from an existing movie and sync it. You will need either a sequencer or the equipment to record live players, one or two VCR machines, a computer (or hard-disc recorder), and a MIDI interface. Choose a scene that has no dialogue, and contains few sound-effects. Then compose your music. If you are using two VCRs, run the original film synchronized with your music to the second VCR. If you have only one VCR, then you must dub the music directly onto the VCR, erasing any sound already there.

Replacing the music in an already existing film is an accepted way to showcase your ability to write for a dramatic situation. As long as you only use this music as a demo, and it is never aired in public, you are not violating copyright laws.

Résumés and Cover Letters

The promo package you create should include stationery, business cards, and a résumé. Some composers also include a photo and reviews of projects they have completed.

Design, or have a professional design, a logo for your name or the name of your production company. Use this logo on your business cards and stationery. That way, the very first visual that a prospective employer sees is pleasing, and implies that you are professional.

Create a résumé, or, if you are a little further along in your career, use a short bio with a list of credits. If you are just starting out and don't have significant credits, use the résumé format. This should reflect what you have done musically—projects completed, important gigs, awards, internships, teaching, software skills, and recordings. Also include prior work experience and your education. This tells the person reading it where you are coming from, and the scope and depth of your skills. Make the résumé look nice, with a pleasing font, and an easy-to-read and logical format.

If you already have some credits, it is common to submit a short bio, accompanied by a list of credits. This is a more direct document than the résumé, for once you have had some experience, the person considering you for a project probably doesn't care where you went to school, or if you won any composition awards. He wants proof of your credibility, to hear and see your competency, and to get to know you as a person.

Finding Work

Once you have all your materials together, you are ready to go out and get the gigs. That means meeting people anywhere you can, circulating, and knocking on doors. Be prepared for a lot of rejection that has nothing to do with your skills as a composer. But most of all, be prepared to talk, schmooze, and play the game.

There are many avenues for the beginning composer, but the most important thing to do is to expand your circle of contacts. Whether you live in Los Angeles, New York, or anywhere else, there are places where people gather. This could be trade organizations like ASCAP, BMI, or the Society of Composers and Lyricists. It could be a local Media Alliance like the one in Boston that includes producers, directors, actors, composers, and everyone else associated with the entertainment business. Hang out with student film makers or people attending film-making seminars. Go to these events, take a stack of your business cards, and don't expect to get offered a gig; just meet some nice people. You'd be surprised how much fun you can have.

You could also get a job as an intern in a trade organization, at a recording studio, or at a production house. Opportunities like these are often posted at colleges or universities, but usually you will need to be resourceful. Make a list, and hit the phones! Put on your best, most confident telephone voice and find out if they ever need interns or entry level assistants. Keep a log of the responses including the names of all the people you talk to, even the receptionists. If they say, "No, but maybe in the future," wait a couple of months and call again. If they say, "No, we never hire unknowns," then cross them off the list.

Many composers in Hollywood need assistants and hire aspiring composers to help them do a variety of tasks ranging from mundane office work to helping write music. Although hard to come by, these jobs include answering phones, making appointments, sequencing music, repairing equipment, doing transcriptions, and helping with paperwork. These can be great entry-level jobs, but there are not very many of them. To land a job like this you should have excellent organizational skills, people skills, computer skills, and have great sequencing chops.

Another approach is to send your tape to producers of low budget films, documentaries, and cable TV shows. Keep in mind that most unsolicited tapes never get played. So the question becomes how to get your tape into the "solicited" mailbox. There are several ways to do this, but the key is to somehow make personal contact with a producer or director. This can happen in any number of ways: You might meet someone at a party, at a seminar, or at an ASCAP or BMI function. You can call and ask the person's secretary if he is accepting any tapes. Then you call again. And again. And again. Eventually, you might get through and make a pitch for him to hear your stuff.

Once you have sent your tape, follow-up is extremely important. Wait about a week, and then call to "make sure that your tape was received." This is somewhat disingenuous, as that is only part of the reason you are calling. The other part is to keep your name in their face. Be careful here, though. There is a fine line between persistence and annoyance. People get busy, and it is sometimes important to remind them of your existence. But it is also possible to become a pest and create a negative association with your name. Oftentimes, the response will be that the producer has not listened to your tape, or if he has, he is not interested. This is very difficult for some composers to hear because most of us want to believe that the world is waiting to hear our musical creations. However, finding work is often a form of self-promotion. The trick is to become thick-skinned, and not to take rejection as a reflection of your musical ability, personality, or worth as a human being. Take it as simply a result of where a particular person is at that particular day. Perhaps they really have no projects going. Perhaps they already have another composer. Perhaps they really didn't like your music. You need to have the confidence that someone else *will* like your music.

In order to survive in the entertainment business, you must develop a strong sense of who you are and what your music is about. Then all the rejections in the world will not phase you, and you can keep on plugging away. Artists in every aspect of the music industry face this same problem. Billy Joel was rejected from over twenty record labels before he got a shot from Columbia Records. Brian Epstein shopped the Beatles' demo to every label in London before he went back to EMI a second time and got George Martin to give them a try. In interviews for this book, composers such as Alan Silvestri, David Raksin, and Alf Clausen spoke about times when they could barely find work even after having had some degree of success and recognition.

Alf Clausen:

> The common thread you will find with composers at any level is that we have all suffered a certain amount of abuse and hard knocks through the growth of a career. My own feeling is that the most successful careers are the ones that are able to keep those abuses in perspective and realize that it is only the music business. We are not looking for a cure for cancer. We can only do the best job we do, and hopefully, sometimes we will be lucky enough to be employed by people who like what we do. And sometimes we might be lucky enough to be employed by people who we really like. It's not going to happen all the time.

> Try to keep a center to the vision. We deal in a product, and they are hiring us for our product. Unfortunately, that goes totally against art, it goes against the artistic tendency, and everything else. But it is part of the business, and as long as you learn how to deal with that, you will be much more successful on a daily basis.

There are many projects involving music happening all over the country, yet the number is finite. And like every other segment of the entertainment industry, there are many more people trying to get work than there are jobs. Who gets what jobs often has nothing to do with who writes the best music or who is most experienced. The important thing is to enjoy writing music and even find a way to enjoy the constant search for work. Composer Lolita Ritmanis speaks about this issue:

> It's hard to know why one person works and another doesn't. You have to stop wondering why because there's no point to it. There are great composers working on projects that have very little visibility. Their music might be brilliant. So why are they not scoring big studio films? It's often not fair, and worrying about it

not being fair doesn't change a thing. I've seen quite a bit of dis-
aster as well as success in this business. If you're only waiting for
the big break, it can be a long wait and you can really get sick
over it. You have to try and enjoy your life, and live a life too.

One thing that young composers should be aware of is *that it takes some time to get established.* There are no overnight success stories; these are all figments of publicists' imaginations. Every composer has paid his dues somewhere, whether it's as an orchestrator, as a studio player, as a rock musician, or as a waiter. If you are just starting out and you don't have the playing skills, or if your cutting-edge band hasn't provided enough income, then you must figure out a way to create an incoming cash flow. Although this might mean getting a "day job" in an office or a restaurant, it is important to create a cushion for yourself so that you can afford to make those demo tapes and CDs, or record a new demo.

Shirley Walker:

You have to be able to afford to be a film composer. I think a lot of
people come here to L.A. and they can't support the pursuit of
their profession. And that's a hard thing to do. So if you have to
make money being a film composer, it's going to be hard for you to
get your career started because unless you're coming in at the very
top, the beginning level isn't conducive to you supporting yourself.

In addition to these economic realities, it is important to remember that the film business is based on personal relationships. Many composers at the top of the field tell stories about producers or directors that they met when they were just starting out. So nurture the relationships that you make all along the way. Enjoy people as human beings first, as business contacts second. The composer that is looking at everyone he meets as a possible "connection" or source of income is creating a lot of stress for himself, as well as very shallow relationships. If you treat people well, if you treat yourself well, then others will pick up on this and want to be around you. The entertainment business can be very difficult and even delusionary, so reaching out to others as people and having a strong personal center and confidence will carry you through the most difficult situations.

William Ross:

> *I approach it from the human point of view. Most people are driven to this business out of love for music and film. They're not out to get rich, at least not when they start. It's a hard thing to come out here to Los Angeles with the uncertainties of the business—to uproot yourself, to challenge yourself. To me, anyone who does that is a success, no matter what happens. I say that with utmost sincerity. I think we are in a business where you are a person first, and somewhere down the line you are a composer and you do all that. But the top of the list for me is what kind of person you are, how you treat people, how do you get along with people. That's got to be in place.*

Finding work is not easy at any level of the entertainment business. Film scoring can be great work, wonderful work, rewarding work. If you love it, if there's nothing else in the world you would rather do, if you are willing to possibly endure several years of struggling and countless rejections, then go for it! There is no single road to the top; it can happen a million different ways. But you will never find out if you can get there until you try.

Interviews

PART V

Elmer Bernstein

Elmer Bernstein has scored over 200 movies, beginning in the early 1950s. He has worked with film makers of every generation, from Cecil B. DeMille to Francis Ford Coppola and Martin Scorsese. He has scored films of wide-ranging subject matter, from *The Ten Commandments* to *Animal House* and *Ghostbusters*. Some of his most well-known scores are *To Kill a Mockingbird*, *The Magnificent Seven*, *The Man With the Golden Arm*, *Airplane!*, and *My Left Foot*. Bernstein also teaches film composing at USC, and conducts performances of his film music with orchestras around the world.

HOW DID YOU FIRST GET INTERESTED IN FILM MUSIC?

I was a concert pianist, at first. I studied composition from the age of twelve, starting with Aaron Copland and finally with Stefan Wolpe. I was always interested in composition. Actually it was curious; I thought I'd be a composer but I never thought of composing for films. It was listening to the work of David Raksin and Bernard Herrmann in the forties—those two composers—that really made me sit up and take notice of what could be done with film music. I think the reason for that was that both Herrmann and Raksin had peculiarly American voices, and I found that voice appealing.

HOW DID YOU GET INTO JAZZ?

Well, the jazz thing came about in my own childhood. My father was a great jazz enthusiast, and I was brought up with the old Dixieland people like King Oliver and going on to people like Bix Beiderbecke and Louis Armstrong. There was a great presence in the house all the time, so I had a sort amateur interest in jazz. I myself was not a jazz player, but it was part of my upbringing.

HOW DO YOU APPROACH THE ACTUAL SCORING FOR A FILM?

Well, it differs from film to film. The first thing I do is spend a week just looking at the film without prejudice. When I say without prejudice, I say to myself, I'm not even going to try to think about music during this week. I just want to look at the film, I want to look at the film until the film talks to me and the film tells me things. So what I want the film to tell me is what it's about, and that's not always on the surface. What is the film about? What is the function of music going to be in this film? Why are we having music in this film and what's it going to do? So I start with those kinds of thoughts. It's a kind of intellectual process rather than a composing process. If the score's going to be based on highly thematic things, then I have to suffer out finding themes, so to speak [laughs]. Sometimes I get into the process and things are not going well for me, or I can't think of what I want to do. If I get desperate about time, I'll look at my 30 or 40 starts until I find a particular start that I can say, "I know what to do with this." Just sneak in the back door, so to speak.

DO YOU USE SYNTHESIZERS AT ALL?

I do. I think every score I've written in the last fifteen years has some synthesizers in it, but I don't use them as an end in themselves. I use them for the obvious factor: they make sounds that other instruments can't.

HOW DID YOU FEEL WHEN THEY FIRST STARTED TO CREEP INTO SCORES IN THE SIXTIES?

Well, oddly enough, I was one of the first people to use them, although people don't generally associate me with that. In the score for *Hawaii*, the very first sound you hear is a Moog synthesizer—way back in 1961.

IT'S REALLY EXPLODED NOW, SO ARE YOU FAIRLY SYNTH SAVVY? CAN YOU FIND YOUR WAY AROUND THEM A LITTLE BIT?

Not hands-on, no. I think about them; in other words, I will think of a use that I want to put a synthesizer to soundwise, and I will depend upon my people who do that kind of thing.

IN GENERAL, HOW DO YOU FEEL ABOUT THE USE OF SYNTHESIZERS IN TODAY'S SCORES?

At the risk of sounding arrogant, I will have to say that film scoring has descended to a lot of gadgetry, in our time. For most people, there are too many gadgets and not enough music.

COULD YOU SPEAK ABOUT THE CONCEPT BEHIND THE SCORE FOR To Kill a Mockingbird?

Funny, before you were asking about the process and I said the first thing I do is to look at a film and try to determine what the role of the music is. Now, I had a big problem with that in *To Kill a Mockingbird*. If you look at the film without music, all you're looking at is a film with a lot of kids in it. But you're also seeing a lot of adult problems—problems of racism, problems of injustice, death and violence, violence to children. It took me the longest time to find where the music was going to go, how it was going to go, and what its specific use would be in the film. I determined, after a long time—it took me about six weeks—that the film is about the adult world seen through the eyes of children. All these problems—what we call adult problems—are seen as the children see them. This led me to childlike things: playing the piano one note at a time, music box sounds, harp, bells, things of that sort. So what really got me into the film was the realization that it was a film about adult issues seen through the eyes of children.

THERE'S SOMETHING ABOUT THAT SCORE THAT IS TIMELESS. IT COULD HAVE BEEN WRITTEN TODAY AS WELL AS ALMOST 40 YEARS AGO.

The thing about *Mockingbird*, and the reason that worked so well, is that it's a wonderful film. It is an absolutely wonderful film—the film is timeless. The film is absolutely timeless. Even though it's about real things, the film has a fable-like quality that makes it timeless. Every once in a while, you get to write a score for something like that.

WHAT ARE SOME MEMORABLE COLLABORATIONS YOU HAVE HAD?

To Kill a Mockingbird was a collaborative effort of director Robert Mulligan and the sadly late Alan Pakula. Those were really enjoyable relationships. I did about five films in a row for them. It was the kind of thing where we would talk about a project long before they even shot a roll of film. So I was constantly collaborating by just talking about it. That was an absolutely wonderful relationship.

If I had to pick the most outstanding relationship with a film maker, it would be with Martin Scorcese. I always said that I wish that every composer could have the privilege of doing at least one film with Scorsese. For him, film making is an art he respects. He's totally dedicated to what he's doing, with no phony ego stuff—no baggage of that kind. He has respect for other artists. It's just the most respectful and interesting collaboration because he's also very knowledgeable. When we were talking about *The Age of Innocence*, we decided that the sound or tenor of the score was sort of Brahmsian. Marty could then start talking about the Brahms sextet and stuff like that because he's so knowledgeable. That was a wonderful relationship—wonderful to work with. It was also wonderful to work with Francis Ford Coppola on *The Rainmaker*. Those were great collaborations.

WHOSE IDEA WAS IT FOR THE 6/8 JAZZ ELEMENT WITH HAMMOND ORGAN IN THE RAINMAKER? WAS THAT YOU OR WAS THAT FRANCIS FORD COPPOLA?

I have to credit Francis with the bluesy 6/8 idea in a roundabout way. What happened was, when I first got on *The Rainmaker*, Francis wasn't going to have a score, as we know a score to be. At first, he was going to go the B.B. King route—in other words, real Memphis stuff with some very minor connective things in scoring. But as he began to develop the film itself, he began to feel that he needed to depend more on score. So it was my decision to use the Hammond B3 organ, but it came out of his idea of Memphis ambience. I retained, out of that ambience, the three instruments you hear a great deal of: the Hammond B3, the muted trumpet, and the guitar. But that came out of Francis's original concept.

When I came on *Rainmaker*, it was in rough-cut form, and the version I finally recorded to was version #26. It went through some amazing changes. The interesting thing about Francis is that each time he changed the film, it was for the better. He wasn't just fooling around; he was just "finding" the film, so to speak.

HOW DO YOU HANDLE A SITUATION WHERE YOU'VE SIGNED ON AND YOU FIND OUT THERE'S A DIRECTOR THAT DOESN'T REALLY COMMUNI-CATE VERY WELL MUSICALLY?

Well, most directors do not communicate well musically. It's rare that they do. You kind of hope they'll let you do your thing, so to speak, and get on with life. But if they're ignorant and invasive you just have a miserable time. There's not much you can do. You try to be as diplomatic as possible, but sometimes you get your score tossed out or you walk out.

WHAT ABOUT WHEN YOU'RE SPOTTING A FILM—WHAT ARE THE KINDS OF THINGS YOU'RE REALLY LOOKING FOR?

I spot a film strictly as a dramatist. I'm not thinking of music at all when I spot a film. I look at the scene and say, Should this scene have music? Why should it have music? If it does have music, what is the music supposed to be doing? So that's my process.

WHAT IS YOUR ADVICE TO ASPIRING FILM COMPOSERS?

Learn everything you possibly can about all kinds of music— ethnic, pop, classical … everything. Be prepared!

Terence Blanchard

Terence Blanchard has dual careers as film composer and jazz performer. He has composed original film scores for *Jungle Fever, Malcolm X, Clockers, Eve's Bayou, Gia, The Promised Land,* and *Till There was You,* and played trumpet on *Mo' Better Blues* and *Malcolm X.* In addition to composing, he keeps a busy touring schedule, appearing around the world with his jazz group.

WHAT'S YOUR COMPOSITION BACKGROUND IN TERMS OF BOTH ORCHESTRAL AND JAZZ COMPOSITION?

I've studied composition and I'm still studying it. I studied when I was in high school and when I was playing with Art Blakey, although I never really had the chance to write for orchestra until I started working in film. But I would write piano pieces and stuff like that. And I was always writing for jazz ensembles.

Studying orchestral music is really great because it helps me understand the relationship between different musical lines, and how those lines define their own harmony. It's different than writing from a jazz perspective where the lines are related to certain chord changes.

HIGH SCHOOL WAS IN NEW ORLEANS?

Yes, I grew up in New Orleans. I moved away from home when I was eighteen and I went to college at Rutgers University. I played with Lionel Hampton while I was in college, joined Art Blakey's band when I was nineteen, and stayed in New York for fifteen years. And then I moved back home.

SO YOUR FIRST FILM-SCORING GIG HAPPENED IN NEW YORK?

Yes. What happened was, I was actually a session player on *Mo' Better Blues* and I had been coaching Denzel Washington. We had to do some pre-records so the actors could play along on the set. One day, while we were taking a break in the studio, I went to the piano and started playing one of my compositions. Spike came over and said, "What is that?" And I said, "This is something I'm working on for one of my albums." He asked if he could use it, if I could write an orchestral arrangement for it. I said yes, even though I had never done one before. When he heard it, he said I had a future writing for film, and he called me to do *Jungle Fever*, which was my first film.

DID YOU KNOW WHAT TO DO ABOUT TIMINGS AND ALL THAT STUFF?

The interesting thing about *Jungle Fever* was that I didn't have a video to write to at the time. Spike didn't really want music to be specific to the scenes. He didn't like it when things happened right on point, right to the frame. There were some mistakes done in *Jungle Fever* in terms of the score because of that. There were certain things that would happen emotionally in the scene where things would shift, but I wasn't given those timings on the original sheets. But he recognized those problems, so for *Malcolm X,* I had a video.

I WAS WONDERING IF YOU COULD TALK A LITTLE BIT ABOUT THE FLASHBACKS IN MALCOLM X, AND WHAT YOU WERE THINKING WHEN YOU HAD TO SCORE THOSE TYPES OF SCENES.

You know, the interesting thing about doing Spike's movies in general is that I never really have to worry too much about period stuff because he covers a lot of that with his source material. What I tried to do with those flashbacks was to have an essence of the period. That's why some of those arrangements are jazz arrangements, a couple of them are big band arrangements. And I tried to make sure that I had a blend of the period music along with the thematic material that we were using throughout the film. Spike is a guy who wants strong melodic content for his scores.

HOW SPECIFIC IS SPIKE IN GIVING YOU DIRECTION OF WHAT THE SOUND SHOULD BE?

In terms of what the sound should be, he's very specific. Spike is a very traditional film maker. He likes big lush orchestral scores. Let's use *Malcolm X* as an example. He said, "I keep hearing orchestra with a choir." So I said, "Okay, fine." And when we got to one of the jail scenes where the camera pans across the faces of the inmates, he said, "I just want to hear the voices right there." So he gives me that kind of direction, but he never really stands over my shoulder while I'm doing it.

AS I REMEMBER IT, THAT WAS A TRADITIONAL CLASSICAL MUSIC SOUNDING CHOIR, NOT A GOSPEL SOUNDING CHOIR.

Right. You know, in Hollywood, and America in general, there's a very limited view of what African-American culture is all about. The thing that we've been always trying to do with Spike's movies is to broaden that, in terms of making people understand that there are many different facets to who we are as a people in this country. And one of the things that was great about that movie is that we used the Boys Choir of Harlem. They're really great. Really professional. Really on top of it.

WAS THAT YOU PLAYING TRUMPET IN MALCOLM X?

Yeah. I play on some of the stuff on *Malcolm X* because it really called for having some kind of jazz improvisation. Branford Marsalis plays on it as well.

WHAT'S YOUR COMPOSING PROCESS? DO YOU WRITE TO PAPER OR ARE YOU USING A SYNTH?

It really depends on how much time I have to write. Lately, I've been doing a bunch of television things, and television doesn't have the luxury of giving you the kind of time you have when you write for films. With television, I generally write from the keyboard because I only have a week and a half or two weeks to write maybe 60 minutes of music. If it's Spike's stuff, I like to use paper and pencil. I like looking at the music.

DO YOU ORCHESTRATE YOURSELF, OR DO YOU USE PEOPLE TO DO THAT?

To me, orchestration is the most joy I have in writing a score. Because coming up with thematic material is one thing, but to me real composition lies in the combination of instruments, creating the textures and colors of the sound. It's not just the notes. It's learning how to paint with those instruments. Whenever I'm writing a cue, I generally hear the orchestration in my head. I'll hear the cello playing the solo, or I'll hear violas carrying the lines in certain spots combined with a bassoon, or English horn—something like that.

DO YOU FIND THAT IT'S EASY TO SWITCH BACK AND FORTH BETWEEN A JAZZ STYLE AND A TRADITIONAL STYLE WHERE YOU'RE WRITING?

The two styles are really in the process of merging. I won't say that it's totally there yet, because I still feel that with my jazz writing there are some issues that I'm trying to work out in terms of form and structure. In terms of how to not be bound to a 32-bar form, a 12-bar blues form, or any of the traditional forms of jazz composition. I'm trying to get to the point where the melody lines really define the structure of the tune.

DO YOU FIND THAT YOU GET LABELED AN AFRICAN-AMERICAN COMPOSER? DOES THAT HAPPEN A LOT?

Yeah. It's a big problem. I suffer from that because the first thing that people wanted to know when I did *Malcolm X* was, "Is he black?" That's what they asked my agent at the time, which I thought was kind of an odd question. And when people began to realize that I am black, then I started to get called for a lot of those types of movies. I turned down a lot of those projects, because frankly, they just weren't things that interested me. I just didn't want to be labeled that. So my agents now have been working really hard to turn that around—which they are accomplishing. I've done a lot of different things like *The Tempest* with Peter Fonda, and *Gia*.

You know, it's not only race and gender, it's also cultural background. And that's the thing that I see that happens a lot in Hollywood, though I know people don't talk about it. I've noticed sometimes when I walk into a meeting, there's a certain kind of tension in the air already. And I'm not that kind of person. I consider myself to be a very easy-going kind of guy, easy to get along with. But I went into a meeting one time with another composer, and I saw immediately how he got hired. He was a great composer, don't get me wrong, but there was a certain type of cultural camaraderie that happened between the director and the composer that immediately made the director feel comfortable. I do understand it to a degree because there's a lot of money on the line in these projects. But at the same time, there's a lot of talented people out there who are probably not getting hired.

I WONDER, COULD IT GO BACK THE OTHER WAY? COULD A WHITE COMPOSER WORK WITH SPIKE?

Oh, I think so, because that's one of the big misconceptions about Spike. People think that Spike is so pro Afro-American that he doesn't hire other folks, but if you ever go to one of his sets you would see that is not true. One of the first things I noticed when I went to the set was the set wasn't full of black people. Not at all. And I was really amazed at that, and it made me feel really happy to be a part of that because it was so inclusive. I'm going to tell you a story. We were doing *Mo' Better Blues* and I had to be on the set everyday. There was a certain crew that didn't do their job and these guys were black. They were gone the next day. They were fired. Spike's thing is that he tries to give the best people the opportunity for the job.

ON ANOTHER NOTE, WHO ARE SOME OF YOUR FAVORITE FILM COMPOSERS?

Elmer Bernstein. I love John Williams. I love Thomas Newman, Jerry Goldsmith, Michael Kamen.

WHAT IS IT THAT MAKES THEIR SCORES SO GREAT?

To me, it's all about the sentiment. It's all about the emotional content and how it matches with the picture and the story. When I watch *Shawshank Redemption,* to me, Thomas Newman's score really elevated that movie. The thing that I always say that's great about Thomas is that he brings both the orchestral and electronic world together in a way that's unique. Because a lot of times, guys will use the electronic world to emulate the acoustic world, and that's a big mistake. He's one of the guys who really understands both worlds and understands that the electronic thing has its own strengths that can be utilized in a unique fashion.

WHAT ADVICE DO YOU HAVE FOR YOUNG COMPOSERS WHO ARE JUST STARTING OUT?

Pray, because everybody I know who got into this business fell into it backwards. You've got to be flexible. The biggest thing that you've got to do is put your ego aside. It's not like working in your own band, or having your own musical situation. The music is there to enhance and support a story. In some cases, the music is there to take a lead role, but more times than not it has a supportive role. You have to put your ego aside and understand the task that you have at hand. And you've got to study. You've got to listen. You've got to do your homework.

Alf Clausen

A lf Clausen began his career playing bass and French horn. He studied at North Dakota State, the University of Wisconsin, and Berklee College of Music before moving to Los Angeles. Well known since 1991 for his music in the television series *The Simpsons* (for which he received two Emmy awards), Clausen has also written the music for *Moonlighting*, *ALF*, *Fame*, *Harry*, *Police Story*, and *The Critic*. His compositions and orchestrations have appeared in feature films such as *Naked Gun*, *Mr. Mom*, *Splash*, *Airplane II: The Sequel*, and *Ferris Bueller's Day Off*. He is also very active as a jazz composer and arranger, with performances by the bands of Ray Charles, Stan Kenton, Buddy Rich, and Thad Jones & Mel Lewis.

LET'S TALK ABOUT YOUR BACKGROUND IN MUSIC, HOW YOU MADE THE JOURNEY FROM NORTH DAKOTA TO HOLLYWOOD.

I grew up in Jamestown, North Dakota. I came up through the concert band and concert choir programs in school as a French horn player. I was exposed at a very early age to some pretty high-quality musical taste, for which I am very, very thankful.

In addition to that, I was basically a rock 'n roller. I grew up with the early roots of rock 'n roll, loved rock 'n roll, loved r&b, I loved Chubby Checker. I loved Little Richard and Elvis Presley and all of those people forming the roots of that music.

I first majored in mechanical engineering at North Dakota State University in Fargo because my college entrance tests all told me that I should be a mechanical engineer! I eventually graduated with a BA degree in Music Theory. I started my master's degree at

Wisconsin, but didn't like it and wound up transferring to Berklee. So I packed my acoustic bass into my VW bug, got a U-Haul trailer for the rest of my belongings, and drove out from Madison to Boston. I didn't know a soul, but I decided that this was going to be the deal. I did all sorts of gigs, and taught at Berklee as well.

I eventually realized that if I was going to make the writing career happen the way I wanted it to, it was not going to happen in Boston. In Boston, you have to have three jobs to make ends meet. So my wife and I decided that L.A. would be a better place to raise kids than New York, and we moved out there. It turned out to be a fortuitous move because a lot of the work at that time was also moving out there. TV variety shows like *The Carol Burnett Show* and *The Merv Griffin Show* moved to L.A. This was the late '60s, when there was a lot of work going on, and I was at the front of the wave as everything started moving here.

So, when I got to Los Angeles, I started working all sorts of kinds of jobs. I played six nights a week playing bass in clubs, and worked as a music copyist quite a bit. I started doing some ghost arranging for a Vegas singer or show, I did some jingles. I just kind of kicked around doing all sorts of stuff.

DURING THAT TIME OF "KICKING AROUND," DID YOU EVER FEEL LIKE YOU WERE LOSING SIGHT OF THE ORIGINAL REASON FOR COMING TO LOS ANGELES?

There were many times when I felt like I was losing sight of why I had originally come here. When I first arrived, somebody had told me that you should give yourself five years and then evaluate your progress. I did re-evaluate, and I thought that maybe I should find another way of doing things. I had gotten some little things thrown my way here and there, but all of a sudden, five years went into ten years. I thought, it's coming along, it's coming along, but it's taking a lot longer than I expected. I just had a lot of faith that things would come the way I wanted them to. I developed a lot of patience and was willing to just wait for the next step to happen.

WHAT WAS THE FIRST SIGNIFICANT THING FOR YOU?

Through a series of strange circumstances I got a gig arranging for the *Donny & Marie Show*. After two seasons with that show, and a season with *The Mary Tyler Moore Variety Hour*, I decided I wanted to get into films. But no one would talk to me. I had gotten pegged as a variety-show arranger/conductor.

So I decided that I would play the game their way, and I would have to start from the bottom again. I had to work my way through the ranks, and start to orchestrate for whatever composer would take me on. I needed some experience, to learn the ropes and see how things were done in that segment of the industry.

Eventually, I started orchestrating for Bill Goldstein. I met him on a recording date where I was doing the booth work. Bill came over and introduced himself and asked me if I had done certain orchestrations. I said yes, and one thing led to another. It turned out he had two pictures going at that time and he asked me to orchestrate on both pictures.

Soon after that, he got the *Fame* series over at MGM, and I started working on that. I did a lot of orchestrating and ghost composing. At the same time, I did some ghost composing for David Rose on *Little House on the Prairie* and *Father Murphy*. One thing led to another. I started orchestrating for Lalo Schifrin and Lee Holdridge. Lee and I struck up a really, really close friendship, which still exists to this day. We worked together on many successful films, including *Splash*, and *Mr. Mom*. His focus with an orchestrator/composer is that if he finds a guy with some talent, he finds a way to help him work his way into the system and get his own gigs. His whole focus was to find a television series, write the theme, and then turn it over to me. This was without me asking!

He called me one day and said, "I've got this pilot over at ABC and it looks really, really good. What I'd like to do is have you orchestrate the pilot, and then let me introduce you to the executive producer so that you can do at least part of the series." This was

Moonlighting. And his plan worked. ABC was very high on the show, public acceptance was very, very good, and I soon ended up as the sole composer on the show. It was a major hit for four seasons. All of a sudden, my identity was established in the film scoring business. That's all it took. Even though I had been slaving away behind the scenes for years, it took the vision and aggressiveness of somebody like Lee to make it happen. I am eternally grateful to him for that.

HOW DID THE SIMPSONS BEGIN FOR YOU? YOU'VE BEEN DOING THAT FOR HOW LONG NOW?

This is my ninth year. Actually, when *Moonlighting* and *ALF* stopped, my career stopped. I went for seven months without a show. Even though I had some income because those shows were in reruns, the cash flow was actually secondary. It was too quiet and I was not a happy camper. The creative mind likes to be busy, the creative mind likes to be assuming the responsibility and the challenge of regular projects. Because I love doing stuff.

Simpsons broke the drought. They had done 13 shows with Danny Elfman's theme and Richard Gibbs doing the underscore. During my dry spell, I was talking with a good friend of mind who is a percussionist, and coincidentally he said that he just had dinner with his nephew who was working on this new show, and they were looking for a different composer. So he gave his nephew my number, he called, we met, and then we spotted the next show—the very first "Treehouse of Horror" episode. I recorded it, and they loved what I did.

IN THAT ORIGINAL MEETING, WHAT WAS THE DISCUSSION LIKE REGARDING THE CONCEPT OF THE MUSIC FOR THE SHOW?

Matt Groening and company told me in that first meeting, "It's not a cartoon, it's a drama where the characters are drawn." And when in doubt, he said to score it like a drama, not like a cartoon, not to mickey-mouse everything. Matt was the one who made the request for the acoustic orchestra. He said, "I hate electronics, I think they cheapen the sound. I want the real orchestra."

WHAT DO YOU SAY TO MUSICIANS WHO ARE JUST GETTING STARTED IN FILM SCORING? DO THEY NEED TO BE IN L.A.?

My own way of doing it was to continue moving up rather than moving down. I started from very humble beginnings and took it step-by-step-by-step. Going from North Dakota to Wisconsin, going to Boston and then to Los Angeles. I know that if I had gone from North Dakota to Los Angeles, I would have been swallowed up, spit out, and I wouldn't have survived without putting in those dues beforehand.

There are a couple of schools of thought about how to get started as a film composer. One is move to where the action is and get involved in doing low-budget films under your own name as a composer. The other is to move to where the action is and start apprenticing with other composers, practicing your craft on a daily basis, which is what I did. I'm a firm believer in the second method. The thing I say to guys who want to do it the first way is: If you can you exist on one or two $500 dollar films a year and not practice your craft in the meantime, then be my guest. The guy who is going to practice his craft on a weekly basis, doing all kinds of stuff, to me is going to end up having much more of an advantage and much stronger chops in the long run.

Cliff Eidelman

After studying composition and orchestration at Santa Monica City College and USC, Cliff Eidelman received his first break at age 22, when he scored the feature film, *Magdalene*, starring Nastassja Kinski. He has gone on to score many feature films including, *One True Thing, Triumph of the Spirit, A Simple Twist of Fate,* and *Star Trek VI: The Undiscovered Country*. Also active as a composer and conductor of concert music, he has appeared with the Royal Scottish National Orchestra, The Munich Symphony and Chorus, and the Toronto Symphony Orchestra.

DO YOU RELY ON AN AGENT TO GET YOU WORK, OR DO YOU DO SOME LEGWORK YOURSELF?

My agent helps, but I also have to do my part in contacting people, having meetings, doing demos. But it's an odd thing, I've never gotten a gig by seeking it out initially. I may have to pitch my music, but someone always finds me; at least the first contact, they seek me out.

Sometimes I get the *Hollywood Reporter* and I circle the projects that look interesting. I may circle five of them, and I'll call my agent and say, "What's going on with this one … this one … that one …" And then my agent will most likely say, "This one's taken … this one's taken … you don't have a chance at that one because the director has a long-standing relationship with another composer … but I'll check on this one, I don't think anyone's on it." That's where it starts.

But I have never actually gotten a gig from doing that. Gigs have come because of other reasons. Because of a previous relationship, or because they heard a score of mine from a previous film, or somebody "temped" my music into some film, and they loved the tempo and the next thing I know they're seeking me out. I personally have never had any luck with seeking out a film and getting it. It's always been the other way around.

For people at the very top of the field, like John Williams or Jerry Goldsmith, I think calls come in for them. Their agents are basically fielding calls, and presenting gigs to them. There is a point where they get offers all the time. But when you're in my position, where there has been some success and high profile projects, but not that one hit, blockbuster film, you really have to continue to pound the dirt yourself. It becomes one of those things where you have to just do the effort.

I think that in order to turn heads it takes a very great film where you can write a fabulous score that gets acknowledged. It has to be an association with a great film that gets great reviews and is also a good moneymaker. So it's a combination. All the pieces have to fit together right.

How do you prepare your score? Do use Cue or Auricle to lay out the score?

I use Auricle to lay out the tempos as I compose to picture. First, I conduct through it a few times with the video, feel the scene, and make sure that all the things that I want to hit are there. Then I create a click that is close to the slight variations of tempo that go with free conducting. If you were to look at my tempo map for a two-minute cue, you might see as many as 20 slight tempo changes. I am very particular about it, about those tempos and about the accelerations and the decelerations and all of that. The click is pushed slightly here, laid back slightly there. In fact, I've got some click maps where it could have been a 24-0 click. But instead, in order to achieve what I was feeling while I conducted to video, the tempo map might end up changing from 24-0 to 23-7, 23-5, 23-1, 24-7.

HOW DO YOU DETERMINE WHAT TO HIT AND WHAT TO LEAVE ALONE?

So much is by feeling. For me, it's whenever the chill occurs and however it's felt. In fact, I think it's detrimental to use a click for music that is more expressive or more lyrical. Especially when the musicians have the clicks in their ears while they're recording, there's a feeling of this perfect click going on. I think that that detracts from the emotion of the music and what the music really wants to do. So I try to conduct with streamers, for that kind of music. I know with *Triumph of the Spirit*, it was all by feel. If I was a little bit early to one streamer, I just knew I had to just slow down slightly so that three streamers later I'd be right on. And I knew it didn't really matter with that picture, because the music was floating, it wasn't commenting on anything specific, it was always floating above.

HOW DO YOU FEEL ABOUT DOING MOCK-UPS?

In many ways they're helpful. If you can give the director mock-ups as you go, and get quick at laying out certain sounds—not flesh out every little detail, just give some good examples—I think that takes away the risk of disagreements when you're on the scoring stage. Mock-ups allow you to finish most of the work at home, and give the director the chance to have some input before the recording session.

WHAT IS YOUR PROCESS IN ARRIVING AT THE CONCEPT FOR A SCORE?

Dramatically, many of my ideas for a picture have to do with color and orchestration, which I have studied in depth. Orchestration is so much a part of music's conceptual design. First I compose the melodic themes, and once the melodies come to me, the orchestration begins to quickly reveal itself.

An example is what I did for the film, *One True Thing*. I had this idea of time changing, the changing of seasons. The feeling of wind passing through trees and then leaves blowing off in another direction. This wasn't music yet; it was just a feeling I wanted to add to the whole effect of the score.

I set individual instruments apart from the orchestra, separated into their own isolation booths. Like three cellos in one room, or three violas with two woodwinds in another. They were off in their own rooms and the orchestra was in the center. Now, my concept was that the piano should be the main idea, accompanied by a small orchestra so that it felt intimate, and never too large. An introverted mood.

I also wanted it to feel like wind was carrying the music this way and out that way, creating different perspectives. The music wasn't just coming from the center of the room. It was coming from over here, and it shifted over there, and then it would come back over here. So, early on, this conceptual approach merged with the themes.

HOW MUCH INPUT DID THE DIRECTOR HAVE AT THIS STAGE OF YOUR PROCESS?

Actually, the reason I got this particular job was because I demoed some thematic ideas for him. That was before I came up with this special idea. So the director was very involved in the creation of the broad emotional and thematic ideas, but less so in terms of the specifics of the orchestration. I mocked up a great many of the cues, but because the ultimate orchestration and setup of the musicians was so unusual, I really wasn't able to demonstrate the final orchestration that included the unique perspective of these isolated groups until we got on the scoring stage with the real players. I didn't want to blow it by trying to make that in my synth studio.

DID YOU EVER HAVE A PROBLEM SEEING EYE-TO-EYE WITH A DIRECTOR?

Did I ever have a real disagreement? I can think of two occasions, where it wasn't so much a disagreement as it was that a director had gotten so used to a temp score that he couldn't hear anything else. I was writing something that took us in a different direction. Once a temp score is thrown into a movie, what tends to happen is that the director gets used to it. To have him get unused to it and then used to something new is difficult. The temp process can be very detrimental. It can be the end of all possible creativity that could have come to that movie through music.

It's gotten to the point where some composers of the final score copy the composers whose music was used in the temp track, sometimes even ripping them off just because the production people get locked into the temp. I've heard thematic ideas from my scores used in other people's scores. It's infuriating. I honestly would never consciously sit there and rip someone off. I wouldn't be able to sleep at night.

WHAT KIND OF TIME FRAME DO YOU NORMALLY WORK UNDER?

I've actually been very lucky in that way. I've had to write a lot of music really fast only a few times. The kind of thing where I had to stay up and do twelve-hour days, seven days a week. On *One True Thing* I had two and half or three months to write it.

HOW WOULD YOU LIKE THE PRODUCTION TEAM TO VIEW YOUR PROCESS?

That they really understand the intense emotional self that I put into it. It's everything I have.

Photo: LM Jones

Danny Elfman

Danny Elfman comes to the world of film composing via the rock band Oingo Boingo. It was through Oingo Boingo that director Tim Burton first heard his music, and ultimately asked him to score *Pee Wee's Great Adventure*. Elfman has gone on to score over 30 films, including *Men In Black, Batman, The Nightmare Before Christmas, Mission Impossible, Midnight Run*, and *Good Will Hunting*, which earned him an Academy Award nomination.

LET'S TALK ABOUT HOW YOU GOT STARTED. DID YOU ALWAYS WANT TO WRITE FOR FILMS?

I was a big Bernard Hermann fan as a kid, in the '60s. I guess what you'd call kind of like a film-music nerd. My training was spending every weekend at the movie theater—I didn't play sports, I didn't really go out in the sun—I hated being out in the sun. I loved being inside a theater; it suited me well, and I lived around the block from one. I loved films and I loved film music. I knew that if Bernard Hermann did the music that it was going to be a great film.

WHAT WAS YOUR ENTREE INTO SCORING FILMS?

It was a fluke, actually. I was with the Mystic Knights of the Oingo Boingo when we were still a musical theatrical troop, between '72 and '78. I was asked to score a midnight film, a cult film for my brother called *Forbidden Zone*, and that was my first time putting music to film, but it was far from a legitimate orchestral film score. It was performed by the Mystic Knights just before they retired, and the rock band Oingo Boingo began.

The fluke was getting asked to do *Pee Wee's Big Adventure*. [Director] Tim Burton was a fan of Oingo Boingo, and he just had a feeling that I could do more than I did with them. Paul Reubens was a fan of the *Forbidden Zone*, so when he heard that score he made a mental note to track me down. My name crossed paths between the two of them and it eventually all tied together.

COMING FROM A ROCK BACKGROUND, HOW DID YOU GO ABOUT DOING THE SCORE? WERE YOU SEQUENCING OR WRITING THINGS DOWN?

I wrote down everything, I didn't start using MIDI notation until '96. In a rock band like Oingo Boingo there's never any point to write music down. I mean, other than basically scribbling out a horn part every now and then, there was no writing involved because that's not the way rock bands work. On the other hand, the Mystic Knights did a lot of original material and it became necessary for me to learn how to notate. The Mystic Knights did a lot of kind of crazy ensemble stuff—real early jazz like Duke Ellington, Cab Calloway, and Django Reinhardt—and I began transcribing some of that stuff. That was my early ear training and from there I began to notate my own original compositions.

When I got offered *Pee Wee's Big Adventure* I knew I could create the music, but I also knew I would need help logistically with the orchestra. I knew what sounds I wanted because I loved orchestral music; I loved Stravinsky, I loved Prokofiev, I loved Charles Ives. So I called Steve Bartek, the guitar player from Oingo Boingo, and I asked him, "Have you ever orchestrated?" And he said, "Umm, I took some classes." And so I said, "Good, you'll do." And we both learned by doing it, as did Tim Burton. It was interesting, *Pee Wee* was Tim's first film, he'd never been to film school. It was my first score, I'd never been to composing school. And Steve orchestrating, he'd only taken a couple of orchestration classes at UCLA. We all learned our craft by doing it and the thing we had in common was we all applied ourselves really intensely to it, and we all had those kind of obsessive personalities. That "If I'm gonna do something, I'm gonna do it really, really well" kind of attitude.

DO YOU HEAR SPECIFIC INSTRUMENTS AS YOU WRITE, OR DO YOU
WRITE SOMETHING AND THEN THINK ABOUT WHO COULD BEST PLAY IT?

I work both ways. Sometimes, when I'm hearing a melody, I'm also hearing the ensemble. In that instance, I look at a scene and I hear all the instruments right away. For example, in the opening sequence of *Mars Attacks*, I heard it dead-on the first time I saw the scene. I mean, I heard it almost note-for-note just like it was playing out of a radio in my head, and I ran home and I wrote it all down. I consider that one of the lucky moments. However, the more usual process of experimentation and working things out by degrees gets me more excited and involved. Although it is a lot more difficult, it can be more rewarding.

In those cases, at first I don't really hear exactly what I'm going to end up with; I get just a vague idea. First I see the film and then I start improvising. I start with a feeling, and I do maybe a dozen improvisations on piano without looking at the picture. Then I start going through the footage and I pull up different scenes to see how the improvisations work. Sometimes I improv for six, seven, eight minutes and then I pull out the ideas I like and focus on them.

And so, if there is any lesson I've learned over 35 scores, it's not to ignore the earliest impulses and not to lose anything. Because what early on seems like the most broad, poorly played, ill-conceived notion sometimes becomes what I'll look back on as one of my best ideas. You know, the raw material.

DO YOU ENJOY WORKING OUT THE MUSICAL DETAILS OF A BIG SCORE?

It's great when I hit a certain section where things get really intricate, and there's a lot of detailing, and I'm satisfied with the way it comes out. That's the hardest work, and when it pays off, it feels really good. I also write songs, and when I'm writing songs, it's all inspiration based. It only takes a moment, once I get inspired to write a song. But writing an orchestral score takes so much time, and it's so easy to get it bungled and to get twisted up. When I start getting into the mode of detailing, and it doesn't turn into a cluttered mess, I'm really happy because I think my biggest weakness as a composer is sometimes I tend to overwrite. Sometimes I don't know when to stop and before I know it, what I thought was a good impulse or a good idea has become clouded into a big mess. I guess it's like when you're painting and you put a few too many layers of colors and suddenly you're looking for the image.

How do you deal thematically with the big picture of doing 30 or 40 cues?

At first, every score is a big puzzle and I have to know where my common links are in that puzzle. There's a start, a middle, and an end—I can't do the in-between stuff unless I know how the melodies are going to work in any situation. I want to know before I start that they can turn quirky, big, sad, melancholy, melodramatic, silly—whatever I'm going to be reaching for in that particular score. In those early improvisations, I'll be taking melodies and fragments of melodies, turning them inside out, and putting them through a rigorous testing to see what they're capable of.

After you come up with your material, do you work chronologically?

In general, I like to work chronologically. However, I usually start working on two or three major scenes that won't be chronological at all. I like to go for the biggies first, and then having those blocked out, I know where my major themes are, how I'm gonna use them. Then I like to go back to the start, and go chronologically from the beginning to the end, if I can.

How many films a year do you do?

Recently, I've been doing four or five a year, but the first ten years I did two films a year because the other months I was touring and recording with Oingo Boingo. Everybody's got their own way of working and I admire people who can get up in the morning, do their day's work and then take off, and, you know, have a family or social life. But I can't do that very well when I'm composing. Composing becomes full-time, there's almost nothing else for me.

DO YOU SEQUENCE EVERYTHING?

When I first started, I was sequencing my ideas, playing them for directors, and then notating them—it was like double work! Even with MIDI take-down making my job a little easier, I still end up spending the first part of my day in organizational work; I'm working with my own performances, I'm working with samples. A lot of people don't realize that a lot of each score is actually me performing. All the percussion in almost all of my scores, all the synth work, and the percussion work is me. That's a lot of extra work because that part of it is neither getting transcribed, nor written down, nor replayed; it's going in the score exactly as I'm playing it. That means that I have to put in the time to tweak all the performances and get them to sound right. So I usually start writing late afternoon into evening, and I try to stop at around two in the morning. But my best hours are really six, seven at night until around two in the morning.

ONCE A ROCK 'N ROLLER ALWAYS A ROCK 'N ROLLER, RIGHT?

Yeah, right!

I HOPE YOU DON'T MIND MY ASKING, WHY DO YOU THINK PEOPLE CAME DOWN ON YOU SO HARD TOWARDS THE BEGINNING OF YOUR CAREER?

Well, there's a lot of jealousy and I totally understand it, by the way. You get somebody like me that comes from nowhere, and I made the mistake of saying in interviews early on that I was self-taught. In music, there's no such thing as self-taught.

It's always been a weird thing about music, unlike any of the other film arts. Because a director can be self-taught, a writer can be self-taught, but a composer can't be, and that's just the way people think. Some people are skeptical, but maintain an open mind. And some people are skeptical and get into this very vicious thing. I don't know what makes music different than the other parts of the process. If a writer who didn't go to film school decides to direct, and does something brilliant, they praise him. They don't sit there and go, "Oh god, he can't direct at all. Obviously he didn't go to film school." But musicians and composers tend to be more hard-core skeptics.

Now that I'm kind of like a veteran, sometimes I hear a new composer who comes out of pop music and I'm incredibly skeptical. I think they must keep a closet full of ghostwriters and stuff. So, I see myself doing the same thing that other people did to me, and I totally understand it. If I see somebody doing an orchestral score, and they came from a rock band or pop music, I don't believe it.

In my case, there was always the smoking gun that everybody was searching for, hoping to prove I wasn't really writing everything. And the thing that was most interesting was that the fingers never pointed at the one person who worked with me for all these years. People were always saying that so-and-so really wrote my stuff. Or that such-and such a person was ghosting all my cues. But of all the names that came up, no one ever mentioned the one person that has done the most, my orchestrator, Steve Bartek. And in the final analysis, I've written over 35 hours of film music, and only fifteen minutes of that was ever written by others when I was in a pinch—and they were always credited. People accused me of not knowing how to write music, but I have a four-foot high stack of sketches that I've done over the years.

ALL OF THIS MUST HAVE BEEN VERY HURTFUL TO YOU.

It was, but at a certain point I just said to myself, "This can't matter to me anymore." I realized I was imitated so much. At that time I did think it was ironic that I was so trashed, but I was also so imitated.

WHAT ADVICE DO YOU HAVE FOR YOUNG COMPOSERS?

Here are some contrary pieces of advice. If you want to be successful, learn to imitate. I think the entire industry right now revolves around plagiarism and imitation, and unless you're willing to plagiarize you may find it difficult to proceed. On the other hand, if you want to be a good composer, or a real composer, learn to resist that tendency. That can be hard, and it can also mean you may not get certain kinds of jobs that you want.

But I could also say this: I think imitation is the easy way out, although it is very tempting, and very seductive. Once you go down that path, it's really hard to turn back. You may say you'll reverse yourself, but it's hard to.

Do your own work, work hard, and be original. I don't regret for a moment that I had to write 20 scores without any kind of help. That work was phenomenally hard for me, especially with being self-taught and writing relatively slowly. But, I think that if I didn't do that, I wouldn't have developed certain skills that I've developed. So, at the risk of sounding like a Quaker or something, I think just the beauty of committing to the hard way out, or the harder road, is usually the best one, and the most rewarding.

Richard Gibbs

Starting his career as a keyboard player for such acts as Chaka Khan, Robert Palmer, and the rock band Oingo Boingo, Richard Gibbs has scored many feature films including *Dr. Dolittle*, *Fatal Instinct*, *Say Anything*, *Ten Things I Hate About You*, and *Natural Born Killers*. He earned a degree in composition from the Berklee College of Music before moving to Los Angeles where he played studio dates, in addition to touring. Gibbs has also scored many television movies and episodic television shows, and served as music director on *The Tracey Ullman Show*, and *Muppets Tonight*.

YOU HAD A CAREER AS A PLAYER BEFORE GETTING INTO FILM SCORING. WHAT WAS YOUR FOCUS?

Keyboards. I always refer to myself as a keyboard player because there are guys who are pianists who I could not pretend to keep up with. I really wanted to be a fusion player, and my heroes were Joe Zawinul and Jan Hammer. Programming and playing on synths was my thing. Plus, at one time, I was a pretty decent trombonist. I graduated from Berklee College of Music with a degree in classical composition, so I had a lot of bases covered.

WHERE ARE YOU FROM, ORIGINALLY?

Daytona Beach, Florida. I'm a surfer boy. That's why I moved out here to L.A. After I graduated from Berklee, I thought, "If I'm going to be a session musician and go try to find bands to hook up with, it's either New York or Los Angeles." And I surf, so it was L.A. It was just that simple. I didn't have any contacts or friends out here, either.

HOW DID YOU GET YOUR FIRST GIGS?

When I got to L.A., I befriended this guy who turned out to be Chaka Khan's little brother, which led to a job as her musical director. The next step was rather bizarre, too. You know, my whole career has been one big serendipity. One day I was sitting in my living room, balancing my checkbook, and discovered I was flat broke. I was wondering what I was going to do about it, and, lo and behold, the phone rang. I answered and the guy on the other end was the musical director for Tom Jones who was looking for a keyboard player to go to Argentina for two weeks, and then go on a world tour. He had literally plucked my name out of a union directory, which, as you know, *never* happens!

Tom Jones was a very nice guy, but after the two weeks in Argentina, and two more in Vegas, I told the music director I simply couldn't play "What's New Pussycat" one more time. The other keyboardist on the gig gave me a number to call when I returned to L.A. It turned out to be Danny Elfman's number.

SO THAT WAS OINGO BOINGO?

Yes. Oingo Boingo preexisted my entrance to the band by probably a good ten years. Danny's older brother, Rick, started the band when they were in high school.

What attracted me to Boingo was that even though they were categorized as New Wave, a rather non-musician's medium in those days; they were extremely musical, energetic, and were trying and succeeding at doing different things, different styles. To me, doing an arrangement of "California Girls" in a blistering 15/8 was fantastic.

WERE YOU INTERESTED IN FILM SCORING AT THIS TIME?

I had no plan for it, but it was a vague idea in the back of my mind. I had taken a class in film scoring at Berklee and figured, maybe I would do it when I turned 50. In the meantime, you know, hey, rock 'n roll, girls, and all that fun!

I got into film scoring through session work. At the same time I was working with Oingo Boingo, I started doing a lot of session playing in town, primarily as a synth player, which was a pretty small category at the time. An engineer friend of mine called me and told me of a feature film from Tristar pictures called *Sweetheart's Dance*. The director was looking for someone who could translate old Elvis songs into score. So my friend arranged a meeting with the director, Robert Greenwald. The first words out of Robert's mouth was, "I don't really like to use a film composer." I said, "That's okay, I'm not a film composer." He hired me on the spot, and eventually, I talked him into letting me score a couple of scenes in addition to the adaptations. The end result was that I had screen credit on a major studio motion picture.

DID THINGS TAKE OFF FOR YOU THEN, IN TERMS OF FILM SCORING?

Not really. It took some time. In the meantime, I got a gig as music director on *The Tracey Ullman Show*. I ended up staying on that show for about three years. That was decent money and became my base of operations. And that show was the beginning of *The Simpsons*. *The Simpsons* started as a one-minute cartoon that would occasionally appear on *The Tracey Ullman Show*.

There was no music in *The Simpsons* at that time, except for every now and then, Matt Groening would want a little circus music, or something like source music. But the cartoon was so short, it didn't really call for me to score it. Eventually, it was spun off as its own series, and coincidentally, Danny Elfman was hired to write the theme. The producers asked me if I wanted to score the individual episodes, and they wanted to know if I could write in a similar style to Danny! They didn't even know that I had been in a band with Danny. So I did the first season of *The Simpsons,* and pretty much set up the template of the orchestra, and the sound of the show. They wanted me to come back and score some more, but by then I had been getting other offers to score movies because of *The Simpsons.* It was a big stepping stone for me. They ended up hiring Alf Clausen, who has done a great job since then.

WHAT WERE THE NEXT PROJECTS THAT CAME YOUR WAY?

At the same time as the beginning of *The Simpsons,* which was also my last year on *The Tracey Ullman Show,* I did a movie called *Say Anything,* directed by Cameron Crowe, and starring John Cusack. That was an interesting situation. They had already hired Ann Dudley to score it and apparently Cameron wanted to keep trying different things, and was asking Ann to rescore and rescore. She got fed up and literally hopped back on a plane to England. The music department at Fox came to me and asked me to help Cameron, who was monkeying around with the music. I tried a bunch of different little things, and Cameron liked what I was doing, so he asked me to look at a scene in which John Mahoney is giving Ione Skye a ring that once belonged to her mom. So we're in a recording studio, Cameron is out in the control room, and I'm sitting at a piano watching a TV monitor, and ad-libbing while I'm watching the scene for the first time. It's not very long, maybe a 30 or 40 second cue. I finish playing, and Cameron says, "Great." I asked him if he liked it, and he just said, "Great." And I said, "Well let me think about it while we're recording and I'll practice it some more." Cameron interjected and said, "No, you don't understand, we *recorded* that!" And that's what ended up in the film, my initial playing.

DID YOU SHARE THE SCREEN CREDIT?

Yeah. That was Cameron's call, so it was "Music by Richard Gibbs/Anne Dudley." I'd never even met Anne, to this day I haven't met her. So it's a little misleading when you look at it. I was using some of her themes and reworking them, in addition to my own writing.

***WHAT IS YOUR COMPOSING PROCESS? DO YOU USE PENCIL AND PAPER,
OR PLAY ALONG TO THE VIDEO?***

A couple of things have happened to radically change my scoring approach. Not in terms of the notes that are written, but how they are written. I always used to write with pencil and paper; that's how I was taught. I would sit at the piano, use a clickbook and a metronome, and work out everything that way. I did everything that way up until two years ago when I was working with writer/director Charlie Peters for the second time. He had a movie called *Music from Another Room*, a small budget picture. Charlie wanted to hear every piece of music in advance of the recording sessions. All I had to sequence with was a primitive Akai MPC-60—it would take forever. Charlie would come over and listen to all the cues, but I was going crazy because after I sequenced it, I still had to sketch it out and give it to an orchestrator. So I was basically writing every cue twice. I finally bought a Mac G3 and hired an assistant to teach me the programs, including Digital Performer.

The next movie I did was *Dr. Dolittle*. This was the first movie I scored where I never held a pencil in my hand. I'd play every part into the computer, and I was nervous as a cat when I got up in front of the orchestra because I wasn't sure if what I had played into my synthesizer was going to come back out through the orchestra. It was a 95-piece orchestra, and it was the first Fox movie to be scored on their new scoring stage.

DO YOU LIKE TO SCORE TO THE SCRIPT?

To be honest, I'm not comfortable doing that. Personally speaking, I'm more of a reactive kind of composer. I'm very much a collaborator. I like to know exactly what I'm dealing with, in terms of picture. I like to have the emotional response to the movie to write to it. The lines may be in the script, but it's when the actors deliver them that I begin to feel the emotion and write the best music.

WHAT ARE SOME OF THE MEMORABLE COLLABORATIONS YOU HAVE HAD?

Working on *Fatal Instinct* with Carl Reiner was a wonderful experience. He was looking around at different composers that were available, and I went and gave an interview. I liked Carl right away; we just hit it off. I could tell we connected, and that I knew how to make him happy. And I could tell he knew it. At the time, I didn't have much of a résumé, but I just felt good walking out of the meeting, and I thought to myself, "I think I got that job."

In that film, we were lampooning so many different films, and I got to score some scenes in the style of Bernard Herrmann. It was hilarious to me. And the irony is that it sounded like I was twisting it and turning it, but I wasn't. I was scoring it as if I was Bernard Herrmann, as if the scene was straight. The comedy was all in the movie; I didn't have to touch on the comedy at all.

There is a postscript to the whole *Fatal Instinct* experience. One day, when we were dubbing the movie, I was hanging out having lunch with Carl. I had to ask him just for my own edification why he hired me. He said, "Well frankly, I hated your tape. I didn't like your music at all, and it was totally inappropriate to what I wanted. But your ideas were great, and I somehow thought it would be fun." And it was fun, it worked out great. We ended up going all over the map, musically. That was one of the more pleasurable experiences I've had.

I'd have to say 95 percent of the work I've done has been a blast. It's been a real pleasure for me. I've talked with a lot of composers who are very bitter, and they think that it's really hard, and people don't appreciate them. They've become tortured souls. Frankly, I don't get it. I'm of the school that thinks, "This is fantastic, I can't believe I'm getting paid to do this."

Elliot Goldenthal

Composer Elliot Goldenthal has created works for the-ater, orchestra, opera, and film. He has received Oscar nomina-tions for his scores to *Michael Collins* and *Interview with a Vampire*. Some of his other well-known film scores are *A Time To Kill, Batman Forever, Heat, Alien 3, Drugstore Cowboy,* and *The Butcher Boy.* His concert work, *Fire Water Paper,* a commemoration of the 20th anniversary of the Vietnam War, has been performed with major symphony orchestras worldwide.

LET'S TALK ABOUT YOUR BACKGROUND AND HOW YOU GOT STARTED IN FILM SCORING.

My musical background is in composition. I got my bachelors and masters degrees at the Manhattan School of Music. I studied with John Corigliano and also unofficially studied with Aaron Copland. From 1978 until Aaron died, we were very close. We would sit together for hours on end, just playing through scores at the piano slowly, and he would look at my compositions. Although he wasn't my official teacher, he certainly spent months and months of time working with me, guiding me through stuff. But my principal teacher was John Corigliano; I studied with him every Wednesday for seven years.

WHAT WERE YOUR EARLY MUSICAL INTERESTS?

I've always been interested in all aspects of composing that include cinema. I remember as a teenager going to see great American and European movies and being really excited about the interrelationship between music and image, getting excited about the work of Prokofiev, Shostakovich, Bernard Herrmann, and Nino Rota, and really thinking of it as yet another medium in which to apply a musical craft. It became a passion of mine, along with theater. I really loved the interaction between acting or dance and music. I got involved working with theater, creating scores on the spot along with actors, doing experimental theater and dance, also composing incidental music for plays throughout the United States in theaters like the ART in Cambridge. I was working in several theaters around the country doing these kinds of things, and at the same time I was composing chamber music. And then I was doing more complicated types of theater, like musicals. I composed three musicals, two of which were performed at Lincoln Center and had extended runs, one of which continues to play throughout the world.

WHAT LED YOU TO YOUR FIRST FILMS?

My first films were back in the 1970s. They happened along with the other alternative kind of stuff back in New York. There were German producers and directors who worked with the Fassbinder school of film making. There was this film that I did with Andy Warhol, I think called *Blank Generation*, about the birth of the punk movement in New York in the seventies. I really had a good time with that score. I was working in film in those days, but chamber music and theater were pushing me in more compelling directions. So I just followed that direction until the late eighties.

SO WHAT HAPPENED THEN? WHAT WAS THE FIRST MAINSTREAM FILM YOU GOT INVOLVED IN?

Drugstore Cowboy, which happened concurrent to working on *Pet Sematary*. Those films were a direct result of Gus Van Sant hearing the scores of my earlier works. At the same time, I was also working on various symphonic works, one of which was for the 70th birthday celebration of Leonard Bernstein. I just felt really comfortable about that *Drugstore Cowboy* situation.

WITH ALL OF YOUR COMPOSITIONAL BACKGROUND AND ALL OF YOUR STUDIES, DO YOU STILL PUT PENCIL TO PAPER?

It depends on the cue. For example, if it's a type of thing where you know there's a theme, a big theme that's going to be used in over 50 types of scenes, then I prefer to be alone with a piano, and a pencil and paper, because I can generally have a feeling for the tone of how the theme is going to work throughout the movie. But with the advent of MIDI synthesis with video lock and all of that kind of thing, if I'm working on a scene that involves tremendous amount of synchronization—an action scene or a scene that you have to make a musical statement on the 21st frame—I find that the actual experience of working with the computer, the synthesizers, and the video all locked up is very, very similar to working with actors live in a studio. Very similar to my theatrical experience.

YOU MEAN THERE'S GIVE AND TAKE.

Yes, it's like I'm moving along with them at the same time. As opposed to pausing, reflecting, and going back to see if it works. The nature and the type of a theme, or the use of that theme, determines the way I like to work.

HOW DO YOU FIRST APPROACH WRITING THE MUSIC?

Well, first of all, let me preface this by saying that before I approach anything, I have a very strong concept of what I want to pull off, whether it works out or not. That might include limiting the choice of pitches or a very clear choice of orchestration. So I don't go into something and just start improvising, I find that if I do that, I just sort of waste my time. I stay away from the piano, away from the computer, away from the pencil. I think about the scene and I say, how can I achieve the dramatic effect that is necessary for the scene and have it still sound fresh? How can I make it sound like you haven't heard that before, you haven't lived that before? Sometimes the answer can be surprisingly simple. In *Alien 3*, for example, I used a solo piano to underline the scene with the little girl because I thought that having a piano way out in space would remind you of the most domestic of all instruments—it would remind you of home. Just things like that. That's a concept.

The other thing is that the study of orchestration is extremely important because it's not just the tunes, it's not just the melody; it's who plays it, what's the concept, what's the orchestral concept. And the sound, the development of electronics is all part of orchestration, of what that thing actually ends up sounding like.

HOW ABOUT A TIME TO KILL WHERE THE SCORE USED TEXTURES THAT WERE VERY DIFFERENT THAN THOSE IN YOUR OTHER WORK?

On *A Time to Kill* I used a lot of thick orchestral clusters that fit the sense of this agonizing racial struggle. But I also used instruments that were very rural, in a sense of folk music, such as harmonica, hammered dulcimer, and also penny whistle. I used those instruments in an unconventional way; they were accompanied with the type of clustery orchestral writing that one would associate with the Polish avant-garde.

WHOSE DECISION WAS IT TO USE THE GOSPEL SONG IN THE SCENE WHERE THE SAMUEL JACKSON CHARACTER GUNS DOWN THE TWO REDNECKS?

Yes, "Precious Lord." [Director] Joel Schumacher and I came up with that. That was three young girls called the Jones Sisters. They were about the same age as the girl that was raped. They were taped down in the Deep South, not in a studio. It was the sound you would hear if you went to a Sunday meeting and heard three girls get up and sing "Precious Lord." So I had this a capella three-girls situation. They were all 11 years old or so. And then I pitted it up against this heavy orchestral, clustery setting. It was almost as if the orchestra swallows up the a capella singing. This was something that was highly conceptualized even before the scene was shot.

WAS THAT WAS PART OF THE SCRIPT?

No, it wasn't part of the script; it was part of the conversation that I had with Joel on how to do the scene.

SO IN THIS CASE, YOU WERE INVOLVED IN THE FILM IN THE SCRIPT STAGE, WHICH I IMAGINE DOESN'T ALWAYS HAPPEN.

It has always been that way in my work with Joel. I would always come on the project in the script stage, or even while we were shooting. Then I'd go down to the set and there would be discussions. This does help me because it gives me a chance for my subconscious to think about concepts of how to approach something so it seems fresh.

WHAT ABOUT THE USE OF TEMP TRACKS?

For a young composer, or a new composer who doesn't have a strong enough background or backbone, it could be dangerous because they'll say, "The temp is working so well. I don't want to lose my job so I'll compose it just like the temp." But if you don't care about losing your job, and you're willing to go your own way as opposed to following something, you can come up with an original solution. There are fifty or sixty things that can work in a scene, so what you have to do is really be clear to the director about how much of this or that you think is right. You have to get intimate with the director so you don't make the mistake of just copying the temp track, which many directors would feel is ridiculous because they hired you to be creative.

WHAT'S YOUR ADVICE TO YOUNG PEOPLE COMING UP IN THIS CRAZY BUSINESS?

My advice is not to keep your head stuck in film. Open your horizons to what you really want to express in music. And no matter what it is, whether it's a rock background or whether it's chamber music, keep those avenues open. When anybody asks me how to develop their chops for movies, I say, do theater. I spent over 10 years doing theater before anything significant happened movie-wise. And that was like 100% preparation. In the situation with *Batman* or *Interview with a Vampire*, where it's the last minute, and you have three or four weeks to do the film, and you know that whatever you write any particular night, an entire orchestra is going to be there in a couple of days. It's going to be recorded and then 2 billion people are going to listen to it. You can't second-guess yourself, you can't backtrack, you can't be afraid. The way that I learned to overcome that fear was in theater, where you have to make those kinds of decisions and you have to be very, very, very clear. You go into rehearsal and it either works or it doesn't. But the theater world, it's sort of a Gold's Gym of dramatic composing.

Michael Gorfaine & Sam Schwartz

Michael Gorfaine and Sam Schwartz are two of the most well-known agents for film composers in Hollywood. The Gorfaine-Schwartz Agency, formed in 1983, represents people such as John Williams, James Horner, Michael Kamen, Elliot Goldenthal, and Ennio Morricone, among others.

HOW DID YOU GET STARTED AS AGENTS FOR FILM COMPOSERS?

SS: From about 1978 to 1982, Michael was the co-director of the West Coast office of ASCAP. In 1980, he hired me to begin a film and television division with the priority of building up the film-music repertoire. While we were at ASCAP, we became familiar with many composers and the process that they live through writing the music and getting work. One thing leads to another, and we decided to go off on our own.

MG: I have always loved films and film music, but I never focused on it until I worked at ASCAP. That is where I started meeting composers, and that is where I met Sam over 17 years ago. I enjoy working with these people. Across the board, film composers are just interesting, good people.

CAN YOU EXPLAIN THE ROLE OF THE AGENT AS IT RELATES TO YOUR WORK?

MG: The way we define it, there are many overlapping duties and roles that the agent performs. It's really a relationship between management and more traditional agenting.

First and foremost, we advise and counsel career direction, and look for opportunities in which our clients can fulfill their career goals. We peruse the film and television world for the jobs for our composers to compose their music. And we also advise our clients about lawyers and business managers with whom they are to work.

Do the jobs always come through you, or does the composer sometimes get them on his own?

MG: Sometimes, if there was a preexisting relationship, a producer or director will approach a composer directly. When you've got people who have worked together and know each other, often that relationship has great communication in it, and they will talk directly to each other. This is a wonderful thing. However, eventually it will come through us so we can hammer out the details of the schedule, the fees—the whole deal.

SS: The way that this is normally operated is through protocol, through the agency. Normally, we sit down with the composer to find the potential creative opportunities, and plan the next move.

MG: It's an overall career-strategy approach that we take. It's not just building momentum, or making deals. It's our job to make sure that, at any point in time, we are manifesting the best possible opportunities for our clients, and advising the best next step. And certainly it's different in different times of an artist's career. In the beginning it about getting opportunities, period. Once you have the momentum it's about choosing properly. The funny thing is, it gets harder and harder once you get established. You want to make sure that the right choices are being made.

Many composers get pegged as doing only one style of music. How do you break them out of that kind of perception?

MG: I don't think any musician I know wants to do the same thing over and over again. No actor wants to play the same part over and over again. No director wants to make the same movie over and over again. The same thing holds true for composers. Any great composer can do a multiplicity of things. We know that. But they can become known for certain things and asked to do those things again and again. One of the things that we want to do is make sure that the people out there that will hire these composers know their multifaceted nature, and what they are able to do. We try to get in very early on projects—as early as the script stage when they are developing a project. We find out whether it's a music-driven project, like an animated musical with songs, or not. Most often it's not; most movies just need a good score. So we find out very early on what the musical requirements are. We get that information to the client we would like to see on the project, and we pitch that client to the project.

WHAT ABOUT PACKAGE DEALS? HOW DO YOU APPROACH THOSE?

SS: In the mid-'80s, around the time of *Airwolf* and *Miami Vice*, we began this process called "packaging." This actually started with television films because of the fact that some of our clients, like Jan Hammer, had their own electronic studios where they could produce all the music. This was unique at that time. We felt that we could take the budgets that were being offered and have the composers just take all the money in exchange for doing all the production in their studios.

Now, 12 years later, almost all television music is done as a package. In the last three years, many of the motion picture projects are packages as well, even if the budgets are rather large. What this does is protect the producer from cost overruns, and it puts the responsibility to maintain a very specific budget on the shoulders of the composer.

MG: Yes. In addition, unless the client is really self-contained with his own facility and is set up to package, we veer away from that. If it's a big orchestral score, there is really little packaging. Especially when you are up against potential changes that almost always occur.

HOW DOES THAT GET HANDLED?

MG: We have a provision in our regular deals and in package deals that any rescoring is the responsibility of the producer's studio. We are very clear about that.

DO YOU SEE ANY DIFFICULTY IN THE BUSINESS FOR SOMEONE WHO IS A MINORITY OR WOMAN COMPOSER?

MG: Not that I am aware of. I think that opportunities are available, and we are not aware of any kind of difficulties. I can't tell you why there are not more women composers, I don't know why.

WHAT KIND OF THINGS ARE YOU LOOKING FOR IN AN UP-AND-COMING COMPOSER? WHAT'S THE COMPLETE PACKAGE?

MG: We are looking for real musical vision, real ability to marry music with images. Thankfully, there are a lot of wonderful musicians, writers, and composers out there. But it is a very special gift, this gift of being able to compose for film.

SS: There are so many talented musicians. But their musical gift is anchored by being film makers first, and their expression is made though music. The musical gift that is necessary to succeed today is to have a great traditional foundation combined with a sense of the abstract future. In other words, being able to express musical thought on computers and machines, on top of a foundation of a classical, traditional gift.

WHAT ARE THE THINGS YOUNG COMPOSERS SHOULD DO TO FURTHER THEIR CAREERS?

SS: In one word: anything. Student opportunities, student film opportunities, student television opportunities, commercials, even local commercials, whatever they can take. I would even suggest that they have their own computer operations going on. That they take videos of some of their favorite and most influential films, shut down the sound, and lay in their own music to show how they would approach a project. And having a CD demo of film music available is important.

But there is one thing that is even more important. In their professional milieu you know their musical gift is a given. What separates those who succeed from those who don't is their ability at the human relationships. It's the way they are perceived by others, and the way they handle meeting any number of people that they encounter—in particular, producers, directors, and studio people. There can't be a better piece of advice than to work on those basic human skills of communication. There are such gifted musicians out there that don't have the burgeoning and remarkable careers that they should at this stage in their lives, just as a result of this area being a complete, utter weakness.

MG: Film and television are collaborative mediums, and it's not one person, it's many people who make a movie or a television show. What Sam is saying is key because it is mainly about collaboration and communication. The composer sits with the director and spots a film, and they determine together where the music goes, and what it is supposed to do. The composer then goes off and uses his musical gift to create the score, but ultimately the score has to be married to the images. I keep repeating it, but it is so important: it is very much a collaboration on many levels.

WHAT DO YOU ENJOY ABOUT WORKING WITH FILM COMPOSERS?

MG: I find them to be great people. With different kinds of musical backgrounds, all of them got to where they are in slightly different ways. Because of the journeys they have taken, they are very responsible and interesting people. Films and television shows provide a wonderful canvas for composers. All that great music would never exist without the kind of inspiration the composers bring.

Photo: Jennifer Lewi

Mark Isham

Mark Isham has a diverse career as jazz artist and film composer. He has composed the scores for over 50 films, including *A River Runs Through It, Nell, Fly Away Home, Quiz Show,* and *Blade.* Beginning his professional career in the Bay Area, Isham played trumpet in the Oakland and San Francisco Symphony Orchestras. He has eight Grammy nominations for his work as a solo artist.

WHAT WAS YOUR MUSICAL BACKGROUND BEFORE YOU GOT INTO FILM SCORING?

When I was a kid growing up in the Bay Area, I wanted to be one of the cool guys in the back of the orchestra, so I picked the trumpet. But then, I think by early teenagerhood, I discovered more popular—not real "pop music"—but I discovered jazz. And I discovered it in two ways. Actually, Henry Mancini was probably the first commercial sound that really sparked my interest. It's only in very long distance hindsight that I realize that his music was for film, also. What was important at the time is that it was jazz-influenced music. That's what I found intriguing. And then, within a year or so, I discovered real jazz: Cannonball Adderly, Miles, and Monk. That was it. My life was over at that point—I was hooked— I was the jazz guy.

Then I discovered Morton Subotnick and the early stuff done with Moog and Buchla synthesizers. This was in the early '70s. That was the other seminal point for me; it defined the next ten to fifteen years of my own musical learning experience. I figured out pretty soon that the average college music department wasn't going to give me what I wanted to know. So I took it upon myself to study privately. I studied with some really excellent trumpet teachers. I even took some private composition lessons for a while from a guy who was sort of a rebel. We would dissect everything from a Herbie Hancock piano solo all the way to the Bartók string quartets.

HOW DID YOUR FIRST FILM-SCORING GIG HAPPEN?

By the end of the '70s, I was a fully eclectic guy with a pretty wide view of music, and a pretty good working knowledge of a lot of it. I was a good professional trumpet player for many years. I was based in San Francisco, and I played in bands that did all sorts of things. I supported myself, and started buying synthesizers when I had some extra money.

In 1982, a director had gotten his hands on a tape of some music that I had written with a friend of mine. It was a project that combined electronics and Chinese instruments. My friend was the Chinese instrument player, and I was the electronica guy. We didn't get that deal, but we made a number of tapes, and one of them was given by my friend to this director. He literally tracked me down and said, "Look, this is the sound I want for my movie." And that was *Never Cry Wolf.*

Understand that this hardly ever happens. I've never actually heard anyone else get their first film out of the blue like this. But to have someone who is totally unknown—I mean, I was not really successful yet making records. I was doing okay, but it wasn't like I had big-selling records or anything. I never set out to be a film composer. And I just happened to write music and someone heard it and said, "I want you to do it for a film." And all of a sudden I had another career.

HOW DID YOU HANDLE THAT FIRST PROJECT?

I had a lot of help. I had two great, experienced music editors to guide me through the process. I did the whole thing on a Prophet

5 with a little hand-held sequencer and multitrack tape. It took about four months to do 60 minutes of music. The idea of doing a film now with that kind of equipment sends shivers down my spine.

YOU HAVE AN EXTENSIVE ELECTRONIC SETUP NOW. DO YOU WRITE AT ALL TO PAPER, OR DO YOU RELY COMPLETELY ON YOUR KEYBOARDS AND SEQUENCER?

I'm still working off of the basic "thrown in the deep end" process of *Never Cry Wolf*, where this guy just said, "I want you to do it." So my basic compositional process at that time was that I would just come up with some ideas looking at the picture. The pictures themselves are always the inspiration.

And that's why I think a lot of us pump so much money back into the sampled sound world—so it's as good as it can be. I wasn't up to par in that regard a number of years back. The accepted level of quality in the demo world had gone quite a bit ahead of me, and I had not been paying attention. There have been a couple of composers in town who have spearheaded this. They use many, many, many samplers and many, many, many high-tech samples. I think it's actually a good thing. I had to rebudget things that year to get back in the game, but getting all that kind of gear has been real helpful for me. I see the difference it makes when it sounds so good that I get certain producers who come in and say, "Why are we spending money on an orchestra?" Yet I would never condone substituting samples for a real orchestra. But if the music is communicating to the extent where people are actually getting that little rush, getting that little tear in the eye even with a sample, then I know I've done it. I go to the scoring session and just have a great time because I'm not worrying whether or not I got the theme right.

DO YOU DO MOCK-UPS FOR EVERY CUE?

Absolutely. I try to mock-up the entire score if time permits. I hate going in front of the orchestra and having the director hear it for the first time. There may be some macho thing about that, and in the old days they had to do it that way. God bless them for surviving. But really, the greatest boon the electronic fake orchestra has given us is the ability to check it out. It gives a sense of what you're doing before any money is spent on musicians and a studio, and you find yourself in that $10,000-an-hour "I've got to fix it right now" scenario.

WHAT ABOUT TEMP TRACKS?

I think a well-done temp, along with a really excellent communication line with the director, is invaluable. Then I really understand when he says things like, "This is what we're learning here in this scene," and, "What I'd like to bring from that scene is another feeling."

I know there are certain composers who hate temp tracks. I understand that point of view. With certain directors temp tracks can be confining, because he will have made up his mind about the music, and unless you do something very similar to the temp, he's not going to be satisfied.

For *A River Runs Through It*, I only had three weeks to do the score. First, I heard a temp score and most of it was unmemorable. But there was one thing in it that validated exactly what I had been thinking. I was sitting there watching the work print, and about half-way through the film I was saying to myself, "I know what this needs. I know what I can do for this." And the last piece in the temp score was exactly that—a Celtic folk song. And I thought, "I'm right. I need to write five or six beautiful folk songs in the Celtic vibe, and choose one for the theme."

DO YOU FIND THAT BEING A JAZZ MUSICIAN INFLUENCES THE WAY YOU APPROACH WRITING FOR FILMS?

Yeah. I have a definite point of view. I mean, this is what composition means to me: Composition is actually being able to get down a great improvisation. It's the same act, as far as I'm concerned. You're making up music. You're creating something. The jazz world puts you in front of an audience, and you create something there with a few signposts that have been put up to guide you.

Composition is the same thing, except that you are allowed to go back and revise and improve and restructure. To me, the high-tech way of composing is great because I can just improvise scads of stuff, and then the music editor in me can come in and just say, "Well, let's rearrange. We've got to get to that point in the film sooner, so let's take those eight bars out." I'm improvising in the style of late Romantic orchestral music. And when I get a good improvisation, I can fine-tune it, and that becomes a composition.

DO YOU CONDUCT YOUR OWN STUFF?

No. First of all, I'm not a conductor. Second of all, I think it's inefficient. The sound in the room is one thing; the sound out of the speakers is usually something very different. And, if for no other reason, contractually I'm paid to write and produce the score. So it's really my responsibility to make sure it sounds right on tape. If I'm out there with the orchestra getting used to the sound of the room and tuning that up, I can come back in the control room and it can sound miles from what it should really sound like. Besides, the director's in there already listening, and already going "Oh god!" I would rather be there holding his hand and saying, "No, no. We're going to do this differently. Engineer, bring that down." So, my orchestrator conducts, because he's the guy that's decided exactly how the bassoons are going to handle that tricky thing there and how to crescendo the cellos. He's made all those decisions, so he should be the one out there handling the orchestral interpretation of that. He knows the score as a written thing much better than I do. I'm the one that has to make sure that the sound on tape is exactly right.

DO YOU ACCEPT PACKAGE DEALS?

I do, it's necessary these days. The important thing to remember is that everything is negotiable. You can negotiate for gross points. You can negotiate for album points. You can negotiate for publishing. You can negotiate for how many musicians you guarantee to employ. Every aspect of a package deal is negotiable. And make sure you do your homework, because if you miscalculate, and you agree contractually to supply 20 strings for 40 minutes of music, you better know what that's going to cost you. And you better do things like go to the director and say, "I will accept this on the terms that you sign off on everything that I play for you in demo form." Sometimes the director is sitting on the scoring stage and says, "What if this were faster?" Then you're looking at writing more music, changing your tempo, and somehow getting new music on the stand while the musicians are waiting for you. That could eat up your profit right there. So it's very crucial that you have a good line of communication with your director. Even if you can't get it in writing that they'll sign-off on the mock-ups, at least, man to man, get them to agree that this is a package deal, and you're going to try to help each other.

YOU SEEM TO FOCUS A LOT ON THE COMMUNICATION BETWEEN THE COMPOSER AND DIRECTOR.

I think more than 50 percent of the gig of the film composer is verbal communication. There are genius composers who couldn't survive in this business if their life depended on it. That is because they're not willing to work in a committee-type environment where you have to discuss, you have to duplicate someone else's point of view, and you have to be willing to create that point of view and somehow fit it in with your own. On the other hand, you can find people who are average composers who have a great ability to work in that environment who are very successful. It's the game. You are working in a group, and you're bringing a musical part to something that isn't all just music. You've got to be able to play in the group, to play in the game by the rules of the game.

Michael Kamen

Michael Kamen's film scores bring the pop, film, and classical music worlds closer together. He has also written several ballets and symphonic works. He is a songwriter and record producer who has worked with artists such as Sting, Eric Clapton, George Harrison, and Bryan Adams. His film credits include *Robin Hood, Prince of Thieves,* the *Lethal Weapon* series, *Don Juan de Marco, Brazil, Mr. Holland's Opus,* and the *Die Hard* series.

HOW DID YOU GET STARTED, MAKING THE JOURNEY FROM BEING AN OBOE STUDENT AT JUILLIARD TO A COMPOSER OF FILM SCORES?

Through a rock 'n roll band—that great archetypal, educational institution. I learned more and got more experience in the New York Rock and Roll Ensemble because it was our own. Because of the time and place we were in, we were, not surprisingly, asked to perform with orchestras. And because nobody else in the band wanted to do it, and I did want to do it, and I didn't know that I couldn't do it, I wrote the orchestra charts. It seemed easy at the time, something I could do. So I wrote bunches of charts for orchestra and found that I really liked it—those were for major orchestras, such as The Boston Pops with Arthur Fiedler.

DID YOU ALWAYS WANT TO COMPOSE FOR FILMS? WAS THAT A GOAL, OR WAS IT JUST SOMETHING THAT HAPPENED ALONG THE WAY?

I would have composed for an ice cream truck. I composed all the time, and I wanted to be a composer when I was a kid. I remember sitting in front of the piano one day when I was eight or nine and looking at all the busts of Beethoven, Schubert, Bach, and Mozart sitting there on the piano, and realizing with much disappointment, "They're all dead! Maybe it's not a job anymore. Maybe it's just one of those things that happened in the olden days, when the world was black and white." It occurred to me that I'd have to do something else; I couldn't be a composer because that job was no longer a job. Then suddenly, through a rock 'n roll band, I wound up being a composer.

How did you get your first gig on a film?

The rock 'n roll band was managed by a guy whose partner made *Dog Day Afternoon* and *Serpico*. He was a film producer named Marty Bregman, and I knew him because we shared offices. I was very visible in the office; I don't have a shy personality, and I suggested that he pick me to do a film score. He asked me to do a film called *The Next Man*. Then I did a film for another friend of mine, and the rock band also did some television films. One was called *Christina's World*, based on an Andrew Wyeth painting. It became easy for me to do these projects because I was able to continue doing what I loved to do: invent music every day.

In those early films, did they want you as a rock 'n roll musician or as a composer?

No, I was always a hybrid character—a classical musician that played rock 'n roll, or a rock 'n roller who was also a classical musician, depending on which end of the street people met me. But it was clear that I was always in both worlds, and I've always brought that feeling into my work. I haven't seen those early films in a long time, but I remember I made a quite classical job out of it, and freely mixed classical music with a set of drums and a rock 'n roll spirit.

HAS YOUR COMPOSING PROCESS CHANGED MUCH OVER THE YEARS, ESPECIALLY WITH THE ADVENT OF NEW TECHNOLOGIES?

Well, technology is more of a memory device for me. In the old days when I used my brain completely to remember things, and pencils to write it down, I felt smarter, but I think everybody feels smarter when they're seventeen. I have an inbred mistrust of technology making the way simpler for us. I don't think it answers questions. I think it provides some solutions and I'm all for it now. I use it all the time. I'm definitely hooked. The difference between banging things out on a shabby piano and banging things out on a shabby Kurzweil is that the shabby Kurzweil remembers what I play.

IN TERMS OF SYNCHRONIZATION, JUST FROM HAVING BEEN AROUND A LITTLE BIT WHILE YOU'VE BEEN WORKING, IT SEEMS LIKE YOU'RE VERY INSTINCTUAL.

Yeah, it's instinctive. I have never depended on any of those devices like Auricle or whatever. They are systems that enable you to look at a piece of film and compute what the best click track would be. But I really hate math so much that I don't get myself involved. For years, I did try to get click tracks right, but inevitably I'd get them wrong, and I just punched my way out of that paper bag.

SO HOW DO YOU SYNCHRONIZE SOMETHING LIKE LETHAL WEAPON OR AN ACTION SEQUENCE THAT REQUIRES A LOT OF SYNCHRONIZATION? ARE YOU STILL JUST FEELING THOSE SPOTS?

Again, I do have an instinct for it, and I have to trust that instinct. That's one of the things you do as a composer: Trust your instincts, and have confidence in what it is you're saying. There are always ways to get it perfect, to refine it, and make sure that that big downbeat hits the explosion or misses the explosion, as the case may be. And certainly there are also music editors who can fix anything that needs fixing. But my job is to make music, and not equations.

WHAT ABOUT THE TIMES THAT YOU'VE CROSSED OVER FROM WRITING MORE CLASSICAL SCORES TO MORE ROCK 'N ROLL THINGS? HOW DOES THE PROCESS WORK WITH ERIC CLAPTON, OR DAVID SANBORN?

It's the same thing. It's just relating to a musician in language that those musicians can understand, so I'm not confused or confusing. Eric is able to carry melody in his head and improvise better than any 15,000 people I know. Same with Sanborn. So when you're working with genius, you just allow them to be themselves. You don't try to constrict them or control them. Every once in a while you'll say, "I really *need* you to play guitar or sax on top of this." When you provide them with a track, they'll figure it out. If they don't figure it out, then you say, "Try this …" and you can demonstrate and so forth.

I WOULD IMAGINE THAT YOUR EXPERIENCE IN BEING A ROCK 'N ROLL MUSICIAN ASSISTS YOU IN THAT WHOLE PROCESS.

That's because I realize the real value in not being educated to death and not being overly regimented in the way you think. Rock 'n roll is a great liberator in that there are no rules, and if there were you'd get rid of them. That's what it's about. That's why it was invented. I was really lucky to be around at that crucial period when it was being invented. It's been a little sad for me to see it go down such a predictable road, as it has done, and become a cash cow where the money is the all-important end product, and the music is secondary.

HAVE YOU EVER WRITTEN A SONG WHERE THE DIRECTOR SAYS TO YOU, "HERE'S A SCENE IN THE MOVIE IN WHICH WE NEED A SONG, NOT UNDERSCORE." HAVE YOU BEEN IN THAT SITUATION, WHERE YOU HAD TO COMPOSE A SONG THAT HAD REALLY DRAMATIC IMPACT?

No, unless it's a montage sequence, I don't think a song is very good news. You're trying to tell a story with action, colors, and characters and you don't need somebody singing in the background telling you what you're seeing. I don't actually agree with that, and very rarely do I think a song contributes positively in that way. There are some notable examples where it does work, however. The songs "Mona Lisa" and "Brazil" are deliberate attempts on the part of the director, not on the part of the composer, to be intrinsic motivations for the characters' actions. That's why we used them. It's not because we wanted a hit record.

Most often, songs in movies are there for commercial reasons. The great lesson of a lifetime was taught to me by Joel Silver, [producer of the *Die Hard* and *Lethal Weapon* series] when I said to him one day, "Joel, you have great taste and wisdom about art and culture. When are you going to make a great film and stop making this shit?" And he said, "I make shit. I buy art!" Movies are art as commerce, and to some people like Joel, that works very well. For me art is art, and commerce is commerce.

WHAT DO YOU THINK MAKES A GREAT SCORE? WHAT MAKES A SCORE STAND OUT IN YOUR MIND?

Melody. A great piece of music is qualified by its melody. There are great scores that are brilliant orchestrations or this and that, but they sound *like* other pieces of music, they're not great pieces of music. There's a difference. A great piece of music is like an invention. It's like a very rare jewel, or a beautiful vista. Even if you create a melody deliberately and say I want it to do this, or I want it to do that, as opposed to conceiving it instinctively, there still must be some degree of inspiration. There's no way on Earth that I could claim to really be in control of the melodies that I write. I'm just inventing stuff. It's a bit like fishing.

SO YOU WOULD NEVER SIT DOWN AND SAY, "I NEED A BITTERSWEET MELODY, SO I'M GOING TO GO UP A MINOR 6TH," OR SOMETHING LIKE THAT.

No, I don't really think of minor 6ths when I'm playing. But I do sit down and improvise a lot. In that sense, improvisation is really a starting point for an idea. I have some training, just enough to get me in trouble, but not enough to screw me up forever. I can recognize somehow what I've done, but I don't define it in musical terms. I never say, "This is serial technique," or "This is a 10th," or anything else. It just has a shape in my mind, and it's very difficult to describe what a shape is. It's blue, yet green. I wouldn't be a very good teacher in that regard, but I would be a very good teacher if I were just able to encourage people to express their own personality. That is what we do, that is the gift of music—being able to express a feeling and an attitude and a vibe confidently, and with some beauty. Believing it to be good enough to make beautiful things.

Do you organize yourself as far as themes are concerned? Do you put it all together at first, or do you just start and see where it takes you?

No, I never list things. However, the spotting process is a very crucial one; I often can see what the architecture of a score will be by talking about it with the director, or the producer, or whoever I'm spotting with. I learn more as I'm working on it, and sometimes I change my mind. But it's really the architecture of a score that you're talking about, and that is a very complicated, and yet quite simplistic design. Nobody goes to the theater to listen to the score. The score is assisting them in watching the film. The score is a component of the story and of the characters. So I don't want people to be sitting there going, "Wow, what a great ii-IV-V progression." That's not what I want, and I don't believe it's an important consideration in making music for films.

As far as themes are concerned, coming up with a theme, having several portions to that theme that you can assign to separate characters in the movie, and being able to bring the theme out with the character is important to me. But that's more mechanical to me than artistic. To say, "If Mel Gibson's on the screen I need the guitar, and if he's being angry and aggressive, I need a big orchestra behind it," that's a no-brainer.

WHAT IS YOUR ADVICE FOR THE UP-AND-COMING FILM STUDENTS, IN TERMS OF GETTING STARTED IN THE BUSINESS?

Getting started in the business is always a dilemma because you can't advise people on getting lucky, and there is a great deal of luck. It's about the work that they do, and it's not about being in the right place or meeting the right people or going to the right party—though all of that can contribute to it. But there is no single thing I could say, other than make the best music you can, and be the best you can be at what it is you do, and what you do uniquely. There is a need for the individuality for each of us to rise to the surface, and for us to take our own work quite seriously. You should have fun while you're doing it. A really great musician doesn't convey their technical brilliance on stage. What they convey is how easy it seems to be playing this incredibly difficult stuff. The more relaxed you are as a human being and as a musician, the more effective your performance will be. This is far short of saying that if you want to work in film do this, do that, do the other thing. I'm afraid that kind of advice is not going to come from me. The kind of advice that I'm going to give you is to be yourself, find your own brand of music to make, and work hard. It's about the work, it's about the work, it's about the work. Your work will come to people's attention, and if you can produce more good work, you're onto something.

Mark Mancina

M ark Mancina composed scores for three of the top-grossing films of recent years: *Speed, Twister,* and *Con Air.* He won a Grammy for his work on *The Lion King,* and was music producer for its Broadway stage version. Additionally, Mancina has led an active career producing songs for such artists as Phil Collins and Elton John.

NOW THAT YOU'VE HAD SOME SUCCESS IN YOUR CAREER, DO YOU HEAR FILM SCORES DIFFERENTLY?

When I first came into film composing I used to be pretty critical of people's scores. I'd listen to some scores and go, "That guy's terrible," or, "This guy's brilliant." Now, I've changed my whole viewpoint. I feel that anyone who does this for a living—successfully completes a score, and goes on to his next score—has accomplished an incredible achievement because there's so much that goes on behind a movie score besides the music. Fielding the politics, the pressures, the emotions, and the wants and desires of some directors who think that they have something on screen that maybe they don't have—all those kinds of emotions are extremely challenging. So I have a huge respect for anybody that does this job. I think it's extremely difficult. In reality, sometimes the music is the *easiest* part, while everything else you have to deal with is really the hardest part of the job.

HAVE YOU EVER BEEN IN A SITUATION WHERE YOU REALLY DISAGREED WITH A DIRECTOR?

Oh yeah, every movie!

[LAUGHING] WHAT HAPPENED?

The majority of the time, we end up with a cue that the director likes better but that I think wasn't as good as my original cue. But that's from *my* perspective. The director probably would say that we ended up with a better piece of music. I would write a cue that I thought was the best that could be for that scene. Then the director comes in and says, "No, I had a completely different thing in mind for this." So where do you go? Who's right, who's wrong?

SO YOU DO MOCK-UPS FOR EVERY CUE?

It depends. I try not to because mock-ups really back you into a corner. But directors and producers are getting much more used to having things mocked up because they can hear what it sounds like before they hire the orchestra to play it.

HOW DID YOU GET STARTED IN FILM SCORING?

I started out as a classical player, as a classical guitarist. I went to school and studied composition—I went through that whole process. I also played in bands and did all kinds of different stuff—playing at night and paying the rent doing music.

When I was 22, a friend who was a cameraman called me and said he was doing a documentary for this guy that does these dog training documentaries; he does dog training, deer gutting, and marlin fishing—and he needs music for these shows. I said, "Absolutely." I had a little sequencer—a Roland—and a couple of keyboards. I put all this stuff in my car and I drove to this guy's production studio and set up. There was no sync or anything. Everything had to be written or clicked, and I had to just freewheel it. I wrote these documentaries, and, for way back then, they came out all right. I had a big orchestral sound in one of them and I wrote some songs, I was singing and playing all the instruments—this was all on an 8-track Fostex. I started to see the magic of putting music up against picture and running them at the same time. That's a whole school; I learned it by doing it. Nobody was there telling me, "That's really stupid what you're doing there." I learned it by doing it, and I did it for years. I really got a sense of what music does, what it can do, what it should and shouldn't do, and all those kind of things.

I did low-budget films and documentaries for nine years. Then Hans Zimmer heard something I did. He called me up and he said, "What part of Europe are you from?" And I said, "I'm not from Europe, I'm from Santa Monica." Then he said, "Well, your writing is really European and I would really love to work with you. Why don't you come down to my studio?" That day I went down to his studio. Trevor Horn was there, and Billy Idol was there, and they were doing this movie called *Days of Thunder*. I just dove right into it as an arranger, writer, and player.

Then *The Lion King* project was looming. Hans was doing the score, and he asked me to produce the songs, and be in charge of that. I said okay, and then dove into that without knowing that it would become the most successful animated motion picture ever made. At the same time I was working on that, I was doing films like *Monkey Trouble* and other little fun family films. While I was finishing up *The Lion King*, Jan De Bont came to me and said, "I want you to do my movie *Speed*, it's just a small movie." This is like a $30-million dollar movie. I told him I'd love to do it. They had me audition cues for them, though. Eventually I got the movie and those two movies—*The Lion King* and *Speed*—came out the same week, and everything just went crazy after that.

WHAT IS YOUR WRITING PROCESS NOW?

Basically what I've been doing now is playing a lot of the instruments myself while writing the cues and playing all the percussion. I collect instruments and any instruments I can get my hands on I'll learn and develop a part and write from that stand-point. Then I'll add the orchestra over the top of it. So, when I play a mock up, it's not really a mock up. What you're really hearing is all of the acoustic instruments that I've recorded, and vocals done myself. The orchestra is the only thing that's mocked up, to a point, or a piano track. Then we go in and record the orchestra and get rid of the synth stuff. So eventually, what you end up having is me playing a series of percussion instruments and a series of stringed instruments, then doing vocals, and then finally an orchestra play-ing. It becomes this hybrid. There is a certain randomness and air that is created when you play an acoustic instrument, and you cannot create it on a keyboard of any kind. I don't care how good your samples are.

How do you handle the business stuff?

At the beginning, when I first start work on a film, I think about the music and what I want to do with it. But there is also a logistical side—a business side—to it. I came from being a producer on records, and an arranger, and that really helped me because part of writing a film score is producing a recording. And producing means being in charge of the entire outcome—the budgets and credits and everything. It can be extremely difficult for the studios to get all that together.

So you're in constant communication with a lot of other people?

You know, it would be wonderful to say that the composer has the final say on everything but that's not the truth. So many times, you'll hear a score and you'll say, "Man! I don't like that cue at all, how could he have written that?" And to be fair, it most likely wasn't the composer's doing. Who knows how it ended up there? Basically, when it all comes down, film composing is a service job, and there isn't a composer out there who would argue that. Everybody has to bend and learn to change things that they don't necessarily want to change because they're not the executive pro-ducer of the film, they're not the director of the film, they're only the composer. It's not the composer's film, it's the director's film. You always have to keep that in mind. And that can make it difficult because sometimes the composer really does know best!

David Newman

David Newman has scored over 55 feature films, including *Hoffa*, *Anastasia*, *Heathers*, *The Nutty Professor*, and *Matilda*. Coming from a Hollywood music family—brother Thomas Newman is also a film composer, and father Alfred Newman was the head of music at 20th Century Fox for many years—David Newman studied violin, and received a degree in conducting from USC.

YOU GREW UP IN A HOLLYWOOD MUSIC FAMILY. WAS THERE ALWAYS MUSIC AROUND AT YOUR HOUSE, OR WAS IT SOMETHING YOUR DAD WOULD LEAVE AT THE OFFICE?

My dad worked at home while we were growing up and there was a lot of music around. Music was a big part of the house, we always heard him banging away on the piano. We were also brought up very traditionally, studying music. My brother Tommy and I, we both grew up studying violin and piano from very young ages. We took theory, counterpoint, and orchestration at 11, 12, 13 years old. A traditional, sort of Germanic musical upbringing.

DID YOU REBEL AGAINST THAT?

No, no. I loved it. I always loved music. It was never a snotty or snooty or upper crust thing around my house. It was something my dad and his brother Lionel talked about with so much love. It wasn't just work for them. It was, in a sense, the only thing that they really talked about. They talked about music with love more than they talked about anything.

DID YOU ALWAYS WANT TO WRITE MUSIC FOR FILMS?

When I was young, I never wanted to write music for film. I didn't start writing until I was 29. I was studying conducting all through my twenties. I had gone to USC as a violin performance major; then, I got a masters there with Dan Lewis in conducting.

For a while after school, I was just doing studio work playing violin. There got to a point in my life when I wanted to change what I was doing. I wanted to be a conductor, but I wasn't doing what it would take to do that. I was just kind of floating around. I was playing violin, I was making a living and everything, but it wasn't satisfying. And film scoring was an option to me. I just decided to do it, and I made a demo, and went through this three or four year process to get going. It took me a really long time.

WHAT'S YOUR COMPOSING PROCESS NOW? ARE YOU SEQUENCING OR USING PENCIL AND PAPER?

For the past three or four years I've been sequencing. But I've done around 60 films, and about 40 of them I wrote directly with piano, and orchestrated at the same time. I never sketched because I was really sloppy. Sketching was really a hard thing for me to do because no one could ever read it.

SO WHAT IS THE PROCEDURE TODAY?

What I do is start to compose and orchestrate into the Erato software program. Then I have to mock-up up everything for the director. I use Logic Audio to sequence the stuff so people can hear it back. I've got several samplers and synthesizers, so I can get a really good sound here in my studio.

DO YOU PREFER TO WAIT FOR A FINISHED WORK PRINT OR DO YOU LIKE TO GET INVOLVED AT THE SCRIPT LEVEL?

I like to be involved early on, if possible. I have a really good relationship with Danny DeVito. I've done all the films he's directed since *Throw Momma From the Train*, and I generally get involved with those earlier on. In general, at that early stage of production, I find that it's better to be intellectually involved—not to start writing—because things tend to change so much. I find that the scripts are very much rough plans for what the movie is going to be. They very often don't pan out. To see the color, the imagery, and the visual sort of ambience of the whole thing is such a big part of conceiving the music that it is best to wait for the work print before writing. This is especially true today, where often the music that is wanted is just colors and tones—more textures than melodies.

WHAT WAS IT LIKE DOING THE UNDERSCORE FOR Anastasia?

I really liked *Anastasia*. I had a great time. I really liked Bluth and Goldman and it was really a fun thing to do. It was scored just like a traditional film. It wasn't quite finished when I got it; it was all animated but it wasn't colorized. So it was all there, a little hard to see, but not really any different from a regular work print.

DID YOU HAVE TO WORK WITH THE SONGWRITERS AT ALL, OR WERE YOU ON YOUR OWN?

I used all material from the songs because I thought that would be the right artistic choice for the movie. That's what my dad (Alfred Newman) would do with all those Rodgers and Hammerstein musicals like *Carousel* and *The King and I*. I really liked how he interwove the score right with the song, and then right out from the song back into the score. It's one of my favorite things. The seamlessness, taking of themes and developing them into other things, and making the movie seem really unified appeals to me a lot.

WHAT ARE SOME OF YOUR THOUGHTS AND EXPERIENCES ON WORKING WITH DIFFERENT DIRECTORS?

Some directors are really good to collaborate with, and some aren't. The ones that are good—you don't always know that they're good to begin with—tend to push you in a way that you end up with something better than you would have. My collaborations with DeVito have been really good and he pushed me to do different things. But more often than not, you find directors saying, "This scene doesn't work, let's put some music in it." Then it becomes non-collaborative. It can be okay, but you're not really adding anything, you're just getting from one place to another. Mostly they're looking for you to write a melody they really like.

WHAT DO YOU DO WHEN A DIRECTOR HEARS THE MOCK-UPS AND DOESN'T LIKE THE DIRECTION YOU'VE GONE?

You just talk to them. Nobody's nasty! But if they say that it's definitely not right, that it just doesn't work, then you must talk to them and listen for clues to tell you what they mean by "doesn't work." They're usually not complicated. Most often, it's something like: It's too fast, or too slow; it's too dark, it's too light; I don't like this instrument, it sounds too sentimental, or it doesn't have enough emotion. It's more stuff like that.

WHAT HAPPENS WHEN YOU GET SOMEBODY WHO IS NOT A MUSICIAN, AND CAN'T MAKE THE LEAP FROM LISTENING TO A STANDARD MOCK-UP TO ENVISIONING HOW IT WILL SOUND WITH A REAL ORCHESTRA?

You have to explain to them. You have to educate them a little bit. It's surprising, the music is so much cleaner than it used to be. It often translates just fine. I don't find so much that directors are shocked when they hear the orchestra. That's the way it used to be—you'd play it on the piano, and when they heard the orchestra it was a complete shock. Now I find that it translates actually pretty well.

What's worse is the temp-music phenomenon, where they get so in love with the temp track. In fact, they might not even like the temp music, but they are so used to hearing it that anything else is completely jarring to them. That's more difficult to deal with, and they often won't admit it's the temp score because it's so unhip to say that. It means that their movie is just the same as everybody else's movie. But you learn to listen between the lines.

IT'S LIKE IN RECORD PRODUCTION WITH THE "ROUGH MIX SYNDROME." EVEN IF THERE ARE WRONG NOTES, THEY'VE HEARD THE ROUGH MIX SO MANY TIMES, THEY DON'T HEAR THEM ANYMORE.

Right. It's the same thing. It takes a really strong director to fight that. Most of them, even the strong ones, can't really fight that. With the temp scores they have so much at stake because that's what they use when they preview their movie. There's no scarier time. Because that's when the studio either signs off or doesn't. The scariest time for them is when they are testing their movie.

But as a composer, you have to deal with it. You can't ignore the temp track. Unless you have a really brave director.

ARE YOU CONTENT? DO YOU LIKE DOING WHAT YOU ARE DOING?

You know, I'm not the most calm, contented person in the world. But, composing to me is a relatively new thing. I really love music, and I really like where I am now. It doesn't mean I wouldn't like to do other things, but I really love writing music. I feel that the choice I made to switch from playing to writing was the right thing to do.

David Raksin

David Raksin has been active writing and teaching film music for over 60 years. His first major project was with Charlie Chaplin on *Modern Times*, and he also composed one of the most well-known songs of all time, "Laura," for the movie of the same title. He was one of the most innovative composers in Hollywood during the 1940s, '50s, and '60s; many composers today are still influenced by his scores, as well as his straight forward, honest, and enthusiastic approach to film scoring.

YOU'VE BEEN INVOLVED IN THIS FIELD SINCE 1935, FROM THE EARLIEST DAYS OF FILM SCORING ...

No, no. Remember, there was music in films all the time. As a matter of fact, I remember when it was accompanied by a piano or an organ. Sometimes the organ players were incredibly brilliant.

Later they had orchestras. My father played in one in Philadelphia, and eventually became a conductor of music for silent films. So I was around this stuff from the time I was seven or eight years old. When sound films came in around 1926 things changed. Music became marginally more sophisticated, but not much. Remember there is a tradition around these things, and when one thing moves forward, it doesn't mean everything else does also. When Henry Ford invented the Model T, it didn't mean that horses stopped running around.

THE "ERAS" WE DESIGNATE FOR CLASSICAL MUSIC STYLES ARE LIKE
THAT. WE TEND TO WANT TO PUT LINES OF DELINEATION AROUND SIG-
NIFICANT EVENTS, BUT IT DOESN'T ALWAYS WORK THAT WAY.

Absolutely. The point is that there were composers who carried
over from the silent days, as would naturally be the case. They
would be accustomed to standing in the pit and playing scores
based upon pieces that were already written, which is what my
father did. And they brought their own predilections for music, so
there was a preponderance of European-derived music. It took a
while for things to begin to look up. Eventually, guys like Max
Steiner came in, and even though his was a European influence, he
started to make some changes. For example, his score to *King Kong*
was way ahead of its time. Then Waxman came in, and Korngold
came in, and there were a number of other guys.

WHAT WERE THE SCHEDULES LIKE UNDER THE OLD STUDIO SYSTEM?

We did tremendous amounts of music. For instance, when I composed the score for *Forever Amber*, that had about 110 minutes of
music—about 100 of those I composed myself. The rest was music
of the story's time. Originally I had twelve weeks to do that, but
they were messing around with the movie, and by the time they
got finished doing that I had eight and a half weeks to do that
tremendous amount of music. And I did it!

There were all kinds of crazy things. For instance, one time they
were doing a picture called *The Goldwyn Follies*, and George
Gershwin was the composer. Right in the middle of it he died, and
they brought in Vernon Duke to complete the score. Vernon wrote
the various songs, and he also wrote a ballet called *Undine* for the
middle of the picture. When Gershwin died, the production had
been effectively stopped; the sets were ready, the company was
ready, but there was no music for George Balanchine, the choreog-
rapher, to work with. So I got a call that afternoon from Eddie
Powell to meet him and Hugo Freidhofer at Zardi's Restaurant.
After dinner, the three of us went into different rooms at the old

United Artists Studio, and overnight we orchestrated that ballet. That was some job. We got done at 3:00 a.m. and it was recorded later that morning.

How did you break in to working at the studios?

Charlie Chaplin had made a movie called *Modern Times*. He was a violinist, and he had plenty of musical ideas, but he didn't really know how to develop them. So he always had a composer working with him, you know, a real composer.

How did you work with him, did he play and you transcribe?

No. He would have ideas, mostly fragments, and then we would discuss them. And he didn't always like that, so after a week and a half of that he fired me. I was brokenhearted and about to go home, when Alfred Newman [head of music at United Artists] said to me, "Don't go home. I've been looking at what you've been doing with his little tunes, and he'd be crazy to fire you." So I got a call from the head of Charlie's studio and he said, "We want to hire you back." I said, "No way, not unless I can have an understanding with him." And we came to that understanding. I told him that I wouldn't work for him if I was just going to be a yes man, and he accepted my terms. So I worked four and a half months on that. It is a co-composed score, and that's what started me off.

I had all kinds of offers after that. I had one from Steiner, who wanted me to be his assistant, but I didn't want to be anybody's assistant, so I turned it down, went back to New York, then went to Europe and worked on a show. Then I got various offers, so I came back.

Were you contracted to a specific studio?

Oh yes, I had several contracts. I was at Fox for quite a while from around 1937 to 1946 when I left. Before that, for about six months, I was under contract to Universal, but we really couldn't stand one another. I thought that their schlock way of doing things was absolutely indefensible. They were very glad to get rid of me, and I was very glad to get the hell out from under.

I also had a contract for a while at MGM, but that was only because I was broke and needed the money. MGM was a hellhole. It was a place where all the bad things said about Hollywood came close to being true. I think that whether it was conscious or not, they wore composers out by pitting the composers against their system.

I'D LIKE TO ASK YOU ABOUT THE SHIFT AWAY FROM THE EUROPEAN STYLE OF COMPOSING TO A MORE MODERN SOUND THAT INCLUDED INFLUENCES OF BARTÓK, STRAVINSKY, AND OTHERS. WHAT WAS YOUR EXPERIENCE OF THIS CHANGE OF STYLES AS IT WAS HAPPENING?

There were other people that influenced it greatly. Our country had a period where it was the world's leading and greatest source of great melodies. It was a time that began in the early twenties and continued into the middle fifties. That was the time of Jerome Kern, and Harold Arlen, and Richard Rodgers, and George Gershwin. There has never been such a time in the history of music anywhere, and I think it is the great glory of our country when that happened, because there has never been such a flowering anywhere else. So we were all influenced very much by these American composers, and we were also influenced by some of the Russian composers, such as Prokofiev, Shostakovich, Rachmaninoff, and people like that. They wrote a kind of music that deserves respect, and we loved it. We would have been idiots not to be affected by it.

And so generally, I am accused of being the guy that started the change going. I doubt very much that I am, but I was one of the very first to do things a completely different way. For instance, in 1936 or 1937 I was working at Universal, and there was a guy there named Lou Forbes, who was so fascinated with what I was doing that he told his brother Leo Forbstein, who was head of music at Warners. And Leo started to employ me there.

WHAT EXACTLY WERE YOU DOING THAT WAS SO DIFFERENT?

The nature of my music was very different. It had all kinds of other influences because I was a guy who loved the music of our time and I was also a jazz player.

I would go over to Warners on the weekends when I wasn't working at Universal, and I would only do chases and fights. I would never see the rest of the picture. One of those was a 58-second montage of boxing. Later, I actually reorchestrated that piece for Leopold Stokowski, who was working at Universal at that time, and he ended up doing it with the Philadelphia Orchestra a few months later. It was probably the first film piece played by a concert orchestra—a jazz piece in $5/4$.

WERE THERE PROBLEMS CONVINCING THE MORE CONSERVATIVE DIRECTORS AND PRODUCERS OF THE VALIDITY OF WHAT YOU WERE DOING?

I was very lucky in that when I was working at Warners, Leo Forbstein was fascinated by what I did. As a matter of fact, I finally got too fascinating for him. I wrote a piece where right in the middle of an *alla breve* meter, I had all these bars of $3/4$, and he couldn't conduct it. He asked me if I could, so I did.

WHEN DID YOU FIRST START TO USE ATONAL AND 12-TONE MUSIC?

I used twelve-tone rows here and there. I did a picture at MGM in 1949 or '50 called *The Man With a Cloak*, and the people at MGM utterly hated the score and wanted to throw it out. Johnny Green, the head of music at the studio, said, "Guys, you don't know what you're doing; this is an extraordinary score." It was also done for a crazy little orchestra. And they wouldn't listen. But all of a sudden, the producer of this film said, "There's something remarkable about this score," and they kept the music in, after a second preview.

Man With a Cloak had a 12-tone row, the first five notes of which spelled E-D-G-A-R. The R became D$^\flat$. I saw Johnny Green the next day and he said, "Gee that's a remarkable score, what's that crazy god-damned tune you've got there?" And I said, "Johnny, it's a 12-tone row." He was astonished, and wanted to know why I used a row. I told it was because in this picture you don't find out until the last 45 seconds or so that the hero, the man in the cloak, is really Edgar Allan Poe. So I thought I would start the main title with those five notes because I had the vision of Dore Schary, the head of MGM, coming out and saying, "Fire that son-of-a-bitch, he gave away the secret of the picture in the Main Title."

I had a great time doing the things I was doing. Sometimes I was motivated by jazz, sometimes by contemporary music. You would have to be deaf not to feel the enormous effect of the music of Stravinsky. For me, it was Stravinsky and Berg. So I wrote just the way I thought I should be writing. It was not unanimously accepted.

How do you see the evolution of film-scoring styles in terms of producers, directors, and audiences accepting new sounds?

The interesting thing about film music is that, as a composer, unless you have some idiot for a producer, which happens about two thirds of the time, you can do things that you could never do in a concert hall. There is a counter-validation between the screen and the music. If they heard it in a concert hall, the audience would run screaming, but when they hear it with a picture, the music and the image counter-validate one another. For example, if you have a really violent sequence and you write something that is really dissonant, they might not like to hear that as a piece of music. But they will accept it if it is the right music for a film sequence. That kind of thing opened up the world for a lot of people. So the first generation that was susceptible to films was prepared for newer music by the scores they heard in movie theaters.

After the success of Laura, were you plagued by people wanting you to do it again?

Oh yes, everybody wanted me to write another Laura, but I would say, "First you have to make me one."

WITHIN A DECADE AFTER LAURA, TV HAD HIT FULL FORCE. HOW DID THIS AFFECT YOU PERSONALLY?

There were times when I wasn't working anywhere else, and I was lucky to get television. I think I did my first television in 1950 on *Life with Father*. We all preferred film because it was much more civilized. I once described television as an industry where they manufacture debris. Television really is sad, although it employed the talents of some very, very good people. Many good composers did it, including Jerry Goldsmith, John Williams, and Johnny Green.

WHAT IS YOUR COMPOSING PROCESS, HOW DO YOU GENERATE IDEAS?

What I'm trying to do is to catch the spirit of a picture. And that means sometimes I go contrary to what's on the screen, and sometimes I go with what's on the screen. It's a matter of instinct. If your instincts are good, it's going to work for you.

Photo: Dana Ross

Lolita Ritmanis

Composer and orchestrator Lolita Ritmanis has worked on more than 30 films and television shows. She has worked as arranger and orchestrator for Michael Kamen, Basil Poledouris, David Benoit, Shirley Walker, and Mark Snow on such projects as *Lethal Weapon 4, X-Files: The Movie,* and *Robin Hood, Prince of Thieves.* She has composed regularly for Warner Bros. animated series, *The New Batman and Superman Adventures,* as well as *Batman Beyond.* Her concert works include choral, solo, ensemble, and orchestral works that have been performed in cities around the world.

WHAT LED YOU TO FILM SCORING?

I grew up in Portland, and the first trip I took down here to Los Angeles was with my parents in my senior year of high school. I had a whole demo tape of songs, and I had stars in my eyes. I wanted the Hollywood experience. I ended up coming down here to go to a small school called The Grove School of Music where I studied jazz arranging and composition. I don't really even know if I ever made a conscious decision, I'm going to be a film composer. I knew I *was* a composer. All my life I was a composer. As a child, when I practiced the piano, I was making up my own little pieces when my mom wasn't looking. After the film-scoring program at Groves I studied composition and orchestration with Mauro Bruno. And I started to get jobs, some more glamorous than others, but to me they were all exciting.

Bruce Babcock gave me a shot at orchestrating a little bit for him on *Matlock*, and that was thrilling. I was also playing in a Top 40 band and working with a community choir. While I was doing all these other things, glad to be making a little bit of money, I got a job at the Warner Bros. music department Xeroxing violin parts. I was thrilled about that. The first day I had to be there, my boss, Joel Franklin, said, "Be here at 9:00 a.m." which is a late call for music library. I was outside the studio gate at about 7:00, with my briefcase and ready to go! From there I progressed to proofreading and orchestrating. All along the way, I had this demo tape I used whenever opportunity presented itself.

AS AN ORCHESTRATOR, WHAT IS IT LIKE WORKING WITH DIFFERENT COMPOSERS WHO HAVE VERY DIFFERENT WORKING STYLES? SOME GIVE YOU VERY COMPLETE SKETCHES, AND SOME ARE BARE-BONES.

It's very different in each individual situation. There are certainly composers that are incredibly gracious and grateful, and they acknowledge you, even at the scoring date. They might announce to the orchestra, "Oh so-and-so orchestrated this cue. Let's hear it for so-and-so." They sometimes acknowledge the soloists in the orchestra, and the good work of many people involved.

There are some orchestrators that tend to think that, because they have been given only melody and chords, they are writing the music. I'm not one of those. Whatever you're going to hum after hearing a particular cue, that's usually, hopefully, the composer's work. Every situation is different. There are many composers who don't really need an orchestrator—their sketches are absolutely complete. And some of the composers who run into the time crunch are also capable of doing very complete sketches. It is merely that the accelerated post-production schedules often do not leave time for detailed sketching.

I am only recently getting into the world of computers—MIDI files and notation programs. When I'm orchestrating from digital files, first I listen to a DAT that the composer provides, and get a feeling of the music. Then it's my job to translate it to make it work for the orchestra. And it's really exciting. I don't think that there is even one step in this whole journey that I've been on that I've really just been pulling out my hair, "Oh, how horrible this is." I've really enjoyed a lot of it, most of it, and I feel very fortunate.

DO YOU STILL USE PENCIL AND PAPER?

That's my favorite way to work. I can't imagine giving it up. It's so much faster for me. I can see the score right under my hands. If you've done it that way I don't know if you can ever completely switch to computers.

HAS DIGITAL TECHNOLOGY AFFECTED THE FINAL PRODUCT?

Yes, and with digital editing for picture, they can makes changes so close up to the last minute, you have to be ready for that, and be able to make changes at the scoring session. It's frustrating though, because many of us try to do things the right way, the proper way, sketch nicely, figure out accurate timings on either Auricle or Performer, and make things right. Not too late, not too early, just right. It can be frustrating when people make changes and your score gets all marked up. A cue gets completely changed around from what you originally thought it would be because the picture has been altered at the last minute.

IT SOUNDS LIKE YOU'VE COME TO A PLACE OF DETACHMENT ABOUT THE WORK THAT YOU DO, KNOWING THAT ANYTHING COULD HAPPEN TO IT.

On some of the really high-profile kind of pandemonium moments, you have to be detached. It's part of the job to apply yourself 100%, and let the chips fall where they may. Because if you get too worried about it, it's not going to do anyone any good. You are hired not only for your orchestration abilities, but for your professionalism in stressful situations.

IT MUST BE A REAL THRILL TO HEAR YOUR MUSIC, AS AN ORCHESTRA-TOR AND AS A COMPOSER, PLAYED BY SUCH INCREDIBLE MUSICIANS.

It is. I forget and sometimes I have to pinch myself and realize "Oh my goodness, this is amazing." These are the best players, and the best sight-readers, in the world. Absolutely the best sight-readers. The mistakes quotient is: there is hardly ever a mistake.

DO YOU ENJOY ORCHESTRATING?

Yes. And I do have to say that I'm not ready to give it up. There usually is a time for a composer where you have to say, "That's enough, I need to be the composer now." But you do say good-bye to quite a bit of income at that point. And I know several people who have done that.

IT'S HARD TO MAKE THE TRANSITION?

Yes, because there are only so many hours in the day. And if you're orchestrating on a feature for a couple weeks, that's full time. If you're under a deadline as a composer, that's full time. What to do? There are only 24 hours in a day.

There are people who will swear to you that if you're a TV composer you'll never get to do features. "Don't do this and don't do that." Well, it's hard because when a gig comes along and it's offered to you, and you have a chance to use your craft and your skills and do something other than waiting tables. And if it's in TV, why not?

DOES BEING A WOMAN IN THIS BUSINESS ENTER INTO THE EQUATION AT ALL?

I do know that, for me as a woman composer, sometimes there has been a request made, "We want a tape from a woman composer." That's been something that people say I should play up more. I should market myself because I'm a woman composer. I have yet to this day, to my face, been discriminated against because of that.

I think that 10 years ago, 15 years ago, there was much more a big deal made out of "Oh, so-and-so is a woman composer." So I do have to thank my predecessors for paving the way.

I think women sometimes get an edge because there are a lot of woman producers and directors out there. But it's still in this phase where some women directors and producers that have climbed up to a pretty high level don't want to be told they should use a woman composer. There's a little of this backlash. Once somebody recommended that I contact this particular woman composer, not Shirley Walker, and she was quite offended that this person said I should call her based on the fact that we're both women composers. She said something like, "What, why does he think I can do something for you just because I'm a woman?"

BUT THAT'S JUST A BACKLASH.

I don't even think about it that much. I think the bigger issue is your family life and how much time you dedicate to making your career happen versus living your life. I mean, at five o'clock, there's not a bell that rings and your career goes on hold. For me, family comes first.

DO YOU THINK THAT PROBLEMS EXIST IN A DIFFERENT DIMENSION FOR YOU AS A WOMAN THAN IT WOULD FOR MEN WITH FAMILIES?

It did more when my kids were babies. My children go to school now. It's a little different from when the kids were infants. I mean, who wants to take a breast pump to Warner Bros. for a session? And tell people you need to pump your milk during a ten-minute break. But I know session players who do it. It's part of life. There are things to consider. Marriage, having a healthy marriage has helped me a great deal. But it takes time. It takes maybe losing a gig here and there, or altering a plan to make it work. For example, during this last Christmas break I was orchestrating a television movie for David Benoit and the deadline kept getting moved. At first it was going to be right before Christmas, and everything would have been wrapped up nice and tidy so I could have my break. Well, it didn't happen that way. I took my Omnifax with me up to Portland to my parent's house. It was snowing the next day, and it was very surreal to be working where I grew up, and having this fax machine and a PowerBook with MIDI files. The kids are playing out in the snow, and Mom's in headphones trying to orchestrate some music and then fax it back to L.A. so it can get copied.

ARE YOU HAPPY WITH WHERE YOU ARE AT AS A COMPOSER?

A personal goal for me is to allow my voice to be heard, and to never stop learning and growing. I've had many great opportunities, and very few regrets. It is easy to sometimes disappear in the Hollywood film-music machine and to forget how wonderful it is to write music—just for the love of writing music.

As a composer it's important to let yourself write what comes to you, and write what inspires you. And not belittle that because people are telling you, "It has to be this way, it has to be that way. You should be doing this, or how can you do that?" You don't have to be what everybody tells you that you have to be. You choose much of your path, I believe.

This business is very exciting, and the people that discourage new composers or any composers that want to come out and give it a try, I think they're wrong. If you want to do it, you can do it. You just have to work really, really hard and be patient. And find little things along the way that will boost your spirits. There are plenty of little things out there, not just the big movies.

William Ross

William Ross is a composer whose work spans feature films, television, and the recording industry. He has composed music for films including *Tin Cup*, *My Fellow Americans*, *The Evening Star*, *The Little Rascals*, and the IMAX film *T-Rex*. His orchestration credits include *Forrest Gump*, *Contact*, *Mouse Hunt*, *The Bodyguard*, *Waiting to Exhale*, and *Father of the Bride*. He continues to work with a remarkable list of artists including Barbra Streisand, Celine Dion, Kenny G., David Foster, and Babyface.

HOW DID YOU DECIDE TO BECOME A FULL-TIME MUSICIAN AND ULTI-MATELY A FILM COMPOSER?

I grew up studying piano, and I was fascinated by it, but I never had any notion that you could do that for a living. My parents were very blue-collar, and from the wrong side of the tracks. The notion of making a living at anything other than work—hard work—was ridiculous. My Mom wanted me to go to college, and my Dad wanted me to go into the Merchant Marines and be the captain of a ship. I decided to go to UCSB where I was pre-med—I always had a fascination with sciences. But there was so much that went on with my life at college—socially, intellectually, personally—trying to figure out, "Oh, wait a minute, now I'm away from home, what is life about, how do I orient myself in this world and make confident decisions for myself in the present and future?" I just kind of broke down. I got to the point where I couldn't go to the labs anymore. The smell of ether just nauseated me. Chemistry class ... just the thought of it ...

I was playing blues piano at fraternities and having fun with it. But I got to the point where I was so unable to determine what step I should take next, that I almost had a nervous breakdown. I came to the conclusion that I have to do today what I really enjoy doing. It sounds like a weird approach, but that's how I got out of it. I didn't look much further beyond "today." Then the next day was great, and I just built on that, one day at a time.

I spoke to a counselor at the school, and knew that there wasn't much future in being a blues piano player. Eventually I switched my major to Anthropology, which is what I got my degree in. So, I'm licensed to dig up your bones!

How did you educate yourself and go from blues piano player to orchestrator?

Just because of the way my mind works, I'm kind of an analytical guy; my way of studying was to get scores and look at them and break them apart. And there was an interesting thing I found. One of the things composers in European conservatories had to do in the past was to be able to write certain key pieces by memory. Like a piece from the *Art of the Fugue* or *The Well-Tempered Clavier*. Many composers mention this thing: that the act of writing it down somehow transformed them. Prokofiev, Ravel, and Mendelssohn all mention it in their writings. Something happens when you are actually forced to sit and write it down; the information comes in and is ordered in a way that you mentally have access to it. When you just buy the book and stick it on your shelf, you don't get the same familiarity with it.

I strongly believe that there is a lot of benefit in trying to understand what has come before, what makes something a masterpiece, what makes something valuable to so many people over a long period of time. I would study anything I could get my hands on. Ravel, Beethoven.

338

I would also take a piece and make myself write something in that style. Ravel talks about taking a great piece as a model being a legitimate way to improve your abilities and skills. Find great pieces, use them as models, and they will pull you up to their level.

How did you get your first orchestration jobs?

Allyn Ferguson got me my first job arranging and conducting for Raquel Welch, and I started getting credits writing charts. I did whatever I could to study film scores in my spare time. My first job orchestrating was for *Dynasty*, a job which came through a friend. Then I hooked up with Dennis McCarthy and started working on *MacGyver*. What a school that was! Dennis was terrific. He would let you take the ball and run with it and compose the cues, and he'd give you full writing credit. So then I had composition and orchestration credit.

I started to get a reputation as a guy who could get the job done and not create problems. The name of the game is to be a problem solver, not a problem creator. That is what a film composer is looking for. The composer wants to be able to say, "I've got so much on my mind, if I can just hand this to this guy and know it's going to work," that's what they're all looking for. There's this giant level of trust. If you get on that list of people that are easy to get along with, does the job, is not a jerk, and can deliver, then your name gets around.

What is the process for you as an orchestrator?

After I get the call, usually the first step is that a meeting is set up. The challenge is to understand the composer's working style, and to figure out how I'm going to fit into that. The composer may know exactly what they want and hand me a sketch where I'm just going to just transfer the notes onto a different sheet of paper and send it to the copyist. Or they may really need a lot of help because they don't have an orchestral background and that's what they've been asked to do. The first thing is to identify what the job really is. That is a big part of it.

Once you identify what the job is, you have to figure out if this job is for you. Are you comfortable doing it? Your pay thing has to work out. Usually when you first start out, you're so glad to be in the meeting and get the credit that the pay is kind of meaningless. My recommendation is to get that taken care of ahead of time. It took me a long time to learn this, but there is nothing wrong with talking about the money.

LET'S TALK ABOUT YOUR COMPOSING PROCESS. DO YOU WRITE TO PAPER, OR ARE YOU SEQUENCING?

That depends on the nature of the score. I relate best to paper. My set-up at home has a lot of different areas to it. My central core is the piano, a piece of paper, and a pencil. I like a period of time when I can sit and germinate ideas, and think about it in an unhurried fashion. Ideally, a week is paradise. Sometimes you get more, most of the time you get less, depending on the schedules.

Those ideas filter through in various ways. I could use a piano, or synthesizers. Auricle is also a great tool, whether it's click or free timing. It's a great way to get the streamers to film. I also have this Erato system, which is a computerized notation system.

WHAT ABOUT THE "MOVE TO L.A." ISSUE FOR YOUNG COMPOSERS?

That's a tough one, and one that I address with a lot of empathy. Most people are driven to this business out of love for music and film; they're not out to get rich, at least when they start. It's a hard thing to come out here, with the uncertainties of the business, to uproot yourself, to challenge yourself. To me, anyone who does that is a success no matter what happens. I say that with utmost sincerity. I've had people call me after years of being out here, they had kicked around the business, they did the best they could, and they were out of money. Or just fed up. And it broke my heart to hear them say they were leaving, they were calling to say goodbye.

I think we are in a business where you are a person first, and somewhere down the line you are a composer. But the top of the list for me is what kind of person you are, how you treat people, do you get along with people. That's got to be in place. So I approach it from the human point of view. That being said, the reality is that most of the people in the business are here in Los Angeles. So it's really an unanswerable question.

Alan Silvestri

A lan Silvestri has provided a distinct melodic voice for many of Hollywood's most well-known films. Starting out as a guitar player, his first regular scoring gig was for the network television series, *CHiPs*. He received Oscar and Golden Globe nominations for his score to *Forrest Gump* and has scored over 60 films, including *Contact, Romancing the Stone, Who Framed Roger Rabbit?, The Bodyguard, Father of the Bride I* and *II, Practical Magic, The Parent Trap*, and the *Back to the Future* series.

How did you get started writing for films?

I had gone to Berklee, got a gig touring, and through a long series of chance events ended up in L.A. My first film happened because of a case of mistaken identity.

I was working with a lyricist as an arranger on a number of songs. He got called to do this film, *The Doberman Gang*, because the producers misread the credits (he was an academy-award nominated lyricist) and mistook him for a film composer. The lyricist in turn called me and asked if I was interested. I said yes, even though I knew nothing about film scoring. This was all happening really fast, and my meeting with the producers was the very next day. So I went out and bought Earl Hagen's book, *Scoring for Film*, and read it cover to cover that night. When I went to this meeting and we watched the film, I found that I had strong opinions about what the music should be. They liked my ideas, and I got the gig. I was a film composer!

My first big break came a few years later, when I came home one day and there was a message from a Harry Lojewski at MGM. So I called this man, a very nice guy, and I said, "What's up Mr. Lojewski?" He said, "Well, there's this show here at the studio, it's been around for a season, it showed promise, but we couldn't say that it did well and the people at the studio here want to take a different approach to it. They've hired a new staff, and they've asked me to find a young guy who can do the score for this show."

Now, this was in the middle of the disco craze, and I had rather long hair, I was about 28, I probably weighed about 120 lbs., I looked perfect. I looked perfect! I'm not some old establishment guy, or any of that; I'm a young guy who's a rhythm-section player.

It turns out that the show he was talking about was CHiPs. They really wanted to see if they could do a disco thing. So I wrote a score for that first episode of their second season—the one where they put Eric Estrada in a John Travolta suit and send him to the disco. Lo and behold, this show takes off almost immediately. I get a call from them that they want me to do the next three episodes, and this was like the end of the world to my wife Sandra and I because this is the closest thing to a steady job in show business that I've ever heard of. So that's how that all came about.

YOUR CONNECTION WITH ROBERT ZEMECKIS SEEMS TO BE VERY SPE-CIAL. HOW DID IT COME ABOUT?

Well, that's kind of interesting. I had done CHiPs for four years, and then it abruptly ended. I was out of work for almost a year, and was starting to go a little crazy. I did a couple of TV episodes for a show that the producers hated, and I started to wonder if I really was going to continue in this business.

In addition, I had a house, and a baby that literally had just arrived! Not only that, but when I got the news about them not caring for the music for the television show, my baby was in intensive care, and we were on the verge of losing her. I got the message while I was in the hospital, if that's not too dramatic for you.

So, after this year of nothing, I was thinking, "It can't get any worse than this." But I get a call one day about writing a piece of spec music for a new series at Warner Bros. I went to see the show, called *Blue Thunder*, and walked out of the theater realizing that I didn't even have a way to go about making a spec piece of music. I had a 2-track tape recorder. How could I even do this without spending a bunch of money? Money I didn't have. So the revelation was, if I'm going to try to make a go of this music thing, I need to find a way to show what I can do. At this point in the mid-'80s, things were just starting to happen in the electronic-music world.

My wife and I had a family meeting, and we decided that I should go out and buy the latest technology: a DX-7, which had only been out a few months and came with a Japanese manual, an 8-track tape recorder, and a Linn drum machine.

So now I've got these three pieces of gear, and one Friday afternoon the phone rings. It's Tom Carlin, who was the music editor on CHiPs. He says, "Al, would you be interested in doing something on spec?" I said, "Absolutely." He then says, "Okay, here's the deal. These guys have a movie. They've listened to a lot of tapes of people, and they still haven't found anything that they feel really works for them. If you'd be interested to try something, then let me introduce you to somebody. The director is a guy named Bob Zemeckis and the film is called *Romancing the Stone*."

So Zemeckis told me about this one scene where they are running through the jungle and it's raining and they're trying to get away from the Federales. I got off the phone, I walked into my new studio. What I had staring in front of me was an 8-track machine, a Linn Drum machine, a DX-7. I'm not a piano player. I had no board to mix with, no work-print to see the film, and I had to bring them a tape the next morning!

I spent all night on this; I actually mixed it by making the RCA cables longer if I wanted a certain track softer. I didn't have to get up the next morning, because it *was* morning, and all I had to do is walk out to the car. I got to the studio and the first thing that happened was that Tom wanted to listen to the cassette, because he had recommended me, now he's on the line. Next thing I know, Bob Zemeckis marches in with his editor. The great coincidence in this story is that Bob and I were wearing the identical Calvin Klein sweater. It was kind of like an omen. It was the beginning of what I consider to be one of my great friendships.

DID THEY OFFER YOU THE GIG RIGHT THEN AND THERE?

No. Michael Douglas, who starred and produced the movie, called me that night. He asked me to send a demo reel. It's kind of interesting that when you're doing this job, you're selling your product, but you're also selling yourself. What counts the most is the impression that people have of you, the level of trust that they have in you, and everything else that goes with it.

The second I hung up the phone that night I realized that I had failed Marketing 101. Even though I felt incredibly empowered and confident that I could get work with my new gear to demo stuff, I was still going up against guys that had more impressive credit sheets and recording histories. I understood, at that point, that the phone call wasn't enough, what I needed to do was get into a room with Michael. That was my only hope.

I somehow got in touch with him, and told him I was going to be nearby Fox the next day and could drop the tape off, as opposed to sending it. He said, "Well, what time are you coming by Fox tomorrow." And I said, "Anytime you want!" Now, Michael is the kind of guy who appreciates somebody who's trying to extend himself for something that he really wants. He said "Okay Al, why don't you come to my office at 11 o'clock tomorrow." So that's what I did. I walked in and brought these tapes. Michael was incredibly gracious to me, and we had the meeting, but the most important thing was that I got to be in the room with him. Whether it was that afternoon or the following day, I don't remember, but the call came through, and I was hired by Michael Douglas to do *Romancing the Stone.*

That is a really interesting cue from several perspectives. The start of that cue was a decision. Many people, including myself, may have started that cue when we first saw the bad boys, they may have started that cue when the rock hit Forrest's head, they may have started that cue after Jenny said, "Run." I didn't want to just jump in there with music. It deserved more than that. So, the question really was, What's this cue ultimately going to be about?" Well, that cue is ultimately about the celebration of someone who thought they had an infirmity, and to their surprise, they discovered that they didn't. When you consider what to do with the music on that level, all bets are off on the obvious stuff.

The cue basically comes in out of nowhere. He's already started to run, but that's okay because this isn't a running cue; this is a cue about the awakening of a realization in Forrest that something he thought was an infirmity, in fact, doesn't exist. Of course, we as an audience are seeing what's going on, we're seeing that this kid can move, we're seeing the braces come off, and we're way ahead of the game. We are getting all this, and were are smart folks. So, the music isn't about the audience seeing that this kid's gonna be able to run without braces; the music is about this kid discovering that he's already been running, and he doesn't need the braces. That's really the emotional release of this whole thing.

That's why the big musical moment has to be on the shot where he looks up with a smile that would just knock people down from coast to coast; this kid has just realized that he does not have this infirmity. That's when we start to celebrate. Boom, we blow the top off of it right then and there. Everything to that point has been a build-up to his awakening to that realization. Physically, then we cut back to the adult Forrest on the bench, and he says, "From that day on, if I was going somewhere, I was running!"

THERE'S A CUE IN CONTACT, WHEN SHE FIRST HEARS THE "SOUND," AND SHE ARRIVES IN THE LAB. AT THAT POINT, THE MUSIC FADES OUT TO SILENCE AND IT'S VERY EFFECTIVE.

That cue in the lab starts to wind down with the physical action. She arrives in the room after frantically driving back to the lab and running up the stairs. She's not running anymore, but the tension is still there. We're building to the moment where we first hear the signal in the lab. So, the music has been very active while she is driving and running, but gradually chills out when she returns to the room with her colleagues and all those computers.

SO YOU'RE TALKING ABOUT CONTRAST HERE.

Contrast, absolutely. That's one of the things that you have to understand about silence. Silence is like any other sense perception, whether it's sight, taste, touch, sound, or whatever it is. If those organs are being stimulated, they are less responsive to a more subtle stimulation. So this is a perfect example. If we are about to introduce a character, and in this case "the sound" is an authentic character, we don't want people's auditory sensibilities to shut down before the introduction.

WHAT ARE THE QUALITIES OF A GREAT FILM COMPOSER?

A film composer needs to understand that this is not music for its own sake, but it is music for a collaborative art. For me, a great film composer is always someone who not only has musical talent, but also a talent for telling a story with music. This is what makes film scoring a unique musical expression. It's all about how the composer can assist the telling of the story as well as write great music.

Mark Snow

Mark Snow is an eclectic composer who has become most well known for his music to the *X-Files* television series. His music for *X-Files* has been nominated for two Emmy's, which bring his total number of nominations—for both orchestral and electronic scores—to eight. Since moving to L.A. in 1974, Mark has scored over 70 television movies, as well as hundreds of weekly episodes for shows such as *Millennium, Hart To Hart,* and *Crazy Like a Fox.*

LET'S TALK A BIT LITTLE BIT ABOUT WHAT GOT YOU INTERESTED IN FILM SCORING.

I went to Juilliard where the oboe was my major instrument and the composing was just something off to the side. But I was very much interested in modern music—this is in the '60s in New York. I never thought about film music as being a good place for really out-there music; I thought it was all songs and schmaltzy love themes and stuff. Then I heard Jerry Goldsmith's *Planet of the Apes* score, which was 12-tone or avant-garde, and way out there for its time. That was really exciting to me and I thought, "Oh man, this is great, I want to do this." I loved that music and that was really the beginning of my interest in it.

SO HOW DID YOU MAKE THE LEAP FROM BEING A STUDENT AT A CON-SERVATORY TO ENDING UP WRITING FOR FILM AND TV?

Well, my roommate in high school and Juilliard was Michael Kamen, and we put together this rock 'n roll band called the New York Rock and Roll Ensemble that played classical music and rock 'n roll. Not a group like Procol Harem, where they combined both styles—we'd play just straight classical and straight rock 'n roll. It was a big deal at the time.

I played drums and oboe in the band, and Michael played keyboard and oboe. We had five albums out. We stayed together for five years, never really had a hit record and weren't one of the big bands, but it was a fun five years. The important thing is that during that time, we all got to hear more about pop music and the music business, and I felt I had much more in me than just being a player. My wife's family was in the business; some of them still are. She suggested, "Why don't we go out to California, and they could introduce you to people, and you could do your thing out there?" So, I decided to take a chance. I had no job in California, nothing, maybe a thousand dollars. We took our two kids, piled into a car, and when we got to California her father helped us out a little bit. Six months after I got there, I got a job doing an episode of a TV series called *The Rookies*. That's where it started for me. I did another episode, and another one, and then I worked a lot for Aaron Spelling in the early days.

How did you learn the technical stuff?

Well, first of all, these were the days before anything electronic. No computers were ever happening then. This was click tracks, frames per minute, Moviolas—no videotape, and really detailed spotting notes. I was able to meet some other composers through some friends and they told me what was up with this stuff and how it's done. I remember my first scoring session. I made all the typical mistakes that newcomers do, where you write all these fragments. When you're starting off, you're so nervous about doing a good job that you think you have to catch all the action. So it sounds like a bad temp score where it's just these little fragments all over the place. That's what separates the men from the boys, when you can write a good piece of music that makes linear sense and also works with the picture.

So it took me a while to get that concept. I overwrote way too much and I was actually fired off a few jobs, which really made me think, What the hell am I doing wrong? I realized there are many, many more approaches than my limited ones at the time, and I started listening like crazy to other film composers and TV composers. That really opened my mind to try new things. I think that was a very important part of my development.

IT SOUNDS ALMOST LIKE YOU NEEDED TO GET FIRED OFF THOSE JOBS AND TAKE A LOOK AROUND.

Absolutely, that's right, because I was getting comfortable and complacent and people were telling me, "You're the greatest." And then one day some producer comes in, he hears it and says, "This sucks, we're getting someone else, you're out!" So, it was a really great learning experience and a good wake-up call.

HOW DO YOU RELATE WITH DIRECTORS AND PRODUCERS WHO ARE NOT MUSICALLY KNOWLEDGEABLE?

In the mid '80s the home studio thing was just starting up, and I bought a Synclavier. When that happened, it was a magical, wonderful learning experience for me because then people could come over and hear the score and make their comments. I learned so much from these people who know nothing about music. It didn't matter that they weren't musicians; they were talking about the drama and the emotional elements of the story. They would say, "Take this out, oh no that's fine, but take out the piano, or try it without the bass," and I would say to myself, "That won't work." Then I'd look at it again and say, "Oh my God, he's right, that's great!" So these people who came in and told me; "I don't know anything about music, but ..."—it never ticked me off. I always thought I could learn something from these guys.

SO, YOU REALLY LEARNED TO LISTEN TO OTHER PEOPLE EVEN IF INITIALLY YOU HAD A DIFFERENT POINT OF VIEW?

Yes. My personality in general is very cooperative and collaborative. I wasn't one with some huge ego who would tell people they were wrong, and it had to be my way. It was important for me to make the people feel comfortable, and that I would basically be doing what they wanted me to do. I might have gone a little over-board in that department when I was younger but it served me well at the time. The wonderful thing about what I'm doing now is that there is much more respect. They now ask me what I think, and often defer to that.

WHAT IS YOUR COMPOSING PROCESS?

With the *X-Files* and this *Millennium* show I do, I just sit here and basically improvise with the picture. These improvisations start to take shape, I start to add more instruments so it sounds less like an improvisation and more like a thought-out piece of music, but noth-ing is written down. I feel very comfortable with it, the results have been very good, it seems to get better all the time, and people dig it.

DO YOU START WITH A MUSICAL IDEA FOR EACH EPISODE THAT YOU FOLLOW THROUGH? DO YOU SCORE THE FIRST SCENE FIRST?

Most of the time, I actually score the last scene first because it seems to have the most music in it and the most stuff going on. It is usually a full piece with different themes and different rhythms and so on. Then I can pull that apart and go backwards and start at the beginning with smaller variations of that big piece. Usually, the last act of these things tends to be more active and more fleshed out dramatically, so then when you do that, it's easier to go backwards and pull things out

WHAT WAS THE CREATION OF THE X-FILES THEME LIKE?

With the *X-Files* theme, Chris Carter, who is very much of a con-trol guy, wanted input on this. He sent over a ton of CDs, a very eclectic group of CDs—rock 'n roll, Philip Glass, classical, jazz, rock—and told me exactly what he liked in each one.

So I did a first version that was okay, but looking back on it, I'd say this is was too predictable, nothing special, kind of loud and fast. Chris gave his feedback, and I tweaked it. So this happened two or three more times. He was very nice, but not quite satisfied, and I wasn't too happy with it either, so I finally said, "Listen, let me just try something on my own. Why don't you go away for a few days and let me see what I can come up with." That's when it started to happen. I put my hand on the keyboard, I had that Echoplex sound. It was there by accident and it sounded like a good accompaniment thing. I knew he didn't like harmony, I knew he liked very minimal sounding things, so I just put this bed, that accompaniment rhythm underneath. I had a melody and was searching for something really weird or interesting, or anti-thematic, whatever you want to call it. I tried every kind of voice imaginable, I tried woodwinds, saxes, guitars, and came upon this whistle thing for the melody, and it seemed just perfect.

DO YOU GET A LOT OF SATISFACTION OUT OF THIS KIND OF SHOW?

I do actually, because the shows are so great. *X-Files* has done so well, it's like doing a mini-movie, and no one tells me not to do anything, so I keep trying. I get a new sandbox, I try new stuff. I'll buy a CD of samples of crazy things, I try it. I got one the other day of nothing but gongs. All kinds of gongs, processed gongs, electronic gongs …

DO YOU HAVE ADVICE FOR YOUNG COMPOSERS JUST STARTING OUT?

The most important thing is a love for it, a fascination, a desire, a love and feel for music. It takes someone who is passionate about film music, who can go to a movie and hear how some music works with the picture and just think, Oh God, that is so cool, I wanna do it. That's the first thing. The second thing—if you have any relatives who know anyone—that's the next part. And if you don't have that, you just go to where the work is, and unfortunately, it's in ugly Hollywood. You knock on every door and you're merciless, you keep persevering like crazy and pray, and one out of ten guys who come to town make it. I don't know, maybe 1 out of 100. Maybe 1 out of 4. I don't know what the exact ratio is but it's not that promising, which is the reality. So just having the desire or being super-talented is not necessarily going to do it. It's having that, plus some good luck and some good breaks.

Photo: Portrait Elegance by Maureeen © 1998-99

Richard Stone

Winner of five Emmy awards for his television music, Richard Stone is best known for his themes and background scores for Warner Bros. cartoons *Animaniacs, Pinky and the Brain,* and the *Sylvester and Tweety Mysteries.* After receiving a degree in music from the University of Indiana, he migrated to Los Angeles and worked as orchestrator and music editor for many film and television projects, including *Witness, Agnes of God, Ferris Bueller's Day Off,* and *Pretty in Pink.*

How did you get started in scoring for animation?

I started out as a music editor, and learned on the way. I did some ghost writing and orchestrating at the same time as I was editing, and I gradually got my feet wet. Then around 1990, *Tiny Toons* was starting up. Bruce Broughton gave me a chance to score one of those, and I've been working exclusively at Warner Brothers ever since.

I became a supervising composer at Warner Bros., and *Tiny Toons* was eventually succeeded by *Animaniacs, Pinky and the Brain, Freakazoid,* and *The Sylvester and Tweety Mysteries.* Now we're doing a show called *Histeria.*

Let's talk about your process from when you first receive the show right up to the recording session.

It's like anything else. We still sit with the producer and have a spotting session. In our case, the music is wall-to-wall; it's not a case of where the music starts and stops, as it would be in a feature film or a live action television show. In our shows the music never stops. The question is always about musical style and what specific things we're going to hit, how loudly, and with what instrumentation. We might talk about which public domain tunes we will use.

The style we use is an extension of Carl Stalling's animation style that he started in the '30s and '40s. I've done a lot of research and study of his work. They have a lot of his scores at the USC archive where they keep old things from Warner Bros. So what we do is an outgrowth of his style that tries to stay in sync with as many things on screen as we can: characters walking across the screen with pizzicato celli and a bassoon, if a boulder falls on somebody it will have a piano glissando on it, the xylophone eye-blink, and all the rest of those clichés. We also try to do musical puns with folk songs—PD tunes that we can use. We quote from the classical literature all the time.

WHAT IS THE SCHEDULE LIKE ON THESE SHOWS?

We have about two weeks to write 20 minutes of music. I say "we" because I can't do this all myself; I supervise a team of composers. If everybody is healthy, each person can manage between two to four minutes per day. We all either work at home or in rented offices.

We get timing notes from the music editor via e-mail. Most of us use the *Cue* software for timing notes. We also use *Performer*. I will take timing notes written in *Cue*, and create a tempo map, which is a specific tempo and a bar layout with meter changes, if necessary. I then export that as a MIDI file and bring it back up in *Performer*. Then I watch it in sync to the video with an audible click-track so I can hear the dialogue and the click while I watch the scene. As I watch it, the music starts to appear in my head and I'll write it out on a six- to eight-line sketch that is very specific as to instrumentation. I write out every note, every voicing; it is an elaborate sketch. Then I'll fax that sketch to the orchestrator who will write out each individual part on a full score. He sends that to the copyist, and then we have the recording session.

HOW IS THIS PROCESS DIFFERENT FROM THE WAY CARL STALLING WOULD HAVE WORKED FIFTY YEARS AGO?

Aside from the technology and the fact that he had an office on the lot at Warner Bros. where he went every day, the musical process is not different at all. He sat at a piano. Most people don't know this, but he never saw the cartoon he was scoring. He scored from exposure sheets. These sheets laid out the action on paper. The director would decide, for instance, how fast a character was walking, and would have this very elaborate sheet saying, for example, "Daffy is walking across the street taking a step every eight frames." This information would be copied onto the exposure sheet giving Stalling a description of all the action and the frame measurements of all the action. That is what he wrote to.

In addition, all the tempos that he used were in even frames because they ran from an optical click loop, and if you look at his scores most of them will say 10-0, 8-0, 12-0, whatever.

WHEN YOU HAVE AS MANY AS 30 OR 40 HITS IN A 30-SECOND CUE, HOW DO YOU HANDLE THAT, BOTH MUSICALLY AND IN TERMS OF THE CLICK?

I often use a variable click. The art of writing for animation is in keeping the music musical, and still hitting the things that need to be hit without being choppy. I've found that sometimes in an effort to hit everything, people come out with something that is meaningless mush. Then it's not entertaining anymore. It becomes like musical sound-effects and that's what you don't want to do.

What you want to do is create a cue to be a piece of music with a beginning, a middle, and an end where every note means something. This will depend on the way things are animated. For instance, if a character gets hit on the head with twelve anvils one after another, they will usually be evenly spaced apart—each anvil hit will be 8, 10, 12 frames apart. You can take the rhythm of that and make it into a piece of music. That's a trick that you can use to make the music really live.

SO, YOU ARE ACTUALLY COMPOSING FORWARD AND BACKWARD FROM ONE PIVOTAL MOMENT?

Yes, that is one possibility. But you can also design your cues so that the start of your new cue is on the first anvil hit, for instance. This will make it even more in sync.

WHAT IS IT LIKE TO BE THE SUPERVISING COMPOSER OVERSEEING A WHOLE TEAM OF PEOPLE?

I have the advantage of being able to cast each segment according to each composer's strength. For instance, some composers handle adventure better than comedy. The disadvantage is that I have to take the responsibility for every cue, whether it works for the producer or not. But I have had the privilege of working with the best group of composers in the universe!

At the peak, when we had three or four different series going, we had five or six composers working steadily, as well as orchestrators. It's actually very similar to the old "studio system," where someone like Max Steiner would have an office at Warner Bros. right near the scoring stage, and next to him would be other composers and orchestrators. What we do today is the closest thing to that, including our wonderful orchestra, who, although they are not under contract as in the old days, are basically the same people week after week.

HOW DOES THE MUSIC ON SOME OF THE OTHER CARTOON SHOWS TODAY DIFFER FROM WHAT YOU DO?

Well, for example, on *Superman* or *Batman*, they don't approach those shows as a comedic cartoon. That's why it works so well, it's very serious business. They choose what they are going to hit very carefully, much the way you would in scoring a feature. Similarly, the people that do the big Disney features, even the comedies, are not hitting eye-blinks. They are painting with a much broader brush.

WHAT ADVICE DO YOU HAVE FOR THE BEGINNING FILM COMPOSER?

My advice is familiar: compose, compose, compose! Have your
music recorded whatever way possible. Score student films, plays,
local commercial spots, anything. It also helps to befriend a working composer and try to arrange a situation where you're assisting
him or her in some way. You can also learn a lot simply by hanging
out at recording sessions.

Photo: Dana Ross Photo

Shirley Walker

Shirley Walker began her film music career as orchestrator, conductor, and synthesist on such films as *Apocalypse Now*, *Batman*, *Days of Thunder*, *A League of Their Own*, *Backdraft*, *The Black Stallion*, and *True Lies*. She has gone on to compose original music for films such as *Escape From L.A.*, *Turbulence*, and *Batman: Mask of the Phantasm*. Walker has written the scores to many television movies and series, including *Batman*, *Superman*, *China Beach*, and *Space: Above and Beyond*.

YOU BEGAN AS A CONCERT AND JAZZ PIANIST AND YOU HAVE A CLASSICAL MUSIC BACKGROUND. HOW DID YOU GET INVOLVED IN FILM COMPOSING?

My very first film experience was industrial scores. And it was fascinating to me. The whole concept of putting music to image was something I just lusted for. I certainly didn't know what I was doing. I didn't have any craft back then. I just had my raw ability as a person who could imagine and create. Because of my training, I knew how to work with other instruments. So I didn't have any problems of getting a recording session done.

DID THAT FIRST PROJECT GO SMOOTHLY?

It was just unbelievable that somebody was going to pay me money to record the music for the film. There was one problem, though. I didn't know it could help to play the music for him in advance of the session, and he didn't know to ask me anything about what it was going to sound like. And at first, the director just hated it. He didn't want to tell me at that time because we were friends and he had been coming regularly to my jazz-trio gig in Haight Ashbury. Then he listened to a cassette of the score for about a week, and he fell passionately in love with it—he just couldn't stop listening to it. He told me all of this way after the fact—how when he heard the way the music sounded he just couldn't imagine it working for the film. Then he finally saw it all put together, and just thought that it was wonderful.

WHAT WAS YOUR MUSICAL TRAINING?

My high-school band teacher had me writing for our jazz band. He also had me transcribing stuff. Count Basie arrangements. Oscar Peterson and Art Tatum solos. What wonderful training. Then I went to San Francisco State College for two years and studied classical composition and performance, but I was too shy for college! Of course, things have progressed since then, or I certainly couldn't be doing what I am doing now.

WHAT HAPPENED AFTER THAT FIRST INDUSTRIAL FILM?

I did some other projects like that, some jingles, and continued playing. My big break was doing some synthesizer stuff and orchestrating for the Francis Ford Coppola projects *Apocalypse Now* and *The Black Stallion*. Then there was a chain of events where one person led to another. On the Coppola projects I met Dan Carlin, Jr., who was conducting the orchestra for some of the stuff I had written. He introduced me to an agent, and I ended up on a TV series. I was very, very fortunate.

HOW DO YOU FEEL ABOUT SYNTHESIZERS TODAY?

If you want to work in the business today, you have to have some technology. There's no way around it unless you're way at the top of things and you just hire it.

I enjoy it now because I finally have gotten good enough with the sequencers and the recording technology to where I can create electronic music that has the same kind of emotional whole that I know how to get with a live orchestra. But I hated it until I got it to this point. At first, I was anti-technology. I resented the notion that I had acquired all these skills as a creative music being, and then here's this whole other thing that comes along that I don't know anything about. People who had those toys were making inroads on the turf that I was establishing myself on. So I had years and years of resenting technology. Now I'm more comfortable.

DO YOU ALWAYS DO MOCK-UPS?

That's such a fascinating area because every film production group that you work with has had different experiences with the mock-ups. For some people, I sit at the piano, I play and sing, and that's enough for them. Other people want to look at every single note. I play a fully-orchestrated sequence for them, and they go, "What's that thing that sounds like an organ, we're not going to have an organ here, are we?" Of course, it's just a synth string pad, and then you've got to talk them through the music.

Here is a good story: I was doing *Turbulence* with producer David Valdez. When we finally got to the scoring stage, on the first day he turned to me and said, "You know, whoever's been inventing those synthesizers should just be shot." And then he explained how scary it was for him to come out to my studio, listen to the mock-ups of the cues, and feel it was kind of okay, but he was not really sure. Then when he heard it with the orchestra, he was so relieved because it sounded as good as he had hoped it would.

When I've worked with someone a lot, they learn to trust me. They know what my dramatic instincts are and we have a vocabulary with each other. Once someone has a good experience with a composer, it's so much easier. It all comes back to the comfort and trust level in your relationship.

WHAT WAS IT LIKE WORKING WITH JOHN CARPENTER, A DIRECTOR WHO IS ALSO A MUSICIAN?

He's very knowledgeable about music in many styles, not just the one that he himself can play. When we did *Escape from L.A.*, he originally did the guitar and the synthesis. After the pressure of shooting and editing the film, it's a way for him of almost decompressing. He likes to get in and musically work with the film. So a lot of the cues were done at his home studio on his synthesizers, and then we redid them with the studio synth guys.

On *Memoirs of an Invisible Man*, it was going to be a total orchestral score. He is not totally comfortable or interested in working in that medium, so that was 100% mine.

WHAT IS YOUR PREFERENCE IN TERMS OF COMING ON THE PROJECT? DO YOU LIKE TO BE INVOLVED AT THE SCRIPT LEVEL?

I look forward to the time when I go in while they're shooting, and then write stuff based on the script. Working on some ideas with some themes as we go along. Some of the people that I've worked with really like that idea.

My favorite way to write for a film is when I get to watch something, and then without the picture, just sitting down and working with whatever emotion I take away from that experience. That becomes my raw material. In the Batman feature length cartoon, *Mask of the Phantasm*, I got to see some test footage from the animation houses—sequences that were not yet assembled into the final film. I just wrote thematic material for scenes I knew were going to take place.

DO YOU SKETCH AND ORCHESTRATE YOURSELF?

I don't transfer my orchestrations to the conductor's score. But when I'm writing, I'm putting everything in—all the dynamics, the phrasing, percussion—everything, it's all there. So I don't physically orchestrate myself, but my sketches are very complete.

WHAT IS IT LIKE SUPERVISING THE BATMAN AND SUPERMAN CARTOONS?

It has been an interesting process on the *Batman* show. From the beginning, I was establishing the musical style of the series. I wrote the first several shows myself just to get the whole thing up and going. I also wrote the themes for the major characters. So for the first number of years of *Batman*, any main theme was mine.

Ultimately all of the composers that are in the rotation now worked their way up from orchestrating on the shows I was writing. Then they got to write a few cues, then maybe a half of the show, and then finally I would give them a whole show of their own. So it's a great way to reward the people who really paid their dues. This season, we started doing *Batman* electronically, but I'm still involved with basically the same team. I like to go to the spotting, and I look at their show once they've got everything on its way. We go through every cue and make sure that there's not a misread somewhere, or something that I think could be handled in a different way. But the composers working for me now are excellent, and it is satisfying to see how they've all come along in their careers.

WHAT IS YOUR ADVICE FOR YOUNG COMPOSERS JUST STARTING OUT?

There's career success, and there's personal, human success. They aren't mutually exclusive, but parallel trains of thought that can both be happening in someone's life. If you focus on career success, you're going to keep your total concentration on, "How do I get myself hired?" You're going to find some way to associate with young film makers that you relate to artistically. You will always be out meeting people, going to film festivals, film schools; you get involved in everything they are doing, whether it's performance art, or theater, or films. You're not concerned so much about your skills; you look at each job as it comes up, and figure out how to do it.

For personal success, you may have some interest in developing your craft, and learning how to compose for film. Then you're going have an educational stream that comes into your life, and you're going to start your research. You're going to look at scores, listen to soundtracks, and note who's doing them. You're going to read everything that you can, and you're going to go to libraries or places where they have film scores. Then you'll be able to put together what you're seeing on a page with what you're hearing. You will develop an enormous respect for the traditions that have gotten the art to where it is today.

END NOTES

Chapter 1
—1.1. Smith, Steven C. *A Heart at Fire's Center*. Berkeley, CA: University of California Press, 1991. Page 122.

Chapter 2
—2.1. Prendergast, Roy M. *Film Music, A Neglected Art*. New York, NY: W.W. Norton & Co. 1977, 1992. Page 23.

Chapter 3
—3.1. Lumet, Sidney. *Making Movies*. New York, NY: Vintage Books, 1996. Page 171.
—3.2. Prendergast, 35.
—3.3. *USA Today*. 12/28/98.
—3.4. Prendergast, 30 to 31.

Chapter 5
—5.1. *Film Music* [Magazine].
—5.2. Prendergast, 122.

Chapter 7
—7.1. Seger, Linda, and Edward Jay Whetmore. *From Script to Screen*. New York, NY: Henry Holt and Company. 1994. Page 1.
—7.2. Seger, 64.
—7.3. Seger, 129.
—7.4. Seger, 129.

Chapter 8
—8.1. Seger, 138.

Chapter 15
—15.1. Baird, Stuart. *Film Music* [Magazine]. February, 1999. Page 37.

Chapter 17
—17.1. Thomas, Tony. *Music for the Movies*. South Brunswick, NJ: A.S. Barnes, 1973. Page 98.

Chapter 19
—19.1. *Boston Globe*, 2/21/99.
—19.2. *Boston Globe*, 2/21/99.

Chapter 20
—20.1. Campbell, Don. *The Mozart Effect*. New York, NY: Avon Books, 1997. Page 11.

Chapter 21
—21.1. Prendergast, 157.
—21.2. Prendergast, 157.

RESOURCES

U.S. Copyright Office, Register of Copyrights

Copyright Office
Library of Congress
Washington, DC 20559
Information: (202) 707-3000
Forms request line: (202) 707-9100

Performing Rights Societies

ASCAP (LA)
7920 Sunset Blvd. Suite 300
Los Angeles, CA 90046
(213) 883-1000
ASCAP (NY)
1 Lincoln Plaza
New York, NY 10023
(212) 621-6000
ASCAP (Nashville)
Two Music Square West
Nashville, TN
(615) 742-5000
BMI (LA)
8730 Sunset Blvd. 3rd floor
Los Angeles, CA 90069
(310) 659-9109
BMI (NY)
320 W. 57th Street
New York, NY 10019
(212) 586-2000
BMI (Nashville)
10 Music Square East
Nashville, TN 37203
(615) 291-6700
SESAC (NY)
421 W. 54th Street
New York, NY 10019
(212) 586-3450
SESAC (Nashville)
55 Music Square East
Nashville, TN 37203
(6115) 320-0055

Composer and Songwriter Organizations

Society of Composers and Lyricists (SCL)
400 South Beverly Drive Suite 214
Beverly Hills, CA 90212
(310) 281-2812

Film Music Network
(818) 771-7778 (LA)
(212) 592-3600 (NY)
www.filmmusic.net

Songwriters Guild of America (SGA)
6430 Sunset Blvd
Hollywood, CA 90028
(213) 462-1108

National Academy of Songwriters (NAS)
6381 Hollywood Blvd. Suite 780
Hollywood, CA 90028
(213) 463-7178

Nashville Songwriters Association International (NSAI)
15 Music Square West
Nashville, TN 37203
(615) 256-3354

Publications

Film Music Magazine
114 N. Central Avenue
Glendale, CA 91202
(888) 678-6158
www.filmmusicmag.com

Film Music Monthly

Education and College Programs in Film Scoring

Berklee College of Music (undergraduate degree program)
1140 Boylston Street
Boston, MA 12215
(617) 266-1400

USC (one year graduate program, certificate)
Graduate Studies Director
(213) 740-3211

North Carolina School of the Arts (Masters program)
School of Music
200 Waughtown Street
P.O. Box 12189
Winston-Salem, NC 27117-2189
(910) 770-3255

UCLA Extension (part-time film scoring courses)
(310) 825-9971

Web Sites

Film Music Network and Film Music Magazine
www.filmmusic.net
Film Music Society
(formerly The Society for the Preservation of Film Music)
www.filmmusicsociety.org/
Society of Composers and Lyricists
www.filmscore.org/
Film Score Monthly
www.filmscoremonthly.com/
ASCAP
www.ascap.com/
BMI
www.bmi.com/home.html

INDEX

• ABOUT THE AUTHOR

Richard Davis is an educator, composer, orchestrator, record producer, performing musician, and author. His film credits include orchestrations and transcriptions for *Robin Hood, Prince of Thieves, The Last Boy Scout,* and *The Fall Guy*; original music for *Monsters, The Cyclist,* and others.

Photo: Mark Babushkin

He has performed with John Denver, Phylicia Rashad, Betty Buckley, Lulu, and Illinois Jacquet. Richard studied composition with Daniel Kessner and Aurelio de la Vega. He is currently an Associate Professor of Film Scoring at Berklee College of Music.

These books feature material developed at the Berklee College of Music

Visit www.berkleepress.com

GUITAR GENERAL INSTRUCTION

A Modern Method for Guitar
by William Leavitt
A practical and comprehensive guitar method in three volumes, designed for the serious student and used as the basic text for the Berklee College of Music guitar program.

Volume 1: Beginner
Guitar and music fundamentals, scales, melodic studies, chord and arpeggio studies, and more.
50449404 Book/CD $22.95

Volume 2: Intermediate
Further study of melody, scales, arpeggios, chords, intervals, chord voicings, improvisation, and rhythm guitar technique.
50449412 Book/Cassette....................................$22.95

Volume 3: Advanced
Includes advanced techniques relating to scales, arpeggios, rhythm guitar, chord/scale relationships, chord construction and voicings.
50449420 Book...$14.95

A Modern Method for Guitar – Volumes 1, 2, 3 Complete
by William Leavitt
Now you can have all three volumes of this classic guitar method in one convenient book. This new book is a complete compilation of the original volumes 1, 2 and 3. Perfect for the serious guitar student and instructor alike.
50449068 Book...$29.95

Berklee Basic Guitar – Phase I
by William Leavitt
An ideal method for the beginning guitar student or guitar class. Technique and reading skills are developed through two-, three-, and four-part ensemble arrangements. An introduction to chords is also included.
50449462 Book/Cassette....................................$14.95

Berklee Basic Guitar – Phase II
by William Leavitt
Building on Phase 1, Phase 2 moves on to solos, two- and three-part ensemble arrangements of music by Bach, Foster, Leavitt, Schumann, and others.
50449470 Book...........$7.95

GENERAL INSTRUCTION

The Reading Drummer
by Dave Vose
Ideal for all drummers interested in learning how to read drum music. A logical sequence of rhythms and drumming patterns with study hints and general practice tips.
50449458 Book $8.95

A Modern Method for Keyboard
by James Progris
Learn how to sight read, develop technical facility, and sharpen your knowledge of harmonic motion, effective chord voicing, and patterns of contemporary chord progression.
50449620 Book – Volume 1 ....$10.95
50449630 Book – Volume 2 ....$10.95
50449640 Book – Volume 3 ....$10.95

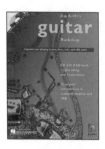  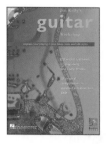 

JIM KELLY'S GUITAR WORKSHOP SERIES

Jim Kelly's Guitar Workshop products are an integrated, interactive, instructional approach to helping guitarists improve their playing through songs and studies in jazz, blues, Latin, R&B, and more. The songs that Jim Kelly has written for this series are designed to help you learn how to play in the style of guitar greats like Jeff Beck, Kenny Burrell, Mike Stern, Pat Metheny, Wes Montgomery, Joe Pass, Stevie Ray Vaughan, and others. Listen to Jim capture the sound of these players, and then use the play-along tracks to develop your own approaches.

With full-band and play-along tracks, learn how to phrase your own solos in new ways by using the techniques of master guitar players.

Valuable to players at all levels, the strong melodies and chord changes are fun to listen to and learn. Jim and his band knock-out each tune so you can hear how it sounds featuring quartet and trio tracks with alto sax, acoustic and electric guitars, bass, and drums. The books provide you with traditional lead sheet music notation and guitar tablature, including style, tempo, form, fingerings, song description, as well as commentary, hints, tips, approach, and practice ideas.

Jim Kelly's Guitar Workshop DVD
63003162 DVD/Booklet......................................$29.95

Jim Kelly's Guitar Workshop
00695230 Book/CD...$14.95

More Guitar Workshop by Jim Kelly
00695306 Book/CD...$14.95

Jim Kelly's Guitar Workshop Video
00320144 Video/Booklet $19.95

More Guitar Workshop Video, by Jim Kelly
00320158 Video/Booklet $19.95

BUSINESS GUIDES

The Self-Promoting Musician
by Peter Spellman
From the Director of Career Development at Berklee College of Music, learn how to become a success in the music business. Complete with tips for writing business plans and press kits; business know-how; using the Internet to promote music; customizing demos for maximum exposure; getting music played on college radio; and a comprehensive musician's resource list.
50449423 Book...$24.95

Complete Guide to Film Scoring
by Richard Davis

Learn the art and business of film scoring, including: the film-making process; preparing and recording a score; contracts and fees; publishing, royalties, and copyrights. Features interviews with 19 film-scoring professionals.

50449417 Book $24.95

Melody in Songwriting
by Jack Perricone

Learn the secrets to writing truly great songs. Unlike most songwriting books, this guide uses examples of HIT SONGS in addition to proven tools and techniques for writing memorable, chart-topping songs. Explore popular songs and learn what makes them work.

50449419 Book $19.95

The New Music Therapist's Handbook – 2nd Edition
by Suzanne B. Hanser

Dr. Hanser's well respected *Music Therapist's Handbook* has been thoroughly updated and revised to reflect the latest developments in the field of music therapy. Includes: an introduction to music therapy; new clinical applications and techniques; case studies; designing, implementing, and evaluating individualized treatment programs, including guidelines for beginning music therapists.

50449424 Book $29.95

Music Notation
by Mark McGrain

Learn the essentials of music notation, from pitch and rhythm placement to meter and voicing alignments. Excellent resource for both written and computer notation software.

50449399 Book. $16.95

Managing

Lyric Structure
by Pat Pattison

This book will help songwriters handle lyric structures more effectively. Equally helpful to both beginning and experienced lyricists, this book features exercises that help you say things better and write better songs.

50481582 Book $11.95

Masters of Music Conversations with Berklee Greats
by Mark Small and Andrew Taylor

An impressive collection of personal interviews with music industry superstars from *Berklee Today*, the alumni magazine of Berklee College of Music. Read about how these luminaries got their breaks, and valuable lessons learned along the way. Paula Cole talks about navigating through the recording industry, George Martin on technology's effect on artistic freedom, Patty Larkin considers the creative process, and Alf Clausen discusses scoring *The Simpsons*. Get the story from these stars and many others.

50449422 Book $24.95

Rhyming Techniques and Strategies
by Pat Pattison

Find better rhymes and use them more effectively. If you have written lyrics before, even professionally, and you crave more insight and control over your craft, this book is for you. Beginners will learn good habits and techniques and how to avoid common mistakes.

50481583 Book $10.95

READING STUDIES

Reading Studies For Guitar
by William Leavitt

A comprehensive collection of studies for improving reading and technical ability. Includes scales, arpeggios, written-out chords, and a variety of rhythms and time signatures. Positions 1 through 7 are covered in all keys. An important method for all guitarists who recognize the advantages of being able to sight-read.

50449490 ....$10.95

Advanced Reading Studies For Guitar
by William Leavitt

For the guitarist who wants to improve reading ability in positions 8 through 12, these progressive studies are written especially for the guitar, in all keys, and consisting of scales, arpeggios, intervals, and notated chords in various time signatures. A special section of multi-position studies is included. An important method for all guitarists who want to learn the entire fingerboard.

50449500 (B-60) $10.95

Reading Contemporary Electric Bass Rhythms
by Rich Appleman

A comprehensive collection of exercises and performance studies designed to enable the student to play in a wide range of musical styles. Includes funk, rock, disco, jazz, top 40, soft rock and country western. Excellent for sight-reading and technical development.

50449770 ....$10.95

About Berklee College of Music

Founded in Boston in 1945, Berklee College of Music is the world's largest independent music college and the premier institution for the study of contemporary music. The college's 3,000 students and 300 faculty members interact in an environment that includes all of the opportunities presented by a career in the contemporary music industry. Our faculty and alumni are among the finest musicians in the world.

About Berklee Press

Berklee Press is the non-profit, educational publishing division of Berklee College of Music. Proceeds from the sales of Berklee Press products are contributed to the scholarship funds of the college. Berklee Press publishes high-quality practical books, videotapes, DVDs, and interactive products for all areas of contemporary music education including performance, ear training, harmony, composition, songwriting, arranging, film scoring, music therapy, production, engineering, music business, synthesis, and music technology. Berklee Press products are dedicated to furthering the enrichment and success of musicians, students, teachers, and hobbyists alike.

For more information about Berklee Press or Berklee College of Music, contact us:

1140 Boylston Street
Boston, MA 02215-3693

www.berkleepress.com

7777 W. BLUEMOUND RD. P.O. BOX 13819 MILWAUKEE, WI 53213

Visit your local music dealer or bookstore, or go to www.berkleepress.com